Praise for *Mind, Value, and Cosmos: On the Relational Nature of Ultimacy*

"If the mystery of existence obsesses you, if that the world works fixates you, then *Mind, Value, and Cosmos* is for you. Andrew M. Davis explores why there is anything at all, why actualities seem shockingly amenable for consciousness, by triangulating John Leslie's value, Keith Ward's idealism, and Alfred North Whitehead's process philosophy—with cameo contributions from Paul Davies, Peter Forrest, Thomas Nagel, John Polkinghorne, Nicholas Rescher, Richard Swinburne, Steven Weinberg, and others. The relational nature of ultimacy, subsuming Mind and Value, is a distinction. (Videos of Leslie, Ward, others on *Closer To Truth*.)"

—**Robert Lawrence Kuhn**, creator, host, writer,
Closer To Truth (www.closertotruth.com)

"Since Darwin, intellectual efforts have been expended primarily in showing the primacy of matter. Many of those who have aimed at comprehensiveness, have thought they could explain a great deal, but they are left with the intractable problem of consciousness. Now attention is shifting to the alternative type of metaphysic, one that gives primacy to mental dimensions. Davis gives promise of being a leader in this much more promising effort. He builds on key contributors and writes about them generously, accurately, and clearly. For one seeking an entry point into this new, or renewed, metaphysical tradition, I recommend this book."

—**John B. Cobb, Jr.**, emeritus professor of philosophy and theology, Claremont School of Theology; co-founder of the Center for Process Studies; member of the American Academy of Arts and Sciences

"In *Mind, Value, and Cosmos*, Davis provides an excellent example of old-fashioned metaphysics and philosophical theology. (Calling it 'old-fashioned' is not a slam, but a compliment.) Dealing with Canadian philosopher John Leslie, British philosopher-and-theologian Keith Ward, and British-American metaphysician Alfred North Whitehead, Davis illustrates three examples of what he calls an 'axianoetic' approach, which regards both value and mind as ultimate in the nature of things through 'mutual immanence.' His thesis is that, rather than trying to determine which of these is *truly* ultimate, we should think in terms of the ultimacy of relationality."

—**David Ray Griffin**, author of *The Christian Gospel for Americans: A Systematic Theology*

"This book brings intellectual rigor to key questions regarding ultimate reality. On Davis's account, it is relationality that is ultimate. His 'axianoetic' approach, which relies heavily on the work of John Leslie, Keith Ward, and especially Alfred North Whitehead, sees both mind and value spread throughout the cosmos. This book is a welcome addition to both process metaphysics and systematic theology."

—**Daniel Dombrowski**, professor of philosophy at Seattle University

"Davis has produced an insightful and widely informed account of one of the key issues of classical metaphysics. It is bound to stimulate further interest in these ever-challenging issues."

—**Nicolas Rescher**, Distinguished University Professor of Philosophy at the University of Pittsburgh; author of *Axiogenesis: An Essay in Metaphysical Optimalism*

"If one wants an idealism, that is, a view that allows an ultimate plurality of related but independent things, Davis is the person for you. He calls this an idealism because of Keith Ward's theory according to which God is a divine mind and because of John Leslie's theory that the world consists of Platonic ideals of various grades, including an identity with the divine mind. Most of all it is an idealism because of Whitehead's cosmology of mutual immanence in which everything actual is a mind, everything in becoming is a mind, and the everlasting creative advance into novelty is mental. Analyzing Ward, Leslie, Whitehead, and many others on the problem of universal possibilities and actualization, Davis develops a wonderfully consistent cosmology. This is one of the several orthodox readings of Whitehead."

—**Robert Cummings Neville**, professor emeritus of Philosophy, Religion, and Theology, Boston University; author of *The Good Is One, Its Manifestations Many*; *Defining Religion*; and *Metaphysics of Goodness*

"What are the ultimates required to understand all things, actual or merely possible? In this impressive work, Davis makes the case for *axionoeticism*, the thesis that mind and values are two mutually dependent ultimates. Axionoeticism has been implicit in the philosophy of many great thinkers, but Davis's contribution is to make it explicit and to defend it by critically examining three recent proponents, Alfred Whitehead, John Leslie, and Keith Ward. I highly recommend this book both to philosophers and theologians."

—**Peter Forrest**, author of *God without the Supernatural: A Defense of Scientific Theism*

Mind, Value, and Cosmos

Contemporary Whitehead Studies

Edited by Roland Faber, Claremont School of Theology, and Brian G. Henning, Gonzaga University

Contemporary Whitehead Studies, cosponsored by the Whitehead Research Project, is an interdisciplinary book series that publishes manuscripts from scholars with contemporary and innovative approaches to Whitehead studies by giving special focus to projects that explore the connections between Whitehead and contemporary Continental philosophy, especially sources, like Heidegger, or contemporary streams like poststructuralism; reconnect Whitehead to pragmatism, analytical philosophy, and philosophy of language; explore creative East/West dialogues facilitated by Whitehead's work; explore the interconnections of the mathematician with the philosopher and the contemporary importance of these parts of Whitehead's work for the dialogue between sciences and humanities; reconnect Whitehead to the wider field of philosophy, the humanities, the sciences, and academic research with Whitehead's pluralistic impulses in the context of a pluralistic world; address Whitehead's philosophy in the midst of contemporary problems facing humanity, such as climate change, war and peace, race, and the future development of civilization.

Recent Titles in This Series

Propositions in the Making: Experiments in a Whiteheadian Laboratory, edited by Roland Faber, Michael Halewood, and Andrew M. Davis

Whitehead and Continental Philosophy in the Twenty-First Century: Dislocations, edited by Jeremy D. Fackenthal

Beyond Whitehead: Recent Advances in Process Thought, edited by Jakub Dziadkowiec and Lukasz Lamza

Tragic Beauty in Whitehead and Japanese Aesthetics, by Steve Odin

Creaturely Cosmologies: Why Metaphysics Matters for Animal and Planetary Liberation, by Brianne Donaldson

Thinking with Whitehead and the American Pragmatists: Experience and Reality, edited by Brian G. Henning, William T. Myers, and Joseph D. John

The Divine Manifold, by Roland Faber

Foundations of Relational Realism: A Topological Approach to Quantum Mechanics and the Philosophy of Nature, by Michael Epperson and Elias Zafiris

Mind, Value, and Cosmos: On the Relational Nature of Ultimacy, by Andrew M. Davis

Mind, Value, and Cosmos

On the Relational Nature of Ultimacy

Andrew M. Davis

LEXINGTON BOOKS
Lanham • Boulder • New York • London

Published by Lexington Books
An imprint of The Rowman & Littlefield Publishing Group, Inc.
4501 Forbes Boulevard, Suite 200, Lanham, Maryland 20706
www.rowman.com

6 Tinworth Street, London SE11 5AL, United Kingdom

Copyright © 2020 The Rowman & Littlefield Publishing Group, Inc.

All rights reserved. No part of this book may be reproduced in any form or by any electronic or mechanical means, including information storage and retrieval systems, without written permission from the publisher, except by a reviewer who may quote passages in a review.

British Library Cataloguing in Publication Information Available

Library of Congress Cataloging-in-Publication Data

Names: Davis, Andrew M., 1987– author.
Title: Mind, value, and cosmos : on the relational nature of ultimacy / Andrew M. Davis.
Description: Lanham : Lexington Books, [2020] | Series: Contemporary Whitehead studies | Includes bibliographical references and index. | Summary: "An engaging dialogue with the modern 'axionoetic' proposals of A.N. Whitehead, Keith Ward, and John Leslie, arguing for the relational nature of ultimacy wherein Mind and Value, Possibility and Actuality, God and the World are affirmed as ultimate only in virtue of their relationality. This relationship Whitehead calls 'mutual immanence.'"—Provided by publisher.
Identifiers: LCCN 2020034233 (print) | LCCN 2020034234 (ebook) |
  ISBN 9781793636393 (cloth) | ISBN 9781793636416 (pbk)
  ISBN 9781793636409 (epub)
Subjects: LCSH: Whitehead, Alfred North, 1861–1947. | Relationism. | Metaphysics.
Classification: LCC B1674.W354 D39 2020 (print) | LCC B1674.W354 (ebook) |
  DDC 110—dc23
LC record available at https://lccn.loc.gov/2020034233
LC ebook record available at https://lccn.loc.gov/2020034234

It is with appreciation, gratitude, and, above all, love that I dedicate this book to my father, Reed C. Davis, whose unyielding support and encouragement undergird every word and every page. Should his long-standing concern for the deeper values of life have developed along a slightly different path, I am confident he might have produced something rather similar. Nietzsche thus utters a truism: "What was silent in the father speaks in the son; and I often found in the son the unveiled secret of the father."

Contents

Abbreviations	ix
Acknowledgments	xiii
Introduction: The Relational Nature of Ultimacy	1
PART I: ANY AND ALL EXISTENCE	**9**
1 Mysteries of Existence	11
2 Ways of Explaining the Mystery	35
PART II: DIVINE NECESSITY AND THE AXIANOETIC TRADITION	**51**
3 Axiarchism: The Creative Supremacy of Value	53
4 Idealism: The Primordiality of Mind	69
5 The Mutual Immanence of Mind and Value	85
PART III: GOD AND THE POSSIBLE	**105**
6 Riddles of the Possible	107
7 Ridding the Possible	129
8 The Mutual Immanence of the Possible and the Actual	143
PART IV: THE WORLD AND ITS ACTUALIZATION	**163**
9 Mind and the Making of Actuality	165

10	The Mutual Immanence of God and the World	191
Conclusion: The Ultimacy of Relationality		213
Bibliography		215
Index		221
About the Author		231

Abbreviations

ALFRED NORTH WHITEHEAD

AI	*Adventures of Ideas.* New York: Free Press, 1967.
AE	*Aims of Education.* New York: Free Press, 1967.
CN	*The Concept of Nature.* Cambridge: Cambridge University Press, 1964.
FR	*The Function of Reason.* Princeton: Princeton University Press, 1929.
Imm.	"Immortality." In *Science and Philosophy.* Paterson: Littlefield, Adams & Co., 1964, 85–104.
MT	*Modes of Thought.* New York: Free Press, 1968.
PR	*Process and Reality.* Corrected edition. Edited by David Ray Griffin and Donald Sherburne. New York: The Free Press, 1978.
"PR"	"Process and Reality." In *Science and Philosophy.* Paterson: Littlefield, Adams & Co., 1964, 122–27.
RM	*Religion in the Making.* Cambridge: Cambridge University Press, 1926.
SMW	*Science and the Modern World.* New York: The Free Press, 1967.
SY	*Symbolism: Its Meaning and Effect.* New York: Fordham University Press, 1985.

KEITH WARD

QSR	*The Big Questions in Science and Religion.* West Conshohocken: Templeton, 2008.
CIG	*The Christian Idea of God: A Philosophical Foundation for Faith.* Cambridge: University Press, 2017.
CG	*Concepts of God: Images of the Divine in Five Religious Traditions.* Oxford: Oneworld, 1998.
EG	*The Evidence for God: The Case for the Existence of a Spiritual Dimension.* London: Darton, Longman and Todd, 2014.
GGP	*God: A Guide for the Perplexed.* London: One World, 2002.
GP	*God and the Philosophers.* Minneapolis: Fortress Press, 2009.
GCN	*God, Chance, Necessity.* Oxford: Oneworld, 1996.
MM	*More Than Matter? Is There More to Life Than Molecules?* Grand Rapids: Eerdmans, 2010.
MJ	"My Journey to the God of Personal Idealism." In *How I Found God in Everyone and Everywhere: An Anthology of Spiritual Memoirs.* Edited by Andrew M. Davis and Philip Clayton. Rhinebeck: Monkfish, 2018.
PF	*Pascal's Fire: Scientific Faith and Religious Understanding.* Oxford: Oneworld, 2006.
RCG	*Rational Theology and the Creativity of God.* Oxford: Basil Blackwell, 1982.
RC	*Religion and Creation.* Oxford: Clarendon, 1996.
RMW	*Religion in the Modern World: Celebrating Pluralism and Diversity.* Cambridge: Cambridge University Press, 2019.
SDN	*Sharing in the Divine Nature: A Personalist Metaphysics.* Eugene: Cascade, 2020.

JOHN LESLIE

EW	*The End of the World: The Science and Ethics of Human Extinction.* New York: Routledge, 1996.
ID	*Immortality Defended.* Malden: Blackwell, 2007.
IM	*Infinite Minds: A Philosophical Cosmology.* Oxford: Clarendon Press, 2001.
U	*Universes.* New York: Routledge, 1996.
VE	*Value and Existence.* Totowa: Rowman and Littlefield, 1979.
ME	*The Mystery of Existence: Why Is There Anything at All?* Edited with Robert Laurence Kuhn. Malden: Wiley-Blackwell, 2013.

OTHER SOURCES

TMG   Davies, Paul. *The Mind of God: The Scientific Basis for a Rational World.* New York: Simon & Schuster Paperbacks, 2005.

VR   Ewing, A. C. *Value and Reality.* London: George Allen & Unwin Ltd., 1973.

TBG   Faber, Roland. *The Becoming of God: Process Theology, Philosophy, and Multireligious Engagement.* Eugene: Cascade, 2017.

TDM   Faber, Roland. *The Divine Manifold.* Lanham: Lexington, 2014.

TGR   Faber, Roland. *The Garden of Reality: Transreligious Relativity in a World of Becoming* Lanham: Lexington, 2018.

GPW   Faber, Roland. *God as Poet of the World: Exploring Process Theologies.* Louisville: WJK, 2008.

BV   Ferré, Frederick. *Being and Value: Toward a Constructive Postmodern Metaphysics.* Albany: SUNY, 1996.

GWS   Forrest, Peter. *God without the Supernatural.* Ithaca and London: Cornell University Press, 1996.

RWS   Griffin, David Ray. *Reenchantment without Supernaturalism: A Process Philosophy of Religion.* Ithaca: Cornell University Press,

DE   Malone-France, Derek. *Deep Empiricism: Kant, Whitehead, and the Necessity of Philosophical Theism.* Lanham: Lexington, 2007.

MC   Nagel, Thomas. *Mind and Cosmos: Why the Materialist Neo-Darwinian Conception of Nature Is Almost Certainly False.* New York: Oxford University Press, 2012.

FP   Polkinghorne, John. *Faith of a Physicist.* Minneapolis: Fortress Press, 1996.

AX   Rescher, Nicolas. *Axiogenesis: An Essay in Metaphysical Optimalism.* Lanham: Lexington, 2010.

MP   Rescher, Nicholas. *Metaphysical Perspectives.* Notre Dame: University of Notre Dame Press, 2017.

GG   Rice, Hugh. *God and Goodness.* Oxford: Oxford University Press, 2000.

GG   Wynn, Mark. *God and Goodness.* New York: Routledge, 1999.

Acknowledgments

A book such as this has no simple genealogy. It is a result of the convergence of a variety of influences, experiences, conversations, and convictions over many years of wonder and wander. I remain deeply indebted to Roland Faber and Philip Clayton, mentors and friends, both of whom encouraged the sources, directions, and conclusions of this work, albeit never without the guidance of discussion and debate. I also remain deeply indebted to Alfred North Whitehead, Keith Ward, and John Leslie whose collective work and shared intuitions are inspiration. I thank Keith Ward and John Leslie, in particular, for valuable personal correspondence on different points requiring clarification throughout the evolution of the project. To my family and friends, I offer a debt of gratitude for their encouragement, patience, and love along the way.

Introduction
The Relational Nature of Ultimacy

This book is an investigation into the nature of ultimacy and explanation, particularly as it relates to the status of, and relationship between, Mind, Value, and Cosmos. In using the term "ultimacy," I am referring to that mode of inquiry pursuing that which is *ultimate* or *necessary* in the nature of things, those *conditions, presuppositions,* or *requirements* without which the universe would not exist at all—and certainly not one giving rise to questioning beings such as ourselves. In using the term "explanation," I am referring to that related mode of inquiry pursuing how such ultimate conditions are *ultimately explanatory,* not simply of any and all reality, but also in and among themselves. A quest for ultimacy and explanation, therefore, is not only concerned with grasping something of those ultimate conditions that ground existence, but also understanding how it is such conditions *relate to one another.* Ultimacy, in this sense, is not a matter of pointing to one thing, reality, or condition as "ultimate"—or, indeed, to many of them—but, rather, a matter of pointing to *the way* in which they are interdependent and mutually supportive. Put differently, an investigation into ultimacy and explanation addresses not only the singular or the plural but also—and perhaps more so—the ultimately *relational.* To find oneself considering the relational nature of ultimacy in this way, I claim, is to move toward affirming the *ultimacy of relationality.* This is my concern in the following pages.

One cannot speak to the kind of *relationality* among ultimate notions, however, without first assuming that these notions are, in some sense, able to be grasped. Considerations of this kind naturally involve a host of perennial questions; and the history of philosophy harbors no shortage of answers rising from diverse metaphysical proposals. Arguably, however, the most long-standing and far-reaching proposals are those surrounding the primordiality of Mind and the supremacy of Value. At the heart of this hypothesis is what I term the *axianoetic* approach to ultimacy. I derive this word from the Greek renderings of *axia* meaning "worth" or "value," on the one hand, and *noētikos*, denoting "mind" or "mental activity," on the other. The roots of these approaches date back to the genius of Plato and Aristotle, and are differently inherited and employed by key figures throughout Western philosophical and theological history. These include thinkers like Plotinus, Anselm, Aquinas, Descartes, Leibniz, Spinoza, Hegel, Whitehead, and—in our current time—Keith Ward and John Leslie. Although diversely expressed throughout the Western intellectual tradition, the axianoetic approach variously insists that *something*, and perhaps *someone*, ultimately mind-like and of immeasurable value necessarily conditions—and is itself necessarily conditioned by—ultimate notions whose collective and reciprocal functions mutually ground the possibility, character, and reason for all existence. For many today, this conviction still remains both luring and haunting. Indeed, as reductive materialist dogmas continue to wane, questions concerning the ultimacy of Mind and Value continue to undergird some of the most exciting philosophical, theological, and scientific proposals of our time.

It is my goal in this book to substantiate these claims by entertaining core facets of the anxianoetic proposals of three eminent modern thinkers, although a constellation of other relevant voices will also be adduced. As referenced above, these thinkers are the British philosopher-giant and mathematician Alfred North Whitehead (1861–1947), whose dynamic metaphysical vision forms the foundations of modern "process philosophy" and "process theology"; the equally British philosopher-priest Keith Ward (b. 1938), whose large corpus has effectively reignited "personal idealism" as a metaphysical option relevant to discussions in philosophy, science, and comparative religion; and the British-Canadian philosopher John Leslie (b. 1940), whose curious, rigorous, and original philosophical contributions have tackled a host of philosophical problems including the mystery of existence, cosmological "fine-tuning," the ethics of human extinction, and the hope for immortality.

Bringing Whitehead, Ward, and Leslie together in terms of the ultimacy and relationality of Mind and Value is not arbitrary. In positive reference to each other, each of them exhibit different, but deeply resonant, intuitions as to the axianoetic nature of divine and worldly things. Differences notwithstanding, Leslie has spoken of Ward's idealistic vision as strikingly similar to his own. Ward too has expressed resonance with Leslie's axiarchic principle that value "requirements" or "needs" might themselves be creatively effectual in and for the cosmos. Far more so than Leslie, Ward is deeply influenced by Whitehead's relational philosophy and praises him for inaugurating a radically novel metaphysical system, one that fosters perhaps the most robust philosophical and theological affirmation of the value of temporality, creativity, and freedom in the history of philosophy. Nevertheless, Ward retains his own reservations and qualifications with respect to "process thought." Leslie also finds in Whitehead vigorous support for his own purposes, namely, an argument for, and defense of, the Platonic reign of Value in the universe.

There remains a fascinating triangulation of insights, emphases, and priorities among these thinkers that has yet to be treated. It is my conviction that questions as to the nature of ultimacy and explanation, and, in particular, those concerning the status of, and relation between, Mind, Value, and Cosmos, constitute the most fertile ground for their meeting. This meeting reveals not only profound echoes but also fascinating deviations between them. In light of their promptings, this book poses a variety of ultimate questions: those surrounding Mind and Value, Possibility and Actuality, God and the World. It does so with fundamentally *relational intuitions*. These intuitions are largely a result of my engagement with Whitehead; and I've come to see that they nicely complement, as well as challenge, the respective proposals of Leslie, Ward, and other relevant thinkers in the tradition.

More than any other philosopher, Whitehead has stressed nothing short of the *ultimacy of relationality*. He has pointed to a *way* in which ultimate notions, from the finite and contingent to the infinite and necessary, live through one another, such that each mutually offer the other factors necessary for their own reality. This mode of relationality Whitehead calls "mutual immanence"; but it is equally that of mutual transcendence. It is this *kind* of relationality, I hold, that can uniquely illuminate some of the most stimulating and challenging questions emerging from serious considerations into ultimacy and explanation. These questions, to be sure, remain steeped in mystery; and even if Whitehead himself did not explicitly pose them (or at least, some of them), doing so ourselves, with attention to his relational intuitions, might admit some manner of novel clarity to the thoroughly foggy disciplines of metaphysics and philosophical theology.

The book is framed by four parts respectively addressing distinctive, but deeply related, mysteries in the axianoetic context of Whitehead, Ward, and Leslie's work. I state these broadly below as well as indicate their directions in the ensuing chapters.

Part I: *The Mystery of Any and All Existence:* Clarifying relevant distinctions, layers, and dimensions inherent in asking fundamental questions (chapter 1), as well as surveying the basic kinds of solutions that have been offered, including those of Value and Mind, respectively (chapter 2).

Part II: *The Mystery of Necessary Divine Existence:* Considering the ways in which the axianoetic tradition of philosophical theology can be read through respective priorities or emphases: on abstract Value as conditioning concrete Mind (chapter 3), or, on concrete Mind as conditioning abstract Value (chapter 4); and raising the question as to how Mind and

Value might reciprocally relate in God such that unique challenges find new resolution and divine necessity new illumination (chapter 5).

Part III: *The Mystery of the Possible:* Engaging key riddles of possibility in terms of their ontological status, whereabouts, and relevance to actuality (chapter 6); looking to possible challenges and alternatives to these riddles (chapter 7), including that of the divine Mind's own possibility, and thus, the question as to how Possibility and Actuality relate in God (chapter 8).

Part IV: *The Mystery of the World:* Inquiring into the actuality of the world, its status, character, and constituents; how it becomes actual from or, in relation to, divine Mentality; what possible challenges this may create (chapter 9), and how these might be addressed through a mutual understanding of the God–World relationship (chapter 10).

These four parts form the primary terrain we will traverse in the following pages. Speaking in more detail to the content and conclusions of each chapter will help further set the stage for the flow of the book.

Drawing upon the axianoetic insights of Whitehead, Ward, and Leslie, as well as other key voices of philosophical influence, Part I lays the groundwork for the book as a whole. Chapter 1 articulates some of relevant distinctions, layers, dimensions, and themes inherent in asking fundamental existential questions, that is, questions about the mystery of any and all existence. We thus navigate from the ontological question to the cosmological question, and from questions of nothingness and necessity to those of contingency, evolution, and beginnings. In doing so, we find that facing the realism of some Platonic-like axiological realities seems utterly inescapable.

Chapter 2 surveys some of the principal *kinds* of "solutions" or answers that have been offered to "solve" the mystery of existence. These include claims as to the absurdity of there ever being "nothing"; rejections of any actual need for explanation; appraisals of chance and quantum probability; affirmations of the ultimacy of abstract Value; and conclusions as to the necessity of concrete Mind. In focusing briefly on each of these "solutions," including some key figures that exemplify them, we also point to acute problems or challenges they may face. Looking respectively to both Value and Mind, as the last of these five kinds of solutions—and the primary focus of the book—we conclude by raising the question as to a *relational solution* between them as possibly distinct from these. A relational solution surrounding Value's relation to Mind and Mind's relation to Value may offer a wider approach to the existential mysteries we face. In particular, it may illuminate key problems that arise from either when taken in abstraction or isolation from the other.

We take up this relational question explicitly in Part II where we look specifically at the ways the axianoetic tradition of philosophical theology affirms *both* Value and Mind as necessary domains of ultimacy, but might also prioritize or emphasize one or the other when approaching the mystery of divine necessity. What is left obscure, however, is how Mind and Value might relate to each other in sustaining such necessity. This is brought to light by attending to the ways in which Leslie, Ward, and Whitehead consider key figures of this tradition. Chapter 3 reveals the ways in which Leslie's reading of the tradition is strongly conditioned by his concerns for "extreme axiarchism," such that the abstract ultimacy of Value is elevated over, and explanatory of, concrete Mind. By contrasting emphasis, chapter 4 shows that Ward's reading of the tradition in terms of "personal idealism" prioritizes the explanatory ultimacy of concrete Mind over abstract Value. Although Leslie and Ward can be seen to approach the tradition with these respective abstract and concrete priorities, they arrive at very similar visions wherein Mind and Value are distinct, but inseparable from each other. Nevertheless, the *kind* of relationality that may obtain between Mind and Value is still left in question.

Chapter 5 reveals how Whitehead's relational vision opens unique spaces for affirming a robust interrelationality between Value and Mind in God such that emphasizing one over the other is abstraction from a wider mutuality between them. This relationality consists not just from Value to Mind (Leslie) or from Mind to Value (Ward), but from each to the other in mutual immanence. Mind and Value thus have equal priority for and to each other. Even if Whitehead did not put it exactly in this way, some thinkers such as A. C. Ewing have done so in ways strikingly similar to his own intuitions. Conceived as "mutual immanence," this relationality sees that Value and Mind offer something essential to each other and thus that their functions cannot be reduced to a unilateral relation from *only* one to the other. In this way, they are not simply mutually immanent but also mutually transcendent to each other in grounding divine necessity. Moreover, it is this unacknowledged kind of relationship that is implicit—if partially explicit—in key figures such as John Polkinghorne, Mark Wynn, Hugh Rice, Peter Forrest, and A. C. Ewing who appraise, critique, and are differently relevant to Leslie's axiarchic contributions. Leslie and Ward themselves do not explicitly recognize this mode of relationality between Mind and Value, but it is arguably just under the surface of their thought as well. We conclude by modestly suggesting that reading the axianoetic tradition in terms of the mutual immanence of Mind and Value may illuminate some of its ambiguities anew.

Part III takes up a central mystery the indications of which are encountered in preceding chapters. This is the mystery of the possible, and the axianoetic riddles they pose when considering ultimacy, explanation, and relation. Chapter 6 begins by looking briefly to key statements and questions undergirding these riddles. These come from different figures and disciplines: from philosophy and theology, to physics, cosmology, and biology. We focus on how possibility is encountered in human experience and principally on how their riddles arise and are differently framed by Leslie, Ward, and Whitehead.

Chapter 7 briefly considers elements of the proposals of W. V. Quine, Frederick Ferré, and David Lewis, three prominent modern figures who differently seek to *rid us* of the riddles possibilities pose. Each of their attempts are unique and challenging, but they are also shortsighted and inadequate, especially against the axianoetic backdrop of Whitehead, Ward, and Leslie's convictions. They are particularly problematic to the extent that they leave no abiding place for ultimate Mind and Value in the cosmos.

Through our engagement with Whitehead, Ward, and Leslie, chapter 8 shows the riddles of possibility to be inherently axianoetic; they are entangled with Mind and Value from the finite spheres of human experience to the infinite spheres of divine Experience. Arguably, only in this way can profound riddles, as to their existential status, locus, and relevance to the world, find resolve. If the possible leads us deeper into the axianoetic nature of God, however, we must also face a robust challenge articulated by Leslie. This challenge concerns God's *own possibility*, and thus a question as to the relationship or priority between the possible and the actual in God. Whitehead, Ward, and Leslie converge and diverge on these points in fascinating ways, but the mutual immanence, and thus also the mutual transcendence, of the possible and the actual in God may offer a unique way forward.

Part IV moves from the riddles of possibility to the mystery of the world as actual. We entertain a variety of related questions concerning the status, character, and constituents of the world in relation to divine Mentality. The respective axianoetic intuitions of Leslie, Ward, and Whitehead draw out resonant, but quite distinctive, proposals surrounding identity, otherness, and relationality between God and the world. Chapter 9 looks to the respective proposals of Leslie and Ward, both of whom insist that divine thought alone is what makes for actuality, albeit with different emphases. Leslie's "pantheism" insists that there is really no reality to the world other than its identity with intricate divine thinking. By contrast, Ward's relational "panentheism" seeks to preserve the real otherness of the world precisely because the value of real otherness allows for the value of real relationship, collaboration, and love between God and the world. Nevertheless, he still holds that the world's reality is only due to divine thought. Some speculative challenges are therefore posed to the plausibility of these proposals with their shared conviction that it is only divine thought that ultimately makes for the actuality of the world. To the extent they both affirm this, but appear to disagree as to whether the world is to be assigned identity or real otherness from divine Mentality, these challenges arise. Through Leslie and Ward's promptings, we also raise the challenge of the inferiority of the world, with its suffering and dissatisfaction. In connecting this to their convictions that it is divine thought alone that makes for actuality, we suggest that these challenges might be avoided by affirming the world as necessarily related to, but always other than, divine Mentality. Moreover, in a truly axianoetic universe, it may really be *more valuable* that the world is necessarily other than God precisely in this way. If so, it may call for an adjusted understanding of the status of the world by Leslie and Ward.

Chapter 10 looks to Whitehead's various concerns for mediation in and among extremes in cosmology and theology. These emerge in his affirmation of what Roland Faber calls "transpantheism," a position distinct from both pantheism and panentheism that affirms both the mutual immanence and transcendence of God and the world for each other. On this vision, Whitehead may evade the challenges put to Leslie and Ward, for the world is never only a result of divine thought, but a genuine, although deeply related, "other" with its own integrity and embodied creativity. In a poetic and collaborative relationship, God does not (and cannot) actualize the world through divine thought alone; rather, the world actualizes divine thought through its own self-creativity. The world requires God for its very possibility and God requires the world for the actualization of divine value. In this way, the world is crowned with purpose, dignity, and grandeur; and suffering is shown to be an inherent shadow-side of the value of co-creation between God and world.

The conclusion briefly revisits the central claims of the book in its concern for ultimacy, explanation, and the mutually immanent and transcendent relationship between Mind and Value, Possibility and Actuality, God and the World. These claims are succinctly captured by the following quotations by Leslie, Ward, Ewing, and Whitehead, which effectively frame the journey ahead:

- *Leslie*: "Necessarily, eternally, there can be ethical requirements for the existence of various things, needs for them to exist" (ME, 130).
- *Ward*: "The deepest reality is mind, eternal and necessary mind" (EG, 75).
- *Whitehead*: "The key to metaphysics is [the] doctrine of mutual immanence, each side lending to the other a factor necessary for its reality" (PR, 126).
- *Ewing*: "It would be as true to say that the [value] principle could not be true without God existing as to say that God could not exist without the [value] principle being true" (VR, 203).
- *Whitehead*: "God does not create eternal [possibilities]; for [the divine] nature requires them in the same degree that they require [the divine nature]" (PR, 257).
- *Whitehead*: "It is as true to say that God transcends the World, as that the World transcends God. It is as true to say that God creates the World, as that the World creates God" (PR, 348).

- *Whitehead*: "Thus the task of philosophy is the understanding of the interfusion of modes of existence" (MT, 71).

The chief aim of the book is to explicate this "interfusion of modes of existence" and thereby add some novel relational insights to a long-standing conversation in Western philosophy and theology. This conversation has been deeply axianoetic, and it shows no signs of ending. Arguably, the need to affirm a place for the ultimacy of Mind, Value, and Cosmos has only increased. To do so, however, necessitates showing how they relationally live through each other. Quests for ultimacy and explanation will continue to point to something of those ultimate conditions without which both God and the world could not be. Mind and Value, Possibility and Actuality, may only begin to name such conditions that are perhaps manifold and without end. It is my conviction, however, that the deeper reality of ultimacy consists in conceiving *how* such conditions relate. The relational nature of ultimacy, I claim, makes for the ultimacy of relationality.

Part I

ANY AND ALL EXISTENCE

Chapter 1

Mysteries of Existence

The notion that a coherent explanation of the nature of things must finally admit something like the primordiality of Mind or the creative supremacy of Value has been a long-standing conviction among some of the most probative thinkers of our species. One should pause here to marvel at such a hypothesis, for it emerges within the context of highly evolved mental lives of truly axiological creatures, those from the genus *Homo*, beings who have somehow awoken to consciousness, baffled and concerned amid what Heidegger described as a kind of clearing (*lichtung*) in the forest of existence. We are and remain *axianoetic* beings; we are creatures of *thought*, and much of our thought is concerned with *value*. How strange and haunting that this should be the case.

Perhaps nowhere else do thought and value come together so meaningfully (and at times dreadfully) than in posing fundamental questions of existence. *Thought* is presupposed in *mentally conceiving* the question and *value* in terms of the *intrinsic worth of knowing* the answer. But what possible answer could one give to the mystery of existence—the mystery of our existence? Offering an answer would in fact *assume* we know *what the question actually is*. When speaking about *any and all reality*, however, this is not quickly the case. And what possible implications of value could there be in approaching an answer (or set of answers) to such questions? Assuming there really is a coherent question, is it really *worthwhile* to know the answer? These are not easy matters and they have been differently assessed and addressed throughout the Western intellectual tradition.

My goal in Part I of this book is to consider some of the necessary distinctions, layers, and dimensions inherent in asking fundamental existential questions. This is the aim of the current chapter. In the following chapter,

I will survey some the principal *kinds* of "solutions" that have been proposed, including some of the problems associated with them. I seek to do so in dialogue with some key voices of the tradition and particularly those of Whitehead, Ward, and Leslie as my guiding resources. These questions are not straightforward and important distinctions and associations need to be made. What is more, the kinds of answers that have been offered are tedious, frustrating, and deeply alluring; and they often overlap in ways that complicate and blur any neat solutions. Nevertheless, we seek to work our way through these layered entanglements with Mind and Value in view as the principal focus of our inquiry into ultimacy and explanation. Situating Whitehead, Ward, and Leslie within their proper contexts on these matters will help set the stage for the unfolding of the book to these ends. We begin with a consideration of our own locus in a universe of questions.

HOMO QUAERENS

The universe remains our embedded context. It is the cosmic arena in which all fundamental questions issue forth and reverberate. The first question ever asked is still "out there," expanding ever faster with the universe itself. This thought is worthy of enduring meditation; and it comes with unique questions of its own: What kind of mind conceived it? What kind of language uttered it? Was it spoken in wonder? Yelled in frustration? Whispered in reverence and awe? What was this question? What did it concern? Perhaps it concerned *everything*.

Ultimate questions are born from the fact of our existence and the shifting layers of our experience; and they extend to the unbounded universe at large. That we have emerged as questioning beings in such a universe is nothing short of astounding. As *Homo sapiens* we are also *Homo Quaerens*; we are questioning beings in a questionable cosmos (AX, 1–2). Consider this for a moment. What does it mean that such a universe houses *our very possibility*? What does it suggest about the nature and character of things that the universe comes to question itself *through us*? Is it plausible that human mentality is purely accidental in such a universe? Or is it perhaps a finite reflection of a kind of infinite and necessary Mentality underlying and giving rise to the cosmos itself? And what of value—that concern for the *worth* of knowing and being, which undergirds all meaningful questions? Is human experience and concern with value fortuitous, or is it an intimation of a kind of axiological ultimacy in the universe? Could Value be the *reason* for the universe itself, the reason for any kind of mentality at all—be it human or divine? While these constitute classical philosophical questions, they are also of much contemporary appeal. They remain central to some of the most compelling philosophical, theological, and scientific discussions at hand.[1] They have consumed my own mind for some time and are the stimulus for the present work.

It is no surprise, of course, that such questions strike many as far too anthropomorphic and, therefore, absurd. This is understandable. Far be it from us to naively project ourselves onto the cosmos. For others, however, these questions emerge naturally—and perhaps inevitably—from our waking to consciousness existence. These are among the most exciting questions our species could ever ask; and we do not ask them without reason. Taking our evolutionary continuity with nature seriously requires that we not simply see ourselves and our experience as *separate* from or *outside* the universe, but, rather, as shocking *exemplifications* (in some sense) of its nature and character. Indeed, we must include ourselves as *data* within the particular *weltanschauung* we are developing. I take this claim to be fundamental, and it is not all that controversial. We have not so much come *into* the world, but *grown out of it*. To say, therefore, that we reflect something of its mysterious nature—however limited—seems rather natural. Every form of inquiry must start from somewhere and with some fundamental convictions. So let me put it bluntly: human existence and experience is a clue to the goings-on of the universe as a whole—its reason, nature, and character. In this way, Whitehead reminds us that "in being ourselves we are more than ourselves: to know that our experience, dim and fragmentary as it is, yet sounds the utmost depths of reality" (SMW, 18).[2] Whatever this bizarre and beautiful universe is up to, we are a part of it and it is part of us. Such a conviction, in fact, may be the first step in mapping the nature of ultimacy.

EXISTENCE AS QUESTION AND PROBLEM

Questions about the nature of existence, experience, and ultimacy are, of course, endless. For many, this may be good reason to not ask them at all. Admittedly, not everyone is a philosopher—and this is probably a good thing. Even so, such questions are deeply tangled in our humanity; they may even constitute our humanity as such. We alone among earthen creatures are privileged (if also cursed) enough to raise such fundamental questions and be concerned with the answers given. "Only to the brutes, who are without thought," Arthur Schopenhauer insists, "does the world and existence appear as a matter of course; to man, on the contrary it is a problem, of which even the most uneducated and narrow-minded becomes vividly conscious in certain brighter moments" (quoted ME, 14). Certain moments are in fact not all that bright as Schopenhauer modeled too well; nevertheless, the question of our existence—of any existence—still emerges, be it out of despair or rejoicing. Heidegger considered these moments carefully.

> The question looms in moments of great despair, when things tend to lose all their weight and all meaning becomes obscured. Perhaps it will strike but once like a muffled bell that rings into our life and gradually dies away. It is present in moments of rejoicing, when all the things around us are transfigured and seen to be there for the first time, as if it might be easier to think they are not than to understand that they are and are as they are. The question is upon us in boredom, when we are equally removed from despair and joy, and everything about us seems so hopelessly commonplace that we no longer care whether anything is or is not—and with this the question "Why are there essents rather than nothing?" is evoked in particular form.[3]

This question does die away for most people. After all, life offers much more with which to busy oneself than the enormity of this question. For others, however, the donning of this question not only leaves an unforgettable impression but also inaugurates a winding philosophical trajectory in their life.[4] Indeed, on a philosophical level, I am tempted to say that a refusal to offer an answer to this question, and those like it, is akin to abbreviating one's humanity, dismissing the wonder of life's mystery, and ignoring one's status as that oddly illuminated clearing within the jungles of reality. One's approach to this question may be winding and answers hard to come by, but the question itself should not be dismissed—and certainly not by philosophers. Assuming the question is coherent, one should at least *want* an answer to it. "I want to know why the universe exists," Henri Bergson states; "Whence comes it, and how can it be understood, that anything exists?"[5] Naturally, all manner of answers have been given to this question and its status as philosophically worthwhile continues to be hotly debated.

Heidegger famously described this question as one that breaks open the ground for all authentic questions. It is this question that is necessarily implicit in all "self-questioning questions"; as such, it is the fundamental question of metaphysics (quoted AX, 7). With Robert Nozick one can appreciate this, saying, "It is possible to think that one cannot answer any question if one cannot answer the question of why there is something rather than nothing. How can we know why something is (or should be) a certain way if we don't know why there is anything at all?"; "the answer to any philosophical question is liable to be overturned or undermined or transformed by the answer to this one" (quoted ME, 214).

The question does cast the largest of philosophical shadows. For Schopenhauer, it is "the pendulum which keeps in motion the clock of metaphysics" (ibid., 14). This "clock" ticks within human experience such that we too might follow Ludwig Wittgenstein in saying, "It always happens that the idea of one particular experience presents itself . . . [and] the best way of describing it is to say that when I have it I wonder at the existence of the world. And I am then inclined to use such phrases as 'how extraordinary that anything should exist' or 'how extraordinary that the world should exist'" (quoted AX, 8). These two statements by Wittgenstein are revealing. They suggest in fact that the question of existence is actually deeply layered.

QUESTIONS OF EXISTENCE: DISTINCTIONS, LAYERS, DIMENSIONS

It is important to grasp relevant distinctions, layers, and dimensions inherent in asking fundamental existential questions. In doing so, we aim to clarify what it is we are actually asking (or should be asking) and what it is we are not. As we continue, it will become apparent that this is by no means straightforward. In approaching these inquiries, I look to some key voices of the tradition and especially to contributions of Whitehead, Ward, and Leslie. This conversation, moreover, aims to set the stage for considering in the next chapter the different *kinds* of answers available to these perennial questions and the ways in which some prominent thinkers have approached them.

Distinguishing the Ontological and Cosmological Questions

In considering the mystery of existence, we are immediately faced with a division between what, on the one hand, can be called the *ontological question* and, on the other, the *cosmological question*. These two questions have been differently expressed throughout the philosophical tradition. For example, Wittgenstein above expressed shock not only that "*anything* should exist" but also that "the *world* should exist." These are in fact not the same thing; a world is certainly *something*, but it is not just *anything*. G. W. Leibniz helps clarify this further. Famously assuming that nothing takes place without sufficient reason, he is adamant that "the first question we have a right to ask will be, *why is there something rather than nothing?* For nothing is simpler and easier than something. Furthermore, assuming that things must exist, we must be able to give a reason for *why they must exist in this way*, and not otherwise" (quoted ME, 13).[6] Questions surrounding nothing and whether or not some things "must exist" will be central to our discussions below. For now, however, Leibniz's distinction between these fundamental questions is clear. This distinction is also put forth by William James. Acknowledging the baffled stares of philosophy on these questions, James states, "Not only that *anything* should be, but that *this* very thing should be is mysterious!

Philosophy stares, but brings no reasoned solution, for from nothing to being there is no logical bridge" (ibid., 14, emphasis his). A more recent voice in Derek Parfit also insists that there are "two questions" involved in the question, "Why does the Universe exist?" "First, why is there a Universe at all? It might have been true that nothing ever existed: no living beings, no stars, no atoms, not even space or time . . . Second, why does *this* Universe exist? Things might have been, in countless ways, different. So why is the Universe as it is" (ibid., 220, emphasis mine)?

From these statements, we see that the ontological question considers the mystery of *any* existence in its utter generality, regardless of its form or mode of being. It does not rush into asking about particularities or contingencies, but rather wonders on a grand scheme: Why is there *anything at all* rather than Absolutely Nothing? The cosmological question, by contrast, seeks not the generality of existent things—whatever they could or might have been and in what possible state—but rather the *particularity* of what they in fact *are*, and the *way* in which they are. Put differently, the question is not simply why *anything* should exist, but why *our particular something* does exists—an *ordered* and *contingent* mode of existence—a *cosmos*. Why indeed this specific kind of cosmic order? Why order at all?

In approaching these two monumental questions, it would seem that even a chaotic state devoid of order—say that of the early universe—would still justify posing the ontological question. Would such a state not also be utterly mysterious against what might have been nothing at all? We realize, however, that we would not be there to ask the question—and this is important. We are, after all, shocking exemplifications of order in the cosmos. Still, it is interesting to imagine a "time" in our cosmic history when something far less ordered did reign. "But there must have been some epoch in which the dominant trend was the formation of protons, electrons, molecules and stars," Whitehead states (FR, 19). In this context, the ontological question itself had yet to be uttered; it was only a latent *possibility* of a universe writhing in chaotic infancy. This is quite a thought. The reason I say this is that such a question can only become *actual* in a *cosmological* context, and did so in *our* particular cosmological context. What we can glean from this is that the ontological question *presupposes* the cosmological context in which it is posed. It is this cosmological context, which *is* the cosmological question.

Does this mean, however, that the cosmological question holds preeminence over the ontological question? Positions among philosophers will naturally differ and individual minds will change over the course of a lifetime wrestling with these questions. Nicholas Rescher is a fine example. He readily acknowledges that "a great deal of milk has been spilled" by him and others over the question "Why is there something rather than nothing?" but he admits that "it now seems to me that the merely fundamental question is not that but rather, 'Why are things as they are rather than otherwise'" (AX, ix). More recently, he confirms this intuition saying, "The crucial question is not 'Why is there something rather than nothing at all?' but 'Why is there something *contingent*—something whose existence is not necessary'" (MP, 9–10). Whether or not one question should be elevated over and against the other is itself an intriguing question. One's answer I suspect will largely depend upon whether or not they think the ontological question is actually legitimate at all. At the heart of this debate is the quandary of Nothingness.

The Allure and Impossibility of Nothingness

Part of the reason the ontological question is so beguiling is because it is posed against the backdrop of *sheer Nothingness*. We have always been fascinated by Nothingness—both its idea and its possibility. It seems to enchant and horrify us at the same time, being at once both strangely comforting and also deeply disturbing. What is more, "it" "is" "something" we in fact love to *reify*, but we will never experience its reality—and for obvious reasons. It is not clear we can even speak of it at all. Keith Ward thus warns of the "reification fallacy" as that error which holds that all nouns must have referent to something, such that "nothing" is really a very odd sort of "something" (GCN, 34). Whitehead too insists that "you cannot approach nothing; for there is nothing to approach" (PR, 93).[7] Does this mean then that the ontological question should not even be uttered? Perhaps it does. Nevertheless, one still tries to imaginatively conceive a point at which there was completely Nothing—an inconceivable Darkness, a Void, a Blank.

Recall the different approaches to "nothing" in the above statements by Leibniz, James, and Parfit. Leibniz assumes that "nothing is simpler and easier than something." James insists that "from nothing to being there is no logical bridge." Parfit claims that it "might have been true that nothing ever existed." We tend to speak rather hastily about nothing. The point I wish make is that the ontological question itself appears stuck in a perhaps false and static bifurcation: that between Being *or* Nothingness. This is principally why Whitehead never explicitly asks the ontological question. It implicitly treats "Something" or "Nothing" as stabilized abstractions.[8]

An example may help here. Suppose you have a card. On one side, the word "Something" is written and, on the other side, the word "Nothing" is written. You continually flip the card, so it oscillates from "Something" to "Nothing" and back again. As soon as you point to "Something," it has become "Nothing"; and as soon as you point to "Nothing," it has become "Something." Only by freezing the oscillation between the two can you point to one as prominent, but it would be an abstraction.

This example is naturally limited. My point is that Reality is not frozen, but oscillates, moves, grows, and becomes in ways blatant to human experience. "The actual world is a process and that process is the becoming of actual entities," Whitehead states (ibid., 22). Alternatively, "Existence" is not something static but "is activity ever moving into the future" (MT, 169). Between the abstractions of Being *or* Nothingness, therefore, is the processual integration of the two in *Becoming*. In this way, Roland Faber insists rightly that becoming is *older than existence* for Whitehead. "Existence is the 'outcome' of a concrescence of an actual world from which something becomes its existence (as ex-sister means coming-to-be from something else)." Indeed, in Whitehead's "chaosmos," the notion of "existence" does not indicate "a binary opposite with 'nothingness' (as non-existence), but is immanent in 'the evolution of new types of order based on new types of dominant societies'" (TDM, 247, quoting PR, 95). The question remains as to whether it is really conceivable that "Nothing" is the flipside of "Something" when the very reality of the world is that of processual becoming.

Robert Lawrence Kuhn has, nonetheless, felt the weight of Nothing and investigated "its" meaning and mystery for years. Guided by "gut feeling" instead of "complex reasoning," he insists that no argument has ever dislodged him from continuing to think, with Leibniz, that "Nothing, no world, is simpler and easier than any world, that Nothing would have been the least arbitrary and 'most natural' state of affairs" (ME, 258).[9] It is by no means clear, however, that we should *privilege* Nothing in this way. The ontological question itself bows toward Nothingness in affirmation, but thinkers like Nozick have been quick to point to this robust and controversial assumption underlying the very framing of the question. Is it not committed unjustly to the notion that Nothing is the *presupposed natural condition* of things, requiring no explanation at all? It certainly seems so.

> To ask "why is there something rather than nothing?" assumes that nothing(ness) is the natural state that does not need to be explained, while deviation or divergences from nothingness have to be explained by the introduction of special causal factors. There is, so to speak, a presumption in favor of nothingness. The problem is so intractable because any special factor that could explain a deviation from nothingness is itself a divergence from nothingness, and so the question seeks its explanation also. (quoted ibid., 241)

It may be then that James is right. It does appear that there is no "logical bridge" we can cross from Nothing to something. Utter Nothingness remains incredibly dizzying to "imagine." Despite sloppy usages of "nothing" by some physicists, it is not just "physical" things that constitute "something," such that they could *ex hypothesi* be subtracted and Nothingness would then obtain. Utter Nothingness would not just be devoid of mass and energy or space or time, but also quantum laws and fluctuations, and any necessary Platonic-like entities. These would include abstract objects and possibilities, numbers and sets, propositions and universals of a logical or axiological nature, as well as any concrete cosmic actualities like that of "God" conceived in terms of Mind or Value (ibid., 260).

There is then nothing about Nothing that appears "simple," logically digestible, or seemingly possible. "The guiding motto in the life of every natural philosopher should be seek simplicity and distrust it," Whitehead tells us (CN, 104). Nothingness may retain its allure, but it also appears utterly absurd. We can affirmatively adjust Nozick's above intuitions: If there was ever utter Nothingness, it should have always remained so. Hence, the long tradition reigns: *Ex nihilo nihil fit.*

The Mystery of Necessity: Platonic Permanence

Is it any easier to grasp something the *nonexistence of which is not possible*, something that *cannot not exist*? It certainly would not be a "thing" by any conventional understanding, but something abstract and, in a sense, indifferent to the turmoil of time. As soon as you admit something *of necessity* in your metaphysics, Utter Nothingness becomes inconceivable. Leslie seems right in saying that "anything able to explain Why There Is Something Rather Than Nothing—why there is even a single existent—couldn't itself have be an existent. It would have to be an abstraction of some kind" (IM, 176). This would even include explanations of the actuality and necessity of "God" conceived in terms of something like infinite Mentality. We will consider this later. For now, however, necessary abstractions are *not* Nothing either. Although it is mind-bending, it does seem we end up with something like nonphysical, Platonic-like phenomena or abstract requirements as candidates for necessity and therefore essential to any inquiry into the why and whence of things—even divine things.

Leslie is adamant that it would be impossible to "get rid of all realities since some are Platonic realities"; indeed, even if "all things had vanished, countless matters would be real" such as rational, aesthetic, and moral possibilities and truths, and perhaps even creative ethical requirements (ibid.; ID, 1). Is it not the case that if 2 + 2 apples were ever to exist in the future, there would necessarily be 4 apples? Or, if there were three sets of five blue birds, should they ever come to exist, there would be as many bluebirds as five sets of three? If anything were ever to exist, moreover, it would have to exist in a certain *way* and not in no way at all. Leslie reasons further that it may also be real that the complete absence of all things is *better* than something horrific that could have been there instead, say perhaps a world of unalloyed misery.

It is a challenge to disagree when considering this deeply. "Couldn't it be genuinely the case, necessarily and eternally," he asks "that a world of people in mental and physical agony would be worse than no world at all, so that in a situation empty of all people and objects it would be a fact, a reality, that the continued non-existence of the world of agony *was needed or required*" (ID, 1–2, emphasis his).[10] This is a worthwhile thought experiment. We will see in another chapter that what Leslie has called "axiarchism" is the position that the world—or a divine Mind—owes its existence to "ethical requirements"—that of Plato's "Good"—that really are creatively effectual in their axiological demand for goodness.[11]

Leslie's above comments surround necessary truths about possibilities and value even if *nothing ever obtained at all*. This is agreeable for Ward also. It would be "a mistake to say that even possibilities of any sort exist, if there is absolutely nothing"; but "since possibilities will always, eternally exist, there never is absolutely nothing" (GCN, 36). For him, these possibilities are Platonic-like realities or requirements presupposed by the existence of any and all worlds. We thus seem to be faced with different Platonic layers that appear rather "shadowy" in nature, but it may be strongly mistaken to say that they are nothing or nonexistent. Despite materialist attempts to vanquish such realities, we will be considering whether or not Ward's intuitions are sound: "The Platonic reminiscence continues to haunt us . . . the possibility of things is not a mere non-being. It is a potentiality to be. It has some form of existence" (RC, 179). But what kind of "existence" would this be and where? We aim to treat such questions in ensuing chapters.

These insights do have a deeply "Platonic reminiscence." Whitehead reminds us that it is Plato who poses the question, "when he points out that non-being is a form of being, that whatever we can say about things which are not-being is a way of saying that they have being." For Whitehead, Plato "is merely thinking about his forms as including alternative possibilities" (PR, 125). With Ward and Leslie, Whitehead too includes the necessity of abstract Platonic-like phenomena as "eternal objects." These remain indispensable to any approach to the nature and character of things, but they are not sufficient by themselves to be existent, explanatory, or efficacious. This is principally due to Whitehead's commitment to the "ontological principle" (or "Aristotelian principle"), which states that "apart from things that are actual, there is nothing—nothing either in fact or in efficacy." It remains a "contradiction in terms to assume that some explanatory fact can float into the actual world out of nonentity," he insists; rather, "Nonentity is nothingness." The ontological principle can thus be summarized: "No actual entity, no reason" (PR, 41, 46).

We will see in another chapter that Ward is close to Whitehead here with his own "Platonic-Augustinian" proposal, while Leslie diverges with his own extreme form of Platonism. Whitehead's ontological principle, however, is deeply significant to the relationship between the ontological and cosmological questions. Faber points to this directly, saying that "Whitehead's 'ontological principle' exemplifies that the 'ontological question of existence' is integrated into the 'cosmological question of chaos and cosmos,' because 'existence' is now a symbol indicating the becoming of something out of something else of which this new becoming has to take account. Thus, the act of 'existence' is always that of a self-creative becoming" (TDM, 247, emphasis his).

It is important to stress at this point that admitting the reality of Platonic-like phenomena need not suggest "Platonism" if by this it is meant that the world of "forms" is any more *real or excellent in nature*. In an immanent and ever-changing world, the *transcendent* and *unchanging* need not be of highest significance. Like the allure of Nothingness, the Unchanging and Permanent also seduce us. What goes wrong with the Platonic world, Ward righty states, is that the forms are seen as the eminent and "truly real world," while "the world of sense-experience, of personal relationships, of beer and skittles and suffering and love is demoted to a shadowy half-reality." Rather, an alternative view on Ward's account would see the Platonic world as providing the "intelligible structures of this and of infinitely many other possible universes" (GCN, 29). Although such "forms" or "ideas" have been praised throughout the tradition for their "independent existence," they must also have an essential and relational referent to process, as was intuited by Plato, albeit only "intermittently," as Whitehead has stated.[12] While the famous "Ideas" were "the glory of Greek thought to have explicitly discovered," Whitehead remarks, they were also "the tragedy of Greek thought to have misconceived in respect to their status in the universe." For Whitehead then, "independent existence" is the principal "misconception which has haunted philosophical literature throughout the centuries." He is adamant that "there is no such mode of existence"; rather, "every entity is only to be understood in terms of the way in which it is interwoven with the rest of the universe." We will see how Whitehead speaks to this relational doctrine of *interwovenness* in due course. For him, it remains clear that this "fundamental philosophical doctrine has not been applied either to the concept of 'God,' nor (in the Greek tradition) to the concept of 'Ideas'" (Imm., 91).

In following chapters, we will be investigating the mystery of necessary Platonic realties in relation to Mind and Value much more deeply, including their need for some manner of proper integration as is required by ideals of coherence. At this point, however, we are left with there *always having been something*—if only by some kind of Platonic-like necessity. These necessities are to be conceived as metaphysical realities or requirements that are crucial to the reality of anything that *could ever be*. But they are also layered, being associated directly with what seem to be still deeper principles, concepts, or variables necessary for the sustenance of any contingent cosmological context, especially one that gives birth to *Homo Quaerens*.

There must be a *way* things are if there is to be anything at all; and if things are such that they allow thinking and questioning beings to exist, they must be in a *particular way* favorable to this. We must naturally be in a cosmos that is friendly to our possibility and catering to our emergence. With this, one need not insist upon the "anthropic cosmological principle" in its tendency to focus narrowly on the emergence of human beings (*anthropos*) alone, but rather upon what John F. Haught has called the "aesthetic cosmological principle" as that tendency in the universe toward the creation of value and beauty of which human subjective emergence is but one possible expression alongside a myriad of others.[13] These deeper principles would seem metaphysically vital to any kind of context such as ours and include (among others) layered dimensions of aesthetic value including: "Order," "Harmony," "Regularity," "Intensity," "Complexity," "Unity, "Variety," "Multiplicity," "Permanence," "Change," "Creativity," and "Process." It would seem that these are a few of the most obvious principles presupposed and exemplified in human experience. They are in fact evocative of Whitehead's own conviction that "the foundations of the world" are to be found "in the aesthetic experience," and that "all order is aesthetic order." Indeed, "the actual world is the outcome" of a more fundamental "aesthetic order" that metaphysically reigns in the nature of things (RM, 91). It is in this sense that Charles Hartshorne expressed his own Whiteheadian intuitions that "the most general principles of harmony and intensity are more ultimate than the laws of physics and are the reasons for there being natural laws."[14] Put differently, the laws of physics sustaining the endurance of electrons, atoms, and molecules in their own repetitions and intensifications appear to reflect aims at a certain kind of value in the nature of things (RWS, 182).

One might naturally be skeptical of such comments and their motivations, but it is important to grasp again the fundamental questions we are dealing with and the kind of equally fundamental axiological answers that may be required in answering them. The existence of a world presupposes certain conditions. The primordiality of the aesthetic is not simply insignificant or wishful, but actually entangled in much of our scientific endeavors. Not only does science assume "the value of seeking truth for its own sake," Ward tells us that "scientists often appeal . . . to a sense of beauty and elegance, in choosing ultimate theories" (GCN, 10). This should make us pause. Whitehead also remarks, for example, that "the feeling, widespread among mathematicians, that some proofs are more beautiful than others, should excite the attention of philosophers" (MT, 60). Why is this? For many reasons no doubt; but perhaps because aesthetic value offers fundamental inklings into the mystery of things.[15]

Ward reasons correctly, I think, when he states that when scientists seek beauty and elegance, "they seem to commit themselves to saying that the universe exists because it is beautiful, and that might be an ultimate reason for its existence" (GCN, 22). Whitehead would seem to agree. In saying that beauty is the "internal conformation" of interrelated items of experience—those of "Reality" and those of "Appearance"—he affirms that "any system of things which in any wide sense is beautiful is to that extent justified in its existence" (AI, 256).[16] Despite, for example, Steven Weinberg's fundamentally tragic view of the human condition, he nevertheless admits, "There is a beauty in these laws that mirrors something that is built into the structure of the universe at a very deep level."[17] Although he does not take the beauty of a theory to be a signifier of its truth, he nevertheless confirms that "we seek beauty in our theories, and use aesthetic judgments as a guide in our research."[18] We will unpack these intuitions as we proceed further, but it certainly does raise suspicion as to the reason, nature, and character of the universe if something like axiological requirements have a mode of ultimacy or necessity, especially of a kind that is discernable and appreciable by human beings.

What we have come to for now is that whether or not there is any "thing" at all, Reality must in some way be utterly *lush* in terms of necessary metaphysical phenomena, inclusive of a host of Platonic-like realities, including some manner of axiological principles conditioning a *way* things *could be*. If one is committed to something like this picture, as Whitehead, Ward, and Leslie are (albeit, differently), then Absolute Nothingness is an absolute impossibility. We realize, of course, that differences between the way things *could be* and the way things *are* seem myriad beyond imagination. It is remarkable that we do (at least in part) intelligibly discriminate an order and contingency in the way of things. Indeed, the contingency of actuality is perhaps as deep a mystery as the permanence of necessity.

The Mystery of Contingency: Order, Intelligibility, Novelty

It is abundantly clear that there is something—and not simply "something," but temporal activity, regularity, and lawfulness that blatantly bespeaks order, intelligibility, and contingency in our cosmos. Does this just happen to be the case? We should be careful here. Whitehead reminds us, "It is not the case that there is an actual world which *accidentally* happens to exhibit an order of nature. There is an actual world *because there is an order in nature*. If there were no order, there would be no world. Also, since there is a world, we know there is an order" (RM, 91, emphasis mine). The world therefore *presupposes* the concept and reality of order; and it is the mystery of this order, and the novel emergence it conditions, that fundamentally captures Whitehead's attention. "We have to explain the aim at forms of order, and the aim at novelty of order, and the measure of success or failure" (MT, 88).

The universe is truly shocking not only in its order and formational potentiality but also in its rational translucency in being comprehensible by human consciousness. "Nature comes to self-consciousness and responsible self-direction," Ward states, "and so discloses that such things have always been potential in the natural order itself" (PF, 39). Our minds can intelligibly map onto the natural world out of which they donned. In this, we again are reminded to *include* ourselves as particularly intense displays of an ordered and intelligible cosmos. This, in fact, is a fundamental assumption without which science cannot even begin. "There can be no living science unless there is widespread instinctive conviction in the existence of an *Order of Things*, and, in particular, of an *Order of Nature*," Whitehead states. This conviction is nothing short of "instinctive faith that there is an Order of Nature which can be traced in every detailed occurrence" (SMW, 3–4, emphasis his). For Leslie, it is worth noting that science seems unable to answer why the structure of the world is an *orderly one*. "Why do events so often develop in fairly simple and familiar ways, leading us to talk of causal laws?" he asks (ME, 126). For Ward, "There is a mystery about the fact that the material stuff of the universe obeys general laws . . . [w]hy should material particles continue to obey such laws as the inverse square law of gravity, or . . . nuclear particles . . . to the restrictions of the Schrodinger's equation" (GCN, 52)? Where are these laws anyway?

Below all these comments is the shock of the world's regular order and intelligibility to human minds. The world of which we ourselves are apart, and from which we derive information from experience, is not only *describable* but also *understandable*. Thomas Nagel thus states rather confidently that the intelligibility of the world is *not an accident*. "Nature is such as to give rise to conscious beings with minds" and be "comprehensible to such beings." Such intelligibility, moreover, is directly related to the laws that science has revealed, and is itself "part of the deepest explanation of why things are as they are" (MC, 17).

That things are a certain *way* as opposed to any other is precisely the mystery of the cosmological question. We can readily imagine how things could have been different, but the cosmological question does not stop here. Paul Davies is right to say that the "great mystery of contingency is not so much that the world could have been otherwise, but that it is contingently *ordered*." Combined with intelligibility, these "features make the mystery much, much deeper" (TMG, 170). Davies statements remind us of what struck Rescher above as the more "crucial" concern when considering the mystery of existence; namely, why it is there is something *contingent*—something whose existence is *not necessary*. What then is it that is *not necessary*? A few examples of contingency will draw out the cosmological mystery further.

Ian Barbour speaks of the ways in which contingency is at least fourfold in our cosmological context. In the first place, the laws that physics describes appear contingent and even habitual in nature. They could have been different, such that Whitehead below calls them "arbitrary" and even "absurdly limited." What is more, the initial cosmological conditions and constants such as the strong and weak force, gravity, and electromagnetism are hauntingly balanced or "fine-tuned," such that if they had been different, perhaps even slightly, the universe would be unfriendly to the emergence of carbon-based intelligent life.[19]

Indeed, Leslie remarks that physicists and cosmologists "are little inclined to treat our universe's early conditions, and the physical and cosmologically important constants, as brute, inexplicable facts which are to be treated as 'natural' just because they characterize Nature as we find her" (U, 184). Rather, they constitute a grand mystery. Quantum mechanics too has revealed what appear to be fundamentally statistical or uncertain elements in the natural world that are, in principle, unknowable. At a minimum, what this reveals is that complete determinism is not entailed in the natural world; there is an openness, Ward states, suggesting "that indeterminism is a basic feature of the physical universe" (PF, 94). Still deeper, however, is the grand existence of the universe itself when it might otherwise not have existed or at least been radically different on a total scale (TMG, 169).

These are no minor contingencies. Davies, however, insists upon yet another mode of contingency in the "higher level" laws associated with the organizational behavior of complex systems. Mendel's laws of genetics, for example, could not be solely derived from the laws describable by physics. Neither do various laws and regularities associated with chaotic or self-organizing systems depend only upon physical laws. "In many cases," Davies states, "the precise form of the patterns of behavior adopted by these systems depends upon some accidental microscopic fluctuation, and must therefore be considered as undetermined in advance. These higher-level laws and regularities thus possess important contingent features over and above the usual laws of physics" (ibid., 169–70).

When Whitehead considers the cosmological landscape, he points to the "arbitrary" nature of the world's conditions, which reflect "general limitations at the base of actual things." These he refers to as "matter of fact determinations—such as the three dimensions of space, and the four dimensions of the spatio-temporal continuum—which are inherent in the course of actual events, but which present themselves as arbitrary in respect to a more abstract possibility" (SMW, 161). It is these arbitrary or "given elements of the laws of nature" that are at the heart of the mystery of the cosmological question, such that Whitehead insists that they "warn us that we are in a special cosmic epoch" (PR, 91). Our epoch "illustrates one special physical type of order" as seen in the "absurdly limited number of three dimensions of space"; these can be nothing other than "a sign that you have got something characteristic of a special order," he states (ibid., 127).

One is liable to agree with Whitehead. Why indeed *these* limitations as opposed to *any other* that could have been in their place? Such contingencies are themselves layered in ways that are striking. Whitehead insists that the "arbitrary features in the order of nature" are not just "confined to the electromagnetic laws," however.

> There are the four dimensions of the spatio-temporal continuum, the geometrical axioms, even the mere dimensional character of the continuum—apart from the particular number of dimensions—and the fact of measurability.... [T]hese properties are additional to the more basic fact of extensiveness; also, that even extensiveness allows for grades of specialization, arbitrarily one way or another, antecedently to the introduction of any of these additional notions. (Ibid., 91)

These varieties of contingency raise the cosmological question in full force. The order and intelligibility of the world are obvious, as are its movements, decays, and resurrections. It seems wildly unlikely that these *had* to be the way they are or that they unfold in purely deterministic ways. It is largely agreed, of course, that the way of things did have to be this way *if* conscious beings such as ourselves were to emerge. But saying this alone does not erase the mystery of our emergence on the planet. The question of our evolutionary emergence is yet another dimension in the cosmological question.

Evolution and Beginnings

It is well known that balanced cosmological conditions make the evolution of complex carbon-based life *possible*. We still face the mystery, however, of why our universe should be such that it not only *welcomes* such processes but may even *compel* them when constraints are ideal. This is naturally controversial, but the world's fruitfulness in giving rise to radical evolutionary novelty—not least in *Homo sapiens*—is one of the great wonders of the cosmos. "While Darwinian explanations are correct," Leslie insists, "they cannot themselves say why our cosmic environment is of a type in which Darwinian processes can lead to things as remarkable as birds, whales, and human beings" (IM, 190). Indeed, for Ward, natural selection certainly plays a necessary role, but "it is by no means a complete explanation of evolution" (GCN, 75). It seems clear that our cosmic and terrestrial environment is of a "type" in which evolutionary "advance" or "progress" has taken place as new forms are actualized. Is it dangerous to even utter this, however? It is for thinkers like Richard Dawkins and Stephen J. Gould, both of whom insist that the process of evolution is "blind" and devoid of "progress" and "purpose," despite appearances to the contrary.[20] There is no inherent reason, however, why materialist neo-Darwinian conceptions of evolution and nature should hold sway when a host of compelling alternatives overcome their inadequacies.[21]

Despite Gould's oft-repeated claim that rewinding evolution would carry no guarantee of our reemergence, Simon Conway Morris has argued at great lengths that "the constraints of evolution and the ubiquity of convergence make the emergence of something like ourselves a near-inevitability." Although it may seem "contrary to received wisdom and the prevailing ethos of despair," he argues that "the contingencies of biological history will make no long-term difference to the outcome."[22] This is an impressive claim about what may be a truly biocentric imperative in the cosmos. Does this mean that one can discern a "progress" or "purpose" in evolution? We are reminded again that we are not separate from the universe, but (in some sense) complex exemplifications of it.[23] Conway Morris does not walk on egg shells with respect to the question of evolutionary progress. "When within the animals we see the emergence of larger and more complicated brains, sophisticated vocalisations, echolocation, electrical perception, advanced social systems including eusociality, viviparity, warm-bloodedness, and agriculture—all of which are convergent—then to me that sounds like progress."[24] It certainly does sound like progress, especially when we remember that we—having emerged as achievements of evolution in the first place—are the ones making these observations. "The plain fact is that consciousness and purpose do exist, at least in the higher animals," Ward states. "It is therefore not absurd to ask whether purpose is not rooted in the physical structure of being itself" (GCN, 138).

One of the great mysteries of evolution in this regard consists in making sense of its *upward innovations*. For Whitehead, the upward trend of the evolutionary process strongly suggests that it is not simply "survival of the fittest," which is at work. He points out that the question "Why has the trend of evolution been upwards?" is "not the least explained by the doctrine of the survival of the fittest" (FR, 4).[25] Rather, "the problem set by the doctrine of evolution," he states, "is to explain how complex organisms with such deficient survival value ever evolved" (ibid., 2).[26] What Whitehead seems to be suggesting is that the evolutionary process is motivated by criteria which *transcend* mere survival. We see in the process not simply the drive "to live" but also "to live well" and "to live better." In this way, evolutionary advance is grounded first in "being alive," second, in being alive in a "satisfactory way," and third, in acquiring an "increase in satisfaction" (ibid., 5). Put differently, what compels the evolutionary process upward is something like the beckoning of intrinsic Value.

The full "mechanisms" of evolution continue to constitute a series of challenging questions. On a different level, one can still wonder why there should be an evolutionary process at all. As far as we know, evolution is the *only way* to have intelligent life, a world, and a cosmos of any kind resembling our own. Our evolutionary lineage transcends the domains of biology. *Homo sapiens* grew out of the Earth, which grew out of the Milky Way, which grew out of Cosmos as a whole. Not only did prebiotic terrestrial evolution reign for some half-billion years prior to the emergence of life on this planet, advances in cosmology have revealed the ways in which evolution is the grand metanarrative of cosmic history. But how grand is it? Did it *begin* at some point and would this help or hinder the explanatory quest? Different models say different things, and I can only make a few comments relevant to the mystery.

The dominant cosmological model surrounds the "Big Bang," according to which the universe "began" some 13.8 billion years ago. From an initial singularity, the universe expanded, cooled, and evolved into an utter plethora of planetary habitats, some (perhaps many) amenable to the evolution of biodiversity and the advent of conscious intelligence. It is fully conceivable that cosmic evolutionary activity *never* had a "beginning"; it may just *be* the metaphysical condition of the universe, which is infinite in its temporal becoming. Whitehead, writing prior to the advent of Big Bang cosmology, held to the intuitions of Plato and Aristotle: "The creation of the world is the incoming of a type of order" and "not the beginning of finite matter of fact" (PR, 96).[27] While it may be said that our *particular* "cosmic epoch" *did* have a beginning in the so-called Big Bang, an evolutionary process of "actual entities" or "actual occasions" embodying Creativity is a prior and metaphysically necessary feature of any and all and cosmic epochs.[28] In this way, time—the very becoming of actuality—may have a primordial foothold in constituting an evolutionary cosmos. This is perhaps not a dominant view, but it is an open question, as Sean Carroll relays.

> The issue of whether or not there actually is a beginning to time remains open. Even though classical general relativity predicts a singularity at the Big Bang, it's completely possible that a fully operational theory of quantum gravity will replace the singularity by a transitional stage in an eternal universe.[29]

These are fantastic questions and we are free to follow the evidence wherever it may lead us. An *absolute beginning* may indeed by hard to establish, but it is not as if its *absence* would be somehow *unproblematic* in terms of explanation. This is important to remember. It has sometimes been suggested that if the universe *did not* have a beginning, then a requirement for its explanation—and particularly any "divine" explanation—lessens. Steven Hawking thus states, "So long as the universe had a beginning, we could suppose it had a creator. But if the universe is really completely self-contained, having no boundary or edge, it would have neither beginning nor end: it would simply be. What place then for a creator?"[30]

Hawking here is being rather shortsighted and unware of a long philosophical and religious tradition, as both Ward and Leslie have pointed out.[31] The question of whether "the time of this universe" had an absolute beginning is not ultimately relevant as to whether the whole universe is "created" or has an explanation. The fundamental question Ward reminds us is, "Does the universe as a whole exist without having any reason or explanation, or because it has to be the way it is, or because it is brought into being and held in being at every moment by a supra-cosmic creator" (GCN, 16–17)? Despite Hawking's shortsightedness with respect to beginnings, he nevertheless queries, "What is it that breaths fire into equations and makes a universe for them to govern? . . . Although science may solve the problem of how the universe began, it cannot answer the question: Why does the universe bother to exist" (quoted ME, 90)?

That is the haunting question: Why, indeed?

NOTES

1. See, for example, the variety of related axiological concerns in recent texts including: Graham Oddie, *Value, Reality, and Desire* (Oxford: Oxford University Press, 2005); Nicolas Rescher, *Axiogenesis* (AX) (Lanham: Lexington, 2010); Thomas Nagel, *Mind and Cosmos: Why the Materialist Neo-Darwinian Conception of Nature is Almost Certainly False* (MC) (Oxford: Oxford University Press, 2012); Fiona Ellis, *God, Value, & Nature* (Oxford: Oxford University Press, 2014); Sharon Hewitt Rawlette, *The Feeling of Value: Moral Realism Grounded in Phenomenal Consciousness* (Dudley & White, 2016); John F. Haught, *The New Cosmos Story: Inside Our Awakening Universe* (New Haven: Yale University Press, 2017); Robin Attfield, *Wonder, Value and God* (New York: Routledge, 2018); Randall B. Bush, *God, Morality, and Beauty: The Trinitarian Shape of Christian Ethics, Aesthetics, and the Problem of Evil* (Lanham: Lexington, 2019); and Robert Cummings Neville, *Metaphysics of Goodness: Harmony and Form, Beauty and Art, Obligation and Personhood, Flourishing and Civilization* (New York: SUNY, 2019).

2. Whitehead remained adamant that human experience must not be omitted from our study of the world. To do so is to abstract the most intense data the world offers. It is this kind of fallacious thinking that divorces fact from value, mind from matter, and objectivity from subjectivity. A recent Tweet by Neil deGrasse Tyson on March 4, 2019, and response by comedian Norm Macdonald exemplifies the two prongs of this thinking. "The universe is blind to our sorrows and indifferent by our pains," Tyson

states, "Have a nice day." Macdonald responds, "Neil, there is a logic flaw in your little aphorism that seems quite telling. Since you and I are part of the Universe, then we would also be indifferent and uncaring. Perhaps you forgot, Neil, that we are not superior to the Universe but merely a fraction of it. Nice day, indeed." Tyson's comment is perhaps deserving of Whitehead's own refrain: "Scientists animated by the purpose of proving they are purposeless constitute an interesting subject for study" (FR, 12).

3. Martin Heidegger, *An Introduction to Metaphysics* (New Haven and London: Yale University Pres, 1987), 1–2.

4. Two examples of note are that of process philosopher and theologian Roland Faber and public intellectual and philosopher Robert Lawrence Kuhn. For Faber, it was in such thought that he found himself confronted at a young age with the mystery of the universe. "It just happened. I remember the awakening, a sudden, intense consciousness of being-in-the-universe, in the face of its speaking to me, raising the questions of its why and whence. How can anything exist? Is it itself or empty or potentially divine? Is the All all there is? Yet, how could Reality be of and, if at all, beyond itself? And can it (and I in it) act in or on itself? I remember vividly having a metaphysical episode in which such a line of questioning led me to an intense apophatic awareness. Stripping everything away from existence, this experimental awareness left me, in the end, with—not darkness, but singing light. I wanted to become a thinker, from early age on; and I have never stopped striving, at one time, to become one." Roland Faber, "My Faith in Baha'u'llah: A Declaration," *Baha'I Studies Review* 20 (2014): 153. In a similar way, Kuhn recounts a sudden realization that struck him with fright the summer of his twelfth year, "My body shuddered with dread; an abyss had yawned open. Five decades on I feel its frigid blast still. *Why not nothing? What if everything had always been Nothing? Not just emptiness, not just blankness, and not just emptiness and blankness forever, but not even the existence of emptiness, not even the meaning of blankness, and no forever. Wouldn't it have been easier, simpler, more logical, to have Nothing rather than something* . . . Why is there 'Something' rather than 'Nothing?' The question would become my life partner . . . I do not pass a day without its disquieting presence" (ME, 246, italics his).

5. Henri Bergson, *Creative Evolution*, trans. A. Mitchell (New York: Modern Library, 1944), 299–301.

6. Rescher frames Leibniz's question as "Why is there anything at all?" and "Why are things as they are" (AX, 5)?

7. Indeed, Roland Faber insists that Whitehead in a deep sense "abhors nothingness." Roland Faber, *Depths as Yet Unspoken: Whiteheadian Excursions in Mysticism, Multiplicity, and Divinity*, Andrew M. Davis (ed.) (Eugene: Pickwick, 2020), 50.

8. William J. Garland underscores this saying, "*All* explanation, whether ultimate explanation or ordinary explanation, is inherently limited in that it presupposes that something is *there to be explained*. Thus, the question of why there is anything at all has no legitimate answer for Whitehead; it should be ruled out from the beginning as a pseudo-question." William J. Garland, "The Ultimacy of Creativity," in *Explorations*

in the Whitehead's Philosophy, Lewis F. Ford and George L. Kline (eds.) (New York: Fordham University Press, 1983), 222.

9. Kuhn continues further, "I cannot rid myself of the conviction that Nothing would have obtained had not something special somehow superseded or counteracted it. Yes, many well-regarded philosophers say, 'So there's a world not a blank; what's in any way surprising about that?' But I just can't help feeling that they are passing right over the problem most probative of ultimate reality" (ME, 258–59). For Kuhn's detailed taxonomy of Nothing, constituting nine levels of Nothingness moving from the simplest to most absolute, refer to ME, 258–61. For a shorter discussion, see Robert Lawrence Kuhn, "Levels of Nothing: There Are Multiple Answers to the Question of Why the Universe Exists," *Skeptic Magazine* 18, no. 2 (2013): 34–37.

10. Although very different thinkers, it is interesting to consider how Albert Camus might answer Leslie's question. In contrast to Heidegger's "fundamental question of metaphysics," namely, "Why are there essents rather than nothing?," Camus pinpoints suicide. "There is but one truly serious philosophical problem, and that is suicide. Judging whether life is or is not worth living amounts to answering the fundamental question of philosophy." Albert Camus, *The Myth of Sisyphus and Other Essays* (New York: Vintage International, 2018), 3. In a deep sense, both Heidegger and Camus's fundamental questions converge in Leslie's concern for the creative supremacy of Value. Value is not only that which ontologically explains the existence of anything but also that which personally undergirds the worthiness of continued existence. Leslie himself can be seen to consider Camu's question writ large in *The End of the World: The Science and Ethics of Human Extinction* (New York: Routledge, 1996). In contrast to Schopenhauer, for example, who might be said to have made "no obvious mistake when he held that life's miseries were inevitably so great that annihilation would be preferable," Leslie insist that "Schopenhauer is seriously mistaken" and not just "trivially mistaken" (ibid., 161). For a short treatment, see John Leslie, "Why Not Let Life Become Extinct?" *Philosophy* 58, no. 225 (1983): 329–38.

11. For an exhaustive treatment, see Leslie's first book on the topic in *Value and Existence* (VE).

12. "This discussion is a belated reminder to Plato that his eternal mathematical forms are essentially referent to process. This is his own doctrine when he refers to the necessity of life and motion. But only intermittently did he keep it in mind. He was apt to identify process with mere appearance, and to conceive of absolute reality as devoid of transitions. For him, in this mood, mathematics belonged to changeless eternity. He then has accepted tautology" (MT, 93). Faber states that Whitehead's vision was a "direct reversal" of Plato (and what many think central to Platonism) by holding that "the forms in becoming are forms *of* becoming, not essences actualizing themselves in the shadow of matter, but potentials of actualizations exhibited by the character of societies" (TBG, 35). So too Didier Debaise states that Whitehead aims not to recover some kind of purified and original "Platonism" but to introduce elements into Platonic thought to effect a rupture, though in the shape of a return . . . Whitehead asserts a Platonic inheritance by completely inverting the theory of ideas." Didier Debaise, *Speculative Empiricism: Revisiting Whitehead* (Edinburgh: Edinburgh University Press, 2007), 95.

13. John F. Haught, *God after Darwin: A Theology of Evolution* (Boulder: Westview Press, 2000), 128. See also, Haught, *The New Cosmic Story*, 139–41. "The aim toward aesthetic intensity is the central theme of the cosmic story, and subjectivity is the most intense concentration of the cosmic aim toward beauty" (ibid., 140).

14. Charles Hartshorne, "A Replay to My Critics," in *The Philosophy of Charles Hartshorne*, Library of Living Philosophers, Lewis Edwin Hahn (ed.) (LaSalle: Open Court, 1991), 590; quoted in RWS, 182. For an engaging treatment of Whitehead's philosophy through his concept of "intensity," see Judith A. Jones, *Intensity: An Essay in Whiteheadian Ontology* (Nashville: Vanderbilt University Press, 1998).

15. Whitehead thus states, "The ultimate motive power, alike in science, in morality, and in religion, is the sense of value, the sense of importance. It takes the various forms of wonder, of curiosity, of reverence, or worship . . . This sense of value imposes on life incredible labours, and apart from it life sinks back into the passivity of its lower types. The most penetrating exhibition of this source is the sense of beauty, the aesthetic sense of realized perfection" (AE, 40).

16. Alternatively, "For Goodness is a qualification belonging to the constitution of reality, which in any of its individual actualizations is better and worse. Good and evil lie in depths and distances below and beyond appearance. They solely concern inter-relations within the real world. The real world is good when it is beautiful" (ibid., 268).

17. Steven Weinberg, *Dreams of a Final Theory* (London: Vintage, 1993), 194.

18. Steven Weinberg, *To Explain the World: The Discovery of Modern Science* (New York: Harper Perennial, 2015), 14. Weinberg's full quote runs: "There remains a poetic element in modern physics. We do not write in poetry; much of the writing of physicists barely reaches the level of prose. But we seek beauty in our theories, and use aesthetic judgments as a guide in our research. Some of us think this works because we have been trained by centuries of success and failure in physics research to anticipate certain aspects of the laws of nature, and through this experience we have come to feel that these features of nature's laws are beautiful. But we do not take the beauty of a theory as convincing evidence of its truth." For a discussion of the evidential nature of the aesthetic, see S. M. Thomas Dubay, *The Evidential Power of Beauty: Science and Theology Meet* (San Francisco: Ignatius Press, 1999). See also Frank Wilczek's fascinating book *A Beautiful Question: Finding Nature's Deep Design* (New York: Penguin, 2015).

19. See John Barrow and Frank Tipler, *The Anthropic Cosmological Principle* (Oxford: Clarendon Press, 1986); John Leslie, *Universes* (U); *Modern Cosmology & Philosophy* (Amherst: Prometheus Books, 1998); and John Polkinghorne, *Reason and Reality* (London: SPCK, 1991).

20. See Richard Dawkins, *The Blind Watchmaker* (Harmondsworth: Penguin, 1986): "The living results of natural selection overwhelmingly impress us with the appearance of design as if by a master watchmaker, impress us with the illusion of design and planning" (ibid., 21, in PF, 56). For Gould, the notion of "progress" is nothing short of "noxious." "Progress is a noxious, culturally embedded, untestable, nonoperational, intractable idea that must be replaced if we wish to understand the patterns of history." Steven J. Gould, "On Replacing the Idea of Progress with an

Operational Notion of Directionality," in *Evolutionary Progress*, M. H. Nitecki (ed.) (Chicago: University Of Chicago Press, 1988), 319.

21. Refer, for example, to Nagel, *Mind and* Cosmos (MC); Simon Conway Morris, *Life's Solution: Inevitable Humans in a Lonely Universe* (Cambridge: Cambridge University Press, 2003); John B. Cobb Jr. (ed.), *Back to Darwin: A Richer Account of Evolution* (Grand Rapids: Eerdmans, 2008); and David Ray Griffin, *Religion and Scientific Naturalism: Overcoming the Conflicts* (Albany: SUNY, 2000), Ch. 8.

22. Conway Morris, *Life's Solution*, 328.

23. Recall footnote 2.

24. Conway Morris, *Life's Solution*, 307.

25. He continues, "The fact that organic species have been produced from inorganic distributions of matter, and the fact that in the laps of time organic species of higher and higher types have evolved are not in the least explained by any doctrine of adaptation to the environment, or of struggle" (ibid.).

26. "They certainly did not appear because they were better at that game than the rocks around them," Whitehead continues. "It may be possible to explain 'the origin of *species*' by the doctrine of the struggle for existence among such organisms. But certainly this struggle throws no light whatever upon the emergence of such a general type of complex organisms. This problem is not solved by dogma, which is the product of abstract thought elaborating its notions of the fitness of things. The solution requires that thought pay full attention to the empirical evidence, and to the whole of that evidence" (ibid., 2–3). Indeed, compare Whitehead's comments with those of Andreas Wagner in his fascinating book, *Arrival of the Fittest: How Nature Innovates* (New York: Current, 2015): "Common wisdom holds that natural selection combined with the magic wand of random change, will produce the falcon's eye in good time. This is the mainstream perspective on Darwinian evolution: A tiny fraction of small and random heritable changes confers a reproductive advantage to the organisms that win this genetic lottery and, accumulating over time, such changes explain the falcon's eye—and, by extension, everything from the falcon itself to all of life's diversity. The power of natural selection is beyond dispute, but this power has limits. Natural selection can *preserve* innovations, but it cannot *create* them. And calling the change that creates them random is just another way of admitting our ignorance about it. Nature's many innovations—some uncannily perfect—call for principles that accelerate life's ability to innovate, its *innovability*." Wagner quotes Hugo de Vries approvingly, "Natural selection may explain the *survival* of the fittest, but it cannot explain the *arrival* of the fittest" (ibid., 4–5, 15; Wagner's emphasis).

27. According to A. H. Johnson, "Whitehead suggests that in all probability there was no 'first day' of creation. The self-creative process of actual entities is occurring *now*. It did in the past, and it is likely to continue in the future. Whitehead seems to believe that, as far as we can tell, the metaphysical situation has always been as it is now." A. H. Johnson, *Whitehead's Theory of Reality* (New York: Dover, 1962), 72.

28. While many have followed Griffin in saying that Whitehead affirmed a single series of "successive universes" such that there is "only one universe at a time," Faber complicates the discussion in terms of "many worlds" and the multiverse. See David

Ray Griffin, *God Exists But Gawd Does Not: From Evil to New Atheism to Fine-Tuning* (Anok: Process Century Press), 297; Roland Faber, *Divine Manifold* (TDM) (Lanham: Lexington, 2014), Ch. 7; *The Garden of Reality: Transreligious Relativity in a World of Becoming* (TGR) (Lanham: Lexington, 2018), 200.

29. Sean Carrol, "Does the Universe Need God?" in *The Blackwell Companion to Science and Christianity*, James B. Stump and Alan G. Padgett (ed.) (Oxford: Wiley-Blackwell, 2012); quoted in Griffin, *God Exists but Gawd Does Not*, 259. For a compelling argument for the ultimacy of time, see Robert Mangabeira Unger and Lee Smolin, *The Singular Universe and the Reality of Time* (Cambridge University Press, 2015). See also, Donald A. Crosby's recent book *Primordial Time: Its Irreducible Reality, Human Significance, and Ecological Import* (Lanham: Lexington, 2020).

30. Stephen Hawking, *A Brief History of Time* (London: Bantam Press, 1989), 141.

31. "This picture that Hawking presents ignores completely the work of all major religious thinkers, who have agreed that what needs explaining is the nature of the universe as a whole, whether or not it had a beginning" (GCN,16). Leslies agrees and adds detail to Ward's comments, saying, "It is sometimes claimed that this or that quantum theoretical model of creation has got rid of the only location at which a divine creator could appear to have been needed, namely, some first moment of cosmic time . . . When, though, we are trying to answer, Why There is Something, Not Nothing, these various maneuvers might be thought to contribute nothing relevant. Why? . . . [P]hilosophers and theologians, whether or not joining Augustine in thinking that God 'created time and the world together' many years ago, have only rarely held that the divine creative activity would be confined to brining the universe into existence at some particular moment. Aquinas . . . wrote that he universe would have been created by God even if it had existed forever. Descartes was merely following scores of other when he held that the universe would immediately vanish were it not for God's action of 'conserving' its existence" (IM, 194–95).

Chapter 2

Ways of Explaining the Mystery

We have been considering some of the tangled distinctions, layers, and dimensions inherent in asking fundamental questions of existence. Asking the questions themselves offers a rare pleasure to creatures who have consciously woken to their wonder. As *Homo Quaerens* we are wedded to this mystery from the *inside*. Certainly, existence affords far more questions than answers—and there is something deeply comforting in this. "Philosophy begins in wonder," Whitehead assures us; "And, at the end, when philosophical thought has done its best, the wonder remains" (MT, 168).

But we still want to know the truth of things to the extent that it can be known. We want to know whether or not there might be an ultimate perspective on things; we want to know what the reason for things might plausibly be, and how it is they fit together. Truth is of utmost value in this regard. We recognize that it is inherently worthwhile to know the truth of things *precisely because it is true*. That something truly is the case is a presupposition of our existence and experience, but what manner of "Truth" might one possibly come to when met with the mystery of *everything*, and how might it relate to what we have considered thus far?

THE LESLIE-KUHN TYPOLOGY

In turning briefly in this chapter to the different kinds of answers that have been proposed, as well as some of the problems associated with them, I rely on the superb resource compiled by John Leslie and Robert Lawrence Kuhn in *The Mystery of Existence* (ME). This text is the first substantial edited volume addressing the principal philosophical, theological, and scientific ways thinkers have approached the mystery of existence. Given that the book includes some fifty reprints from Plato to Hawking, we will naturally only focus upon a select few core examples and figures exemplifying the kinds of answers available.

Leslie and Kuhn locate a host of thinkers along a typology of five kinds of solutions:

1. A Blank is Absurd
2. No Explanation Needed
3. Chance
4. Value/Perfection as Ultimate
5. Mind/Consciousness as Ultimate

As editors, Leslie and Kuhn readily acknowledge the difficulty of locating particular thinkers along this typology. These basic categories are insufficient to house the complexity and relationality among different attempts to answer fundamental questions of existence. Philosophical and theological history offers all manner of "solutions" to these questions and they often intersect in ways that obscure and haze any clean distinctions. "Attempts to answer '*Why Existence?*' overlap in many intricate ways. They strongly resist being forced into tidy boxes . . . the process of picking the correct section for a particular writer was often little better than tossing a coin, so please attach no great importance to the section headings" (ME, 6). We will begin to point to this "overlap" between the solutions of Value and Mind in particular as we proceed. Despite its categorical limitations, the Leslie-Kuhn typology is nonetheless helpful as an orienting guide into the different kinds of answers available in approaching the ontological and cosmological questions. In briefly treating each in turn, our chief aim is to set the stage for a deeper look into the axianoetic tradition which affirms the ultimacy of both Mind *and* Value in the nature of things, albeit with the possibility of different emphasis or priorities between them. Locating Leslie, Ward, and Whitehead in this tradition will be our principal focus in Part II. For now, however, we survey the five principal "solutions" of the Leslie-Kuhn typology, some figures that exemplify them, as well as some of the concerns or questions they raise for our prime sources.[1]

A Blank Is Absurd: There Had to Be Something

We concluded in the last chapter that a complete Blank, Absolutely Nothing, appears absolutely impossible. There is Nothing here to approach as Whitehead reminded us; and reifying "Nothing" as "Something" through inevitable uses of language only traps us in a fallacy, as Ward highlighted. These convictions are shared by the likes of Henri Bergson and David Lewis, albeit quite differently.

Bergson insists that "part of metaphysics moves, consciously or not, around the question of knowing why anything exists—why matter, or spirit, or God, rather than nothing at all?" With Parfit, he agrees that the ontological question "presupposes that reality fills a void, that underneath Being lies nothingness, that *de jure* there should be nothing, that we must therefore explain why there is *de facto* something." Not only is this presupposition "pure illusion" for Bergson, but absolute nothingness has "not one more meaning than a square circle," such that the "abolition of everything is self-destructive, inconceivable," a "pseudo-idea, a mirage conjured up by our imagination" (quoted ME, 24). There has, therefore, never been an absence of all things. There had to be something, but what is it there had to be?

For David Lewis's "modal realism," what there had to be is *the actuality of absolutely every logically conceivable thing*—albeit not in our world. In collapsing any distinction between the *purely possible* and *actually existing*, Lewis insists that all possibilities conceivable in our world are really *actualities* in countless infinities of other isolated worlds. "There are so many other worlds," he states, "that absolutely *every* way that a world could possibly be is a way that some world *is*" (ibid., 27). This is a remarkably plentitudinous proposal. Far from Nothing being a viable alternative to Something, Something finds ultimate reason in the bewildering fact that everything actually exists somewhere. It seems a large step from the absurdity of Nothingness to the reality of utterly everything conceivable. One is tempted to proclaim that both Absolute Nothingness and the Absolute Existence of Every Conceivable World seem equally absurd and also equally horrific, such that no criterion of Value either releases worlds of beatitude or hinders those of utmost horror from coming into existence.

While Whitehead, Ward, and Leslie agree with Bergson that a blank is indeed absurd, we will see that their fundamental axianoetic commitments deter them from insisting that *all possibilities* are really actualized somewhere. They each hold vital distinctions between the possible and the actual adjudicated by criteria of Value that are operative in their actualization in and as the world. Possibilities are not simply "useful fictions," but Platonic-like necessities in some sense governed toward actualization by virtue of their worth. This holds for human beings as well as for God. While Nothing remains absurd in the face of necessarily existing realities, and ethically dubious in face of the beatitude of what *might have been*, the actualization of all possibilities is nightmarish. We will return to the riddles of the possible and the place of Mind and Value in Part III specifically.

No Explanation Needed: Submission to Brute Fact

Not only is a blank absurd, some have insisted that what there *had to be*—a universe such as ours—has no explanation whatsoever. What could account for this? The answer, it has been argued, is nothing at all. No reason and no explanation are needed. Does it not seem plausible, after all, that something having *always existed* throughout infinite epochs is, *ipso facto*, not requiring of explanation? Both David Hume and Bertrand Russell famously exemplify shades of this kind of approach to the mystery of things.

Hume is adamant that there is no contradiction in the notion that a thing or set of things can begin to exist without reason or cause. It is plausible, he states, "to conceive any object to be non-existent this moment, and existent the next, without conjoining to it the distinct idea of a cause or productive principle" (ibid., 48). What is more, should something have always existed by virtue of an eternal succession of causes, what need then for a big "C" cause? "In such a chain too, or succession of objects, each part is caused by that which preceded it, and causes that which succeeds it" (ibid., 49). For Hume, the "WHOLE" does not need some external cause, since appealing to antecedent causes—even if *ad infinitum*—is sufficient to explain it. If, for example, we were shown the "particular cause of each individual in a collection of twenty particles of matter," Hume thinks "it very unreasonable" should someone then ask after "the cause of the whole twenty." The cause of the whole twenty "is sufficiently explained in explaining the cause of parts" (ibid.). Should it make any significant difference if that "twenty" become an infinity of successive causes that is the unfolding universe itself?

Bertrand Russell holds a similar position on these points. Not only is the question as to the mystery of the universe really without meaning and illegitimate to even pose, he can find no compelling reason why the totality of the universe should require a cause or have a beginning at all. His famous debate with F. C. Copleston reveals a position resonate with that of Hume. "The whole concept of cause," Russell states, "is one we derive from our observation of particular things. I see no reason to suppose that the total has any cause whatsoever." If indeed "the concept of cause is not applicable to the total," then Russell can conclude that "the universe is just there, and that is all" (ibid., 54). The idea that the world must have a cause or must have a beginning, moreover, is simply "due to the poverty of our imagination."[2] It need not require any of these. In the final analysis of things, therefore, both Hume and Russell mandate our submission to Brute Fact.

The problem, however, is that a brute fact is also a "brutal fact" as Michael Heller has provocatively stated. It is brutal because it violates the very endeavors of rationality; namely, "that we should go on asking questions for as long as there is still something left to explain" (ibid., 278). Russell in fact boldly stated that physical science was becoming rather "uninteresting" precisely because it was nearing a complete grasp of the world. "Physical science is thus approaching the stage when it will be complete, and therefore uninteresting. Given the laws governing the motions of electrons and protons, the rest is merely geography—a collection of particular facts telling their distribution throughout some portion of the world's history." "Of this world, uninteresting in itself," Russell states, "man is a part."[3] Yet, if man too is a part of the world, it seems to follow that much in man is also *uninteresting* for Russell. One senses a connection between such a conviction and the illegitimacy he heaps upon questions of ultimate explanation. Indeed, such statements may add some clarity to Whitehead's own claim that despite Russell's giftedness, he was nonetheless "simple minded."[4]

It has hardly been the case that the philosophical tradition easily accepts the sentiments of Hume and Russell on these matters. Hume's account of causality and explanation has been rejected by many philosophers. In him, Whitehead states, we reached the "high watermark of anti-rationalism in philosophy" (PR, 153).[5] Very few physicists would also subscribe to the notion that something like the Big Bang might happen for no particular reason and have no explanation at all. Ward thus speaks deeper to the brutality of brute fact for science.

> To say that such a very complex and well-ordered universe came into being without any cause or reason is equivalent to throwing one's hands up in the air and just saying that anything at all might happen, that it is hardly worth bothering to look for reasons at all. And that is the death of science. . . . The whole of science proceeds on the assumption that a reason can be found for why things are the way they are, that it is the end of science if one finds an "uncaused" event, or one for which there is no reason at all. (GCN, 19)

Ward righty reasons that it seems "odd to think that there is a reason for everything, except for that most important item of all—that is, the existence of *everything*, the universe itself" (ibid., 23). But this is precisely what Human and Russell maintain. The principle of sufficient reason is ultimately groundless against the totality of the cosmos.

As suggested already, the Big Bang may have been preceded by an infinitude of other epochs, contractions, and oscillations. This is held by a variety of physicists today, including Sean Carroll and Roger Penrose. Yet, Leslie is still adamant that these scenarios do not easily escape "a Leibizian reaction." By this, he means that even the existence of an "infinite series of past events couldn't be made self-explaining through each event being explained by an earlier one" (IM, 193).

Leibniz himself offered a helpful example. Suppose a book of geometry owes is particular pattern to the fact that it was copied from an earlier book, which was also copied from an earlier text. If this continued backward infinitely, would we then know *why* the book is about geometry? Clearly, we would not. The whole series of geometry books remains unexplained. Rescher too has stated that it is "deeply problematic—not to say wrong," to think that a *distributive* explanation takes away the need for a *collective* explanation. "After all, to explain the existence and indeed even the placement of the individual bricks," he states, "is not automatically to achieve an explanation of the wall"; this would require explanation not only of "those bricks distributively but also their coordinate copresence in the structure at issue. Only by addressing the aggregate coordination of those bricks can we put onto the agenda the wall that they collectively constitute" (AX, 24). Alternatively, it has even been suggested that the universe could somehow explain itself through some kind of temporal self-creating loop. Leslie, however, uses the example of a time machine in response to these kind of "nonsensical" explanations. "Think of a time machine that travels into the past so that nobody need ever have designed and manufactured it," he states; "Its existence forms a self-explaining temporal loop! Even if time travel made sense, this would surely be nonsense" (IM, 194).

Chance: Wild Assortments of Quantum Probability

Perhaps everything can be accounted for by virtue of chance probabilities associated with quantum fluctuations, gravity, and cosmic inflation. Our massive universe may have emerged from sparse amounts of particulate matter-energy, fragments of "space-time foam," or a single point, all governed by the pseudo-providence of statistical law and probability. Physicists and cosmologists have suggested a variety of these kinds of proposals (ME, 71). They have supposed, moreover, that the universe was likely subject to quantum effects in its infancy. Having been minute enough, it very well may have been propelled into existence by the determinations of probabilistic laws and quantum fluctuations. Having at one point zero net energy, chance fluctuations could have very well granted it existence out of the "nothingness" of quantum vacuum fields in extremely low-energy states (GCN, 39).

There is no fundamental consensus on these proposals. The cosmological model of Hawking and Hartle supposes that the universe arises boundary-free "quite literally out of nothing" due to initial net zero energies, coupled with quantum gravity, inflation, and the majestic mathematical background of "imaginary time." These are no simple matters and they are certainly not "nothing." Ward remarks that it requires "pre-existent Hilbert spaces, quantum operators, Hamiltonians, imaginary numbers and other mathematical entities which are, if anything, more mysterious than the existence of the space-time universe itself" (ibid., 41). Where Leslie admits that the notion of time zero inflation producing a no-boundary universe *ex nihilo* is "altogether questionable," Ward insists that the "conceptual problems of such a model are enormous" (ME, 73; GCN, 41).

What is essential for the Hawking-Hartle model is the claim that the universe is self-contained as a whole such that there is no external event or Divine cause needed to set it off. We touched on the problems with these assumptions in the last chapter. We saw that Hawking still asks after the fire-breathing mystery of equations applicable to reality, and that "ultimate beginnings" are beside the point. There is no doubt that chance and probability will play an essential role in a universe which appears freely creative and not utterly determined by antecedent causes, but this does not answer the question as to why all the cosmological ingredients—timeless mathematical entities, quantum laws and events, infinitudes of possibility, and aesthetic domains of order—should already be there. The operations of probability and chance already presuppose lush realities rendering a universe such as ours possible.

Alex Vilenkin is quite confident that the universe could be produced out of the "nothing" of quantum chance and quantum tunneling. Such a "nothing," however, must already bow in obedience to the laws of quantum physics (ME, 74). Vilenkin himself admits that the picture he paints of "quantum tunneling from nothing" effectively raises this deeper question. "The tunneling process is governed by the same fundamental laws that describe the subsequent evolution of the universe. It follows that the laws should be 'there' even prior to the universe itself," he states. Put differently, these laws may not simply be *descriptive* in nature, but have a *prescriptive independence* of their own. Vilenkin is right to recognize something of a *mysterium tremendum et fascinans* here. Many scientists, philosophers, and theologians have recognized this. "In the absence of space, time, and matter, what tablets could" such laws "be written on?" Valenkin quires. "The laws are expressed in the form of mathematical equations. If the medium of mathematics is the mind, does this mean that mind should predate the universe? This takes us far into the unknown, all the way to the abyss of great mystery" (quoted ME, 97–98).

The Ultimacy of Value: Creative Axiological Requirements

Yet another solution to the mystery of existence involves something like the creative supremacy of Value. Leslie asks us to consider deeply whether or not "good" and "bad" transcend subjective matters of individual taste. Could it not be that these are in some sense metaphysically preeminent in the nature of things and not simply clever *inventions* in a world otherwise devoid of objective values and ideals? Could "better and worse" or "importance," as Whitehead states, involve "ultimate notions as they occur in daily life" (MT, 1)? If so, this would not be insignificant for attempts to pierce the mystery of existence. Leslie reasons that it could truly be a reality that "a thing, if it were to exist all by itself, could in some cases be *absolutely better than a blank*: than an absence of all things." Whether something existed or not, "the need for one or more good things—the need for a divine mind, perhaps, or the need for a good cosmos—might then always be 'there,' eternally and unconditionally real," he states (ME, 101). Nevertheless, could "ethical needs" or abstract notions of "Goodness" or "Value" really be *creatively responsible* either for the necessity of "God" or the Universe, or indeed, both? Could such things exist simply because it is supremely good that they should—the *need* itself eternally procuring the reality needed? In this way, the ultimate reason for something to exist may be grounded in the fact that it is "intrinsically valuable that it should exist," as Ward has stated (RC, 195), or because it is metaphysically "best," as Rescher holds (AX, 36).

This is a compelling, but also deeply challenging, axiological proposal with a long-standing place within Western philosophical and theological thought.[6] The creative supremacy of Value can be traced back to the Greeks, particularly to Plato's notion of "The Good," which reigns supreme among the forms as that which is *beyond* existence, but nevertheless *bestows* existence on all things. The Good "not only infuses the power of being known into all things known," Plato tells us, "but also bestows upon them their own being and existence, and yet The Good is not existence, but lies far beyond it in dignity and power" (quoted ME, 109). Plato argued, moreover, that "if anyone desired to find out the cause of the generation or destruction or existence of anything, he must find out what state of being or doing ... was best for that thing." They must "look for the power which in arranging things as they are arranges them for the best" (ibid., 109–10). In considering the mystery of things, Aristotle thinks it unlikely that "fire or earth or any such element should be the reason why things manifest goodness and beauty both in their being and in their coming to be." Neither is the spontaneity of chance compelling in considering "so great a matter"; rather, "the cause of all good is the good itself." On the principle of The Good "depend the heavens and the world of nature," he states (ibid., 110–11). Plotinus too continues his own elaborate version of this tradition where The Good or One is "that on which all else depends as to their source and their need, while Itself is without need" (ibid., 111).

Such a perspective, as Leslie presents it, banks not only upon the notion that there are *objective axiological domains* framing existence and experience but also that some are *creatively effectual* in actually bringing things about. Both of these notions are hotly debated. On the one hand, objective values have been dismissed on both ontological and epistemological levels as far too "queer" to exist, let alone be grasped by purely physical human creatures. On the other hand, even if they did exist, one does struggle to see how something as abstract as the "Good" or "Value" could *do* anything at all, such that *reasons* might plausibly be associated with them. A variety of thinkers have offered these critiques, not least, Whitehead and Ward. For many philosophers, it is not *prima facie* clear that "ethical needs," "the best," or other abstract axiological needs or requirements can be creatively effective *on their own*. Regardless, Leslie insists that although "logic could never prove it, the [ethical] requirement has a creative success that is necessary in an absolute fashion." "What gives it success?" he asks; the answer: "Nothing" (ID, 87). Still, one wonders whether ethical abstractions are any more liable to act creatively than abstractions of mathematics. Does not fire need to be breathed into them as well? "The idea seems strange," Davies admits; "how can 'ethical requirement' create a universe" (TMG, 171)? However strange, we will see in Part II that the creative supremacy of Value has a long and venerable tradition, of which Leslie, Ward, and Whitehead are all part. But it has *not* been so clear that it stands on its own or is "without need."

The Necessity of Mind: The Noetic Rootedness of All Reality

Is there a place in reality for a permanent Mentality, the eternal necessity of which grounds (in some way) not only its own existence but also the existence of all things—even abstract Platonic-like things of a presumably nonphysical and ideational character? Does "God" in this sense exist? If so, what is the nature of divine necessity? If God is the ultimate reason, then what reasons or explains God, and what is God's nature like? Such questions have been diversely expressed throughout the philosophical and religious tradition. Contrary to popular belief, Ward has argued correctly that the Western classical tradition has, on the whole, accepted the reality of God's existence as a kind of nonphysical Mentality or Spirit whose necessity erects the stop sign of explanation (refer to GP; GGP). Yet, while the notion of "necessary existence" appears essential to any approach to ultimate explanation in this regard, it has not always been clear what "necessary existence" actually involves.

Richard Swinburne has argued that God is "a non-embodied person" and "spirit" whose nature is utterly simple. This divine person *cannot not exist* due to the eternal necessity of the divine nature. "Theism postulates God as a person with intentions, beliefs, and basic powers, but ones of a very simple kind, so simple that it postulates the simplest kind of person that there could be," he states (quoted ME, 147). For Swinburne, to say that God's existence is *necessary* is to insist that the "existence of God is a brute fact that is inexplicable—not in the sense that we do not know its explanation, but in the sense that it does not have one" (ibid., 149). Indeed, an "ultimate explanation," he states, is a complete explanation whose ultimate terms have "no explanation either full or partial in terms of any other factors." They are "ultimate brute facts."[7]

Neither divine simplicity nor reasonless brute explanation, as Swinburne pronounces them, seems very helpful in the quest for ultimate explanation. Although he insists that the simple is more likely to obtain than the complex, Ward can "find no reason whatever to suppose that is true, in absence of some prior presupposition." Could there not have been still simpler explanations than a cosmic mental "person" who brings the world into being—especially if Brute Fact has a place in the scheme of things? Is there any more simple a hypothesis, for example, "than that there are one or two ultimate physical laws and an initial state such as is posited by the big bang theory, from which all things develop by random" (RCG, 97)? Not only does it seem implausible to say that the "necessary and incomprehensibly great creator of all is a very simple being," it is not clear for Ward that it would "not be simpler to eliminate him from the scene altogether" (ibid.).

Leslie also shares these general sentiments. A "divine person" knowing omnisciently the infinitude of mathematical facts is "*in some sense at least* infinitely more complex than any human mind.*" Despite how one defines "simplicity," he points out that God, according to Swinburne, is "less simple than a blank." What is "simple" on Swinburne's account is really what is *next simplest* following the utter simplicity of a blank. Leslie concludes, therefore, that Swinburne's deity is not all that simple after all (ME, 143). This all assumes, of course, that a Blank truly is simple—let alone possible—which is not obviously the case, as discussed already. Whitehead would remind us that it is *not only* in scientific or philosophical matters that we should "seek simplicity and distrust it" but also in theological matters; for "the various doctrines of God," he insists, "have not suffered chiefly from their complexity. They have represented extremes of simplicity, so far as they have been formulated by the great rationalistic religions" (RM, 65).[8]

The brutality of brute fact for science should not be *any less* brutal for theology. Why should God be the great exception to explanation in this regard? Leslie has argued unwavering against the conclusion that the existence of the world can be explained by pointing to a "divine person" whose own existence and attributes *have no reason or explanation at all* (ID, 83). Indeed, it is not clear that this can help us in any way. Weinberg thus asks, "If you believe God is the creator, well, why is God that way?" He insists that the "religious person is left with a mystery which is no less than the mystery with which science leaves us."[9] Nagel makes a similar point, saying, "So long as the divine mind just has to be accepted as a stopping point in the pursuit of understanding, it leaves the process incomplete, just as the purely descriptive materialist account does" (MC, 21). What then are we left with? Ward would give us two options: either God cannot at all be accounted for, such that the existence and nature of God "just happens to be the case" without reason or explanation, or the divine nature in some way reasons its own existence so that the callousness of brute fact is avoided (RC, 195). This is a question as to the proper understanding of explanation and necessity, and it is applicable to both physics and theology. For a comprehensive understanding of the world, Nagel insists that "it would have to be the case that either the laws of physics, or the existence and properties of God . . . cannot be conceivably other than they are." He states, moreover, that "the interests of theism even to an atheist is that it tries to explain in another way what does not seem capable of explanation by physical science" (MC, 21–22).

When Whitehead considers the layers of enduring stability forming the order of nature, he is not impressed with summary answers that refer nature to some transcendent and unexplained divine reality lying behind it. Instead, it may be that attention to *what* nature is can actually offer insight into the depths of its *why*.

> This reality occurs in the history of thought under many names, The Absolute, Brahma, The Order of Heaven, God . . . any summary conclusions jumping from our conviction of the existence of such an order of nature to the easy assumption that there is an ultimate reality which, in some unexplained way, is to be appealed to for the removal of perplexity, constitutes the great refusal of rationality to assert its rights. We have to search whether nature does not in its very being show itself as self-explanatory. By this I mean, that the sheer statement, of *what* things are, may contain elements explanatory of *why* things are. Such elements may be expected to refer to depths beyond anything which we can grasp with a clear apprehension. (SMW, 92; emphasis mine)[10]

These statements are worthy of careful consideration. What could these explanatory *depths* possibly be? Whitehead's use of "nature" here appears inclusive of the tangled reality of all things in his cosmology. The "total metaphysical situation" includes the Universe of Actualities, Inherent Creativity, Platonic Realities, and God. We are drawn back to ourselves and our own experience yet again; for if *what* things are—if what *we are*—are *value-expressions* of the universe, might not this suggest that axiological "elements"—even if abstract—do carry a kind of ultimate explanatory role in *why* things are—even of why God is? Might not Bernard Loomer be correct when he reasons that "our deepest and dearest convictions concerning value and the 'way of things'" might "penetrate to the very heart and mind of the 'why of things,'" such that the "innermost secret of the world is decisively disclosed in the very structure of the world"—a structure presupposing some depth of axiological order?[11] Whitehead, Ward, and Leslie, as we will later see, are rather close here.

As mentioned above, it has not always been clear how abstract realities or requirements might aid or hinder the explanatory quest, and how they might relate to a divine Mind. William Lane Craig has argued that God is a transcendent Mentality, which creates the universe and which carries its own explanation "in the necessity of its own nature" (quoted ME, 158). For Craig, the universe is by definition inclusive of all physical reality such that the "cause" of the universe must be understood as transcending space, temporality, and physicality. As such, there seem to be only two candidates of things under which such a description would fall: "either an abstract object (like a number) or else a mind (a soul, a self)." Craig, however, insists that "abstract objects don't stand in causal relations. This is what it means to be abstract." The number 9, for example, does not seem capable of doing anything at all. "So if the universe has an explanation of its existence," Craig concludes, "that explanation must be a transcendent, unembodied Mind which created the universe—which is what most people have traditionally meant by the world 'God'" (ibid., 157).

Nevertheless, Leslie points out that when Craig insists that God is explainable by *the necessity of the divine nature*, he seems to be introducing something "markedly abstract." He appears "to have in mind an absolute requirement, a requirement whose power was inevitable, that a being having God's characteristics *be more than a mere possibility*" (ME, 144–45). Such a requirement, it does seem, would be likened to something like an abstract requirement. The question would then surround how such abstract realities relate to this divine Mind. Leslie's own extreme axiarchic Platonism does not ultimately view mathematical truths, or truths about possibilities of value, as dependent upon divine Mentality (or any mentality for that matter). They would be just as true even if no minds existed at all. Only in this way does he hold that God finds some manner of eternal axiological explanation. This position, however, is strongly objectionable to Craig and particularly questionable for both Ward and Whitehead, as we will see.[12] What is more, it raises a still deeper question as to the *relationship* between Mind and Value that has yet to be posed.

RELATIONALITY AND ULTIMACY

In both this and the previous chapter, we have focused principally upon the different distinctions, layers, and dimensions inherent in asking fundamental questions of existence. From the ontological question to the cosmological question, and from questions of nothingness and necessity to those of contingency, evolution, and beginnings, the mysteries of existence continue to persist for *Homo Quaerens*. These mysteries are not without proposed solutions—and some appear more compelling than others. In surveying the principal kinds of solutions, as well as some key problems associated with them, we have found our way into the mysteries of Mind and Value as the central focus of our inquiry into ultimacy and explanation. The question as to their *mode* of relationality must now be briefly posed as it frames the journey ahead.

We can approach this question in the following way: If abstract axiological requirements are in some sense conceptually grounded in and as dimensions of the divine Mind itself—even if not identical to it—then one might still plausibly make sense of the notion that God lives by an abstract necessity of the divine nature. Leslie readily admits, after all, that the necessity of a divine Mind may be due to the *eternal success* of an abstract ethical requirement for this Mind to exist. Although distinct, the abstract ethical requirement *for the existence of this Mind* and *the success of this Mind actually existing* are *never actually separable*. The question then emerges as to how they relate and why it is we should privilege an axiological requirement over the Mind? Could we not just as well insist upon the Mind as essential for the requirement *just as the requirement is essential for the Mind*? If so, might this not help address the difficulties thinkers have raised as to how abstract objects or requirements *can exist and be creatively effectual*, on the one hand, and how the necessity of God's existence *can be explained or reasoned*, on the other? If so, privileging either one or the other may itself be *abstraction* from a more fundamental kind of *mutuality* that obtains between them. Indeed, while Leslie tends to privilege abstract Value for the existence of a divine Mind—even infinite Minds—Ward tends to privilege concrete divine Mentality for the existence and efficacy of Value. We will see in Part II that these are, in fact, two different ways of *reading* or *emphasizing* fundamental intuitions of the philosophical tradition. Whitehead, however, may be able to remedy these abstract tendencies by pointing to a kind of *relationality* between Mind and Value, such that they are *equally requiring of the other for their own existence*.

That the mystery of God, the Universe, and existence might find "solution" not simply in the ultimacy of *one* thing, reality, condition, or the other but rather in a *kind of relationality* among these is not overtly treated in Leslie and Kuhn's typology. Nevertheless, this is yet another kind of robust answer to the mystery of things that deserves careful attention. Not only might it shed light on the reason and mystery of "God" but also on the reason and mystery of the world, and how it relates to God. In fact, the theological depths of the philosophical tradition have, on the whole, recognized that the reign of both Value and Mind *together* is in some way essential to approaching the mystery of divine necessity. This relationship, however, has not always been expressed clearly. Whitehead, Ward, and Leslie are a part of this tradition. We turn now to the ways in which they mutually cast new light upon old insight.

NOTES

1. For an interactive discussion of these "solutions," refer to Kuhn's *Closer to Truth* Episode # 1213, titled "Why Anything at All?"
2. Bertrand Russell, *Why I am Not a Christian* (New York: Touchstone, 1957), 7.
3. Ibid., 49.
4. Despite a mutual respect emerging from their ten-year collaborating on *Principia Mathematica*, Whitehead and Russell would have a falling-out and develop drastically different worldviews. Charles Hartshorne gives a sense of their clash when he cites Whitehead saying, "Russell is the most gifted English man alive. Russell doesn't understand the importance of the past, or of tradition, and—he *won't* qualify. Bertie says that I am muddle headed, but I say that he is simple minded. Seek simplicity and mistrust it." Charles Hartshorne, *Insights and Oversights of the Great Thinkers: An Evaluation of Western Philosophy* (Albany: SUNY, 1983), 255.
5. "But Hume, in so far as he is to be construed as remaining content with two uncoordinated set of beliefs, one based upon the uncritical examination of our sources of knowledge, and the other on the uncritical examination of beliefs involved in 'practice,' reaches the high watermark of anti-rationalism in philosophy; for 'explanation' is the analysis of coordination" (ibid).
6. See, for example, the different proposals in Scott MacDonald (ed.), *Being and Goodness: The Concept of Goodness in Metaphysics and Philosophical Theology* (Ithaca: Cornell University Press, 1991).
7. Richard Swinburne, *The Existence of God*, second edition (Oxford: Clarendon, 2004), 79; Cf. Ward, RCG, 7.
8. Whitehead had a rather complicated relationship with theology. Lucian Price reports that, over nearly a decade, during his Cambridge period, "he was reading theology. This was all extracurricular, but so thorough that he amassed a sizable theological library. At the expiry of these eight years he dismissed the subject and sold the books. A Cambridge bookdealer was willing to give quite a handsome figure for the collection. It then appeared that the pay must be taken in books at his shop. So he went on an orgy of book-buying until he had overdrawn his account." Lucian Price, *Dialogues of Alfred North Whitehead* (Jaffrey: David R. Godine, 2001), 6. However long Whitehead's "dismissal" of theology lasted, he would nevertheless return to theological conviction. For insight into this journey, refer to Victor Lowe, "A.N.W.: A Biographical Perspective," *Process Studies* 12/3 (1982): 137–47.
9. "Steven Weinberg, on *Closer to Truth: Cosmos, Consciousness, God* (PBS/public television episodes "Why is there Something Rather than Nothing?" and "Arguing God's Existence," at https://www.closertotruth.com/contributor/steven-weinberg/profile.
10. Speaking alternatively on the grounds of explanation, Whitehead states, "Any proof which commences with the consideration of the character of the world cannot rise above the actuality of this world. It can only discover all the factors disclosed in the world as experienced. In other words, it may discover an immanent God, but not a God wholly transcendent. The difficulty can be put this way: by considering the world we can find all the factors required by the total metaphysical situation; but we cannot

discover anything not included in this totality of actual fact, and yet explanatory of it" (RM, 59–60). Thomas Hosinski states that this "can be regarded as Whitehead's revision of the principle of sufficient reason." In his own words, "To seek 'behind' the system for some one radically transcendent 'ground' of the whole system (e.g., God as creator in an absolute sense) is to abandon the rational hope for metaphysical coherence." Thomas Hosinski, *Stubborn Fact and Creative Advance: An Introduction to the Metaphysics of Alfred North Whitehead* (Lanham: Rowman and Littlefield, 1993), 213, 223, n. 7.

11. William Dean and Larry E. Axel (eds.), *The Size of God: The Theology of Bernard Loomer in Context* (Georgia: Mercer University Press, 1987), 25.

12. For Craig's treatment of abstract objects and the challenges of "Platonism," see William Lane Craig, *God and Abstract Objects: The Coherence of Theism: Aseity* (Cham: Springer: 2017); William Lane Craig, *God over All: Divine Aseity and the Challenge of Platonism* (Oxford: Oxford University Press, 2016).

Part II

DIVINE NECESSITY AND THE AXIANOETIC TRADITION

Chapter 3

Axiarchism

The Creative Supremacy of Value

What John Leslie has termed "axiarchism" refers to those traditions or theories that conceive the universe as "ruled largely or entirely by Value" (ME, 6).[1] This designation is admittedly vague and covers a variety of axiologically based doctrines as to the existence and nature of things. These could range from positions espousing the existence of a creative and benevolent deity to those that simply see things as in some way enlivened by desires for goodness. Leslie's own contribution has been to see the "universe as a product of a directly active ethical requirement, a requirement which *as a matter of fact* proved sufficient to create things" (ibid., emphasis his). While this may seem the most "straightforward" or "thoroughgoing" variety of axiarchism, Leslie has also spoken to its deep theological appeal and the ways it casts new light upon a long-standing tradition of philosophical theology.

Should axiarchism include talk of "God," it can do so in different ways. One way is that of "extreme axiarchism," which, at a minimum, might only refer to the "principle that some set of ethical needs is creatively powerful." The notion of "God-as-a-person" would, in this case, only be a kind of theopoetic mythology personifying this abstract principle. But this is not the only "theological" touchstone of extreme axiarchism, and certainly not the most dominant in the tradition. Beyond this reductionist rendering, is a still deeper dimension of theological relevance. Leslie grants that "extreme axiarchism" might well be *joined* with the belief in God, conceived not as an abstract principle, but as an individual supreme in perfection—a divine Mind—whose own existence "might be supremely needful." Conceiving this Individual or Mind as having an "ethical side to it," he states, might render plausible a long tradition insisting that the necessity of divine existence consists, in some way, in God having the eternally sufficient ground for divine existence *within* the divine Self. In this case, God's existence is required ethically because the divine nature *is what it is* (ibid., emphasis mine). Put differently, this ethical requiredness "would have its sources *in* that mind's own tremendously rich nature," so that it would be misleading to say that something outside or exterior to God rendered God existent (IM, 156; emphasis mine). Leslie's insights here are ingenious and may truly render the notion of necessary divine existence cogent in ways that inexplicability, brute power, or logic simply cannot. Nevertheless, compelling questions still remain.

THE QUESTION OF RELATIONALITY

Key questions in particular surround the mode of relationship between Mind and Value in God. It seems to me that once one insists with Leslie that the divine nature "is what it is," or that abstract Value requirements or needs *interior* to divine Mentality are *inseparable* from the eternal reality of that Mind's actual existence, then the question as to the *relationality* and *priority* between Value and Mind can be explicitly posed. My goal in this and next two chapters is to pose such questions by showing the ways in which much of the tradition of Western philosophical theology is *axianoetic* in nature, insisting upon the necessity of *both Value and Mind* when facing the mystery of divine necessity. This tradition, however, is rather ambiguous as to the *kind of relationship* these two divine domains have to each other. I base this discussion in the distinctive ways in which Leslie, Ward, and Whitehead attend to this tradition.

In this chapter, we find that Leslie's concern for "extreme axiarchism" tends to tilt his interpretation of the tradition toward the ultimacy of Value (including his reading of both Ward and Whitehead). In the following chapter, we find that Ward's concern for "Idealism" tends to tilt his interpretation of the tradition toward the ultimacy of Mind (including his reading of both Leslie and Whitehead). The "tend to" in these comments is important, for Leslie also has an essential place for Mind, just as Ward has an essential place for Value. Both recognize the ways that Value and Mind complement each other. Both also express resonances and appreciation (if also some criticism) of each other's work, and also that of Whitehead. Still, we will see that their foundations are carved from respective axiarchic and idealistic *priorities*. Arguably, these emphases are equally present in the tradition and are brought together in the question of Value's relation to Mind and Mind's relation to Value. The tradition, I claim, can be read more *relationally* and *holistically* in terms of this relation: not as axiarchic or idealistic but as *axianoetic*.

But what kind of relationship might obtain between Value and Mind and how might it be expressed? Coupled with Leslie and Ward's insights, chapter 5 then looks to Whitehead's profoundly relational vision and the way it aids us in conceiving how it is that Value and Mind might reciprocally relate in God. This ultimate metaphysical relationship he names "mutual immanence." Insight into this relationship, he claims, is nothing short of a metaphysical gift (and discovery) of the theological tradition, but also broadly applicable outside it. Even if Whitehead himself did not express the relation of Value and Mind explicitly in this way, we will find that thinkers like A. C. Ewing have done so in ways I think strongly acceptable to Whitehead, as well as to Ward, and perhaps also Leslie. What is more, it is this relationality that arguably undergirds the proposals of John Polkinghorne, Mark Wynn, Hugh Rice, and Peter Forrest who have also entered the discussion. What emerges from an affirmation of mutual immanence, I suggest, is a deeper vision into the mystery of divine necessity, founded *neither* on the Abstract priority of Value over Mind (Leslie) *nor* on the Concrete priority of Mind over Value (Ward), but rather in their mutually reinforcing entanglement. We will find, moreover, that this entanglement is not only one of mutual immanence but also that of mutual transcendence in terms of the respective functions Mind and Value each offer each other.

While Part I principally targeted some of the different distinctions, layers, and dimensions inherent in *any mode of existence*, as well as surveyed some of the "solutions" offered, Part II now specifically targets the mystery of *divine existence* in terms of the relationality between Mind and Value. Leslie, Ward, and Whitehead remain differently wedded to a diversely axianoetic tradition of philosophical theology. The mutual immanence of Value and Mind might aid us not only in grasping theirs and others intuitions regarding divine necessity more deeply; it might also illuminate this tradition anew. We turn first to Leslie.

LESLIE'S AXIARCHIC PRIORITY

John Leslie's principle contribution to philosophical theology has been a robust argument for—and defense of—the notion that Platonic "Value," "Goodness," or "ethical needs" and "requirements" might themselves be effectual in "creating" the entirety of things: those diversely terrestrial, those cosmic and multiversal, and those noetically divine. Using language of Value "creating" as Leslie does can be misleading. Popular perspectives often portray "creation" as essentially meaning: *before which something was not*. Despite some suggestive statements in this regard, this is not at all what Leslie intends. As we saw in the Part I, "creation" rather has a wider hierarchical meaning in reference to *ultimate priority* and *not chronology*.[2] To speak of "creation" of the divine Mind by Value then is simply a way of making sense of the divine Mind's "necessary existence" and the ultimate status of Value in eternally grounding this existence. Such a notion, Leslie rightly claims, is "unoriginal" and far from new. Indeed, in his own way, he details the "huge influence which the doctrine of a Reign of Value" has exerted both in previous centuries and in modern developments. Axiarchism, he insists, "has immensely influenced both religion and philosophy," but "nobody stands out as having done special justice to it" (VE, 195). Leslie's own contributions aim to fill this lacuna. Below, we look briefly to key figures he locates in the Axiarchic tradition, from Greek philosophical lineage, to medieval theological expression, to an amalgam of modern voices, including those of Whitehead and Ward.

The Greek Axiarchic Lineage

Plato holds a preeminent place in Leslie's axiarchic universe. The *Republic* as Leslie interprets it can strongly suggest that The Good by itself, although far transcending existence in both its "dignity and power"—even that of Mind's existence—is that which "bestows existence on all known things" (quoted ME, 109). This, for Leslie, can certainly sound as if Plato "is suggesting that ethical needs—needs for good things to exist, realities which are themselves too abstract to be 'things that exist'—directly account for why there is a cosmos, not a blank" (ibid., 101). In the *Timaeus*, we are told that "God wished all to be good" in bringing order to chaos in the creation of the world. That which God *wills*, however, might very well be that *through which* God exists. Indeed, the upmost goodness of God's existence could be a "factor that itself explained why God exists," Leslie states (ibid., 102).

In interpreting the *Phaedo*—particularly Plato's comments on Anaxagoras—Leslie finds the ethically "best" rising to the top. Here, Plato recounts his delight in Anaxagoras's notion that "mind was the disposer and cause of all." If this was the case, Plato reasons that "mind will dispose all for the best." He stresses that he could not imagine that Anaxagoras "would give any other account" of the being of things, "except that this was best." Nevertheless, Anaxagoras, "altogether forsaking mind," made recourse not to the best, but to air, ether, water, and "many other eccentricities." He in fact failed to "look for the power which in arranging" things, "arranges them for the best," and he never reflected that it "is really the good and the right which holds and binds things together" (quoted ME, 108). With this, Leslie can return to the *Republic*, which he insists "makes clear that goodness, rather than minds loves of it can be immediately effective" in infusing all things with the "power of being" (VE, 209).

In reading Plato in this heavily axiarchic way, Leslie also readily acknowledges other "charitable" readings of his works. It's well known that Plato's thought is not clearly systematized and open to a variety of emphases and interpretations. Leslie's reading is certainly not wrong; to the contrary, it is ingenious. Still, it is strongly colored by his concerns for what he *wants* Plato to say. He's not alone here either; Plato's words have led "hundreds of philosophers" (including perhaps Ward and Whitehead) "to think the sorts of things that they certainly sound as if suggesting," namely that "ethical" or "axiological" reasons for the existence of things could be a reality even if "there existed nobody who could do anything about it" (ME, 102). This, however, may be quite different from saying that ethical realities can themselves be *creatively efficacious* such that reasons can be attached to them. These ethical realities may very well ground the existence of God, but in Leslie's reading of Plato, they also transcend the domain of mind.

He draws similar conclusions in the thought of Aristotle. Aristotle continues and transforms the insights of Plato, picturing all movement and generation as finding proper end in "purpose and the good." The good is an essential factor in Aristotle's fourfold causal scheme and "the cause of all good is The Good itself" (quoted ME, 210). In contrast to Plato, however, Leslie states, "The Good, which is 'the First Mover,' becomes identified with a God who is nothing so abstract as The Good of Plato." Whereas Plato's cosmic principle of benevolence "was too abstract to be an existent, Aristotle's God is a divine mind" whose supreme reality consists in Thinking Itself (VE, 210; ME, 102). Being changeless and self-sufficient, this Mind nonetheless attracts all things toward their final good in its own contemplative self-reflection. "The act of contemplation is what is more pleasant and best," Aristotle insists. "If then God is always in that good state in which we sometimes are, this compels our wonder; and if in a better this compels it yet more"; for "the actuality of thought is life, and God is that . . . self-dependent actuality," which is "life most good and eternal" (quoted ME, 111).

In saying that the necessity of God is that of "a principle whose very essence is actuality," Leslie highlights a difficulty Aristotle himself recognized. It had been said that "potentiality is prior, in which case nothing has necessary existence, for it might be that all things were capable of existing without existing in fact" (quoted VE, 210). To overcoming this difficulty, Leslie remarks that the *essence* of God can be understood not so much as *existence*, but as *that* existence which *supreme perfection exemplifies*. Through this, Leslie again reaches the ultimacy of Value as the axiarchic foundation of divine necessity. Perfect Value is not simply completeness, but an existence that is supremely and ethically required with eternal success. In this way, clarity might be added to the vagueness of Aristotle's comments that "The First Mover exists necessarily; and in as much as he exists by necessity his mode of existence is good." Such necessity, Aristotle tells us, cannot be otherwise and is in fact "essential from the viewpoint of goodness" (ibid., 211). While differences remain from Plato, especially concerning the overtness of a divine Mind Thinking Itself, there are also "strong echoes" in the idea that there is an "ethical aspect" to this necessary Mentality (ME, 102).

For Leslie, these Platonic "echoes" are even stronger in Plotinus, whose own "Good" is entirely beyond Being and necessarily generative of all existent realities. "The One" or "The Good," he insists, "is that on which all depends, toward which all Existences aspire as to their source and their need." As "Term of all," the Good is utterly self-sufficient and without need; nevertheless, from it flows Mind (*Nous*), the "intellectual-Principle and Existence and Soul and Life and all Intellective-Act" (quoted ME, 111). The universe has come into being not through "purpose" or "judgment establishing its desirability," but rather through "sheer necessity." Yet, Plotinus fully admits that "even if a considered plan [had] brought it into being it would still be no disgrace to its maker" (ibid., 6). For Leslie, the claim that "effort and search play no part in the creative process" can still be held by modern axiarchists of this more "Neoplatonic" persuasion. A divine Mind, after all, need not be like human minds in seeking, searching, and choosing; to the contrary, it might eternally possess all thoughts worthy of possessing as is dictated by the goodness of its own nature (IM, 164). That such a position be designated "Neoplatonic" or "Platonic" is, for Leslie, largely a matter of personal preference. Should one have concern for the vital standing of Plotinus, they may want to reserve the word "Neoplatonic" for the notion "that absolutely everything owns its existence to a creative ethical requirement," he states. Should "such a requirement create only a divine person," however, "it being left up to him whether anything else got created," then this might be labeled "Platonism" and not "Neoplatonism." One might just as well reserve "Neoplatonic" solely for a "creation story" that positively rejects affirmation of a "divine person." Of these alternatives, Leslie implores us to choose as we will (ibid., 188).

In Plato, Aristotle, and Plotinus, Leslie rightly finds the supremacy of Value operative, but the clarity of its unilateral priority can also appear questionable in light of the ways Mind also appears in their complex metaphysics. Even if ambiguous, each of these thinkers also holds an essential place for Mentality in their scheme of things. In contrasting emphasis, Ward's reading of these famous Greek figures in the next chapter will reveal how they can (and perhaps should) be read in terms of the priority of Mind.

Medieval Expressions

Turning to the medieval theological giants in Anselm and Aquinas, Leslie also highlights strongly axiarchic leanings such that "Perfection" or "Goodness" is the foundation of divine existence. Anselm famously inspired a host of "ontological arguments" grounded in the notion that a being of Maximal

Greatness or Supreme Value, "than which nothing greater can be conceived," must exist not simply in the "understanding alone" but also in reality; for it is *more valuable* to exist in reality than only in the understanding alone. Similarly, Anselm reasons that it is "possible to conceive of a being which cannot be conceived not to exist," and that this is greater or *more valuable* than "one which can be conceived not to exist." If that "than which nothing greater can be conceived" can be conceived *not to exist*, then it cannot be said to be Supremely Valuable beyond all conception (quoted ME, 113–14).

The ontological argument has had great critics and supporters throughout the tradition, and it continues to be rethought today.[3] In maintaining, "not only that *existence* is part of the perfection which God possesses by definition, but also that *necessary existence* is part of this perfection," Leslie locates Anselm in the axiarchic tradition dating back perhaps to Aristotle's own insights (IM, 183, emphasis his). But here too we see not only a relationship between mind and value on a human level, as we attempt to *conceive* of the *greatest* possible being, but also presumably on a divine level such that divine existence is also *aware* of its own Maximal Value.

Thomas Aquinas was steeped in the Aristotelian tradition and the conviction that The Good is that at which all things aim. Aquinas even states that "nonexistent things seek a good, namely to exist." Although this may be odd when interpreted literally, Leslie nonetheless insists that it is "not odd, if read as an axiarchist's recognition that a good's absence gives rise to a requirement." Aquinas, after all, also insists that "Goodness, as a cause is prior to being" (quoted ME, 211). In support of absolute divine simplicity, he insists that "Goodness and being are really the same and differ only in idea"; for "God to be good," therefore, is "identical with God," such that God is "his goodness" (ibid., 112). While Leslie is not impressed by Thomistic proclamations of divine simplicity, he does uncover much extreme axiarchic potential when Aquinas distinguishes God as *Being* (*ipsum esse subsistens*) from all other *beings*. In saying, for example, that the "divine will" exists "outside the order of being" as that cause productive of "the whole of being and all its differences," Leslie thinks Aquinas might very well be expressing a "Platonic theory that God is an ethical requirement that a good world exist," one that "is itself creatively effective instead of needing to be put into effect" by a divine person who knows, wills, and possesses creative power. This might also be more satisfactory from the perspective of simplicity Leslie thinks; even if equally mysterious, creative ethical requirements are *less complex* than some cogitating divine person (ME, 102). Aquinas then, for Leslie, can be read in support of Platonic or Neoplatonic theory that the name "God" refers not to any being but to "a creative force whose power is inseparable from its goodness, a force in no need of guidance from any complexly structured mind" (IM, 14).

Nevertheless, one should not forget that, for Aquinas, Mind *does* hold an essential place, particularly in relation to the "Forms" or "Ideas." Aquinas is merely agreeing with Augustine and the Middle Platonic lineage centuries before him when he insists that it is "necessary" to posit the reality of Ideas *within* the divine Mind and not external to it. It is through these ideas that the forms of things exist, even apart from those very things. In God, forms function both as *exemplars* of particularly formed things and as *principles of knowledge* whereby they are known in their proper *likeness*. In both senses, the "Ideas" are necessarily in God for Aquinas. The world as such is a result of "God acting by His intellect."[4]

Modern Voices

In surveying the spectrum of modern philosophy, Leslie finds a diversity of axiarchic depths in the work of several key thinkers. These include, among many others, Descartes, Leibniz, Spinoza, Hegel, and even Whitehead and Ward. A brief treatment of his reading of each of these figures sheds further light on his axiarchic interpretive lens.

Descartes axiarchic "vacillations" are readily apparent for Leslie. In praising God for willing what is best, Descartes had also clarified that "some reason of good" did not precede "God's preordination of things"; rather, "their goodness is the fact that he willed them" (quoted VE, 195). For Descartes, all existents spring either from a cause exterior to and other than themselves or interior and immanent to themselves. As long as efficient causation is not simply reduced to meaning a cause "prior in time," it is conceivable that a thing can in fact "be its own sufficient cause." In the case of God, this is a reality; for God "was never non-existent," and can therefore be "named the cause of his own existence." Revealing his Anselmian intuitions, Descartes insists that "I cannot conceive a God without existence, a being supremely perfect and yet lacking absolute perfection" (ibid.).

In calling existence a perfection, Leslie remarks that Descartes "seems to mean that to exist combines *ethical desirability* with some degree of *greatness or completeness of being*." Descartes appears to suggest this directly, saying that "the more perfect contains in itself more reality" (quoted ibid., 196). Nevertheless, Leslie points out that it is not simply *mere existence*, but *necessary existence* that is vital to divine perfection. In drawing a connection between God's supreme perfection or value, and God's own necessity, Leslie claims that "Descartes has in mind that there are for God's existence ethical grounds of overwhelming strength" such that one is tempted to suggest that "ethical requiredness" bears direct responsibility "for an actual fact of existence." This would presumably flow from "clear and distinct insight into God's nature" (ibid., 198). While Leslie admits that Descartes does not have a "tidy axiarchism," "ethical perfection" and "effectively required existence" can nevertheless converge in his understanding of God. Leslie is adamant, however, that Descartes does not tells us *why* this is the case; as such, he "misrepresents how perfect goodness could be involved in being required or necessary." This notwithstanding, such Cartesian insights remain firmly grounded in the notion that there are requirements that the "ethically perfect exist" (ibid.). Little is said by Leslie, however, as to the "ethically perfect" being a divine Mind for Descartes.

Leibniz can be read as a foremost exponent of axiarchic conviction. While he is not always clear or consistent, the preeminence of the ethically best reigns supreme in his view of things. Leibniz strongly denies "that God's works are good only because he created them." This might falsely suggest that The Good was arbitrarily linked to whatever God decides. "Why praise God for his deeds," Leibniz asks, "if he would be as praiseworthy in doing the contrary?" Rather, Leibniz insists that a violation of the "rule of the best" would in fact "destroy divinity" (quoted VE, 200). Rather, God must be "bound by moral necessity" such that God "cannot help acting for the best" (ibid., 204).

For Leslie, Leibniz often seems to view ethical requirements as creatively efficacious of the *totality of things*, and not just God's existence. "Unless in the very nature of essence there was some inclination to exist nothing would," Leibniz states. "From the fact that there exists something rather than nothing it follows that in possibility or essence itself there is a need of existence, a claim to exist" (ibid.). This "need" or "claim" is that of the Good, such that what *is* Best will be what *Is*. Leslie admits, however, that Leibniz "never says outright that the creative factor is *the ethical requiredness of the total scheme of things*, the existence of God and of all else resulting from it"; rather, much of what he says might also suggest the contrary. One example Leslie gives involves the status of possibility, a question we will take up explicitly in Part III. Leibniz makes possibilities *depend upon* divine thought, but in doing this, Leslie insists that he is "forgetting that God's *own possibility* could hardly result from God's ideas on the subject" (ibid., 203; emphasis mine). On Leibniz's account, various possibilities clash like the conflicting quarrels of heavy bodies, each vying for existence. But he realizes an honest difficulty in linking "reasons" to abstract realities like possibilities. One may object that while heavy bodies do exist, possibilities "anterior to existence or apart from it are imaginary or fictitious and therefore no reason of existence is to be sought in them" (quoted ME, 121). For Leibniz, the only "existence" such possibilities or essences have is in the Mind of God. "I reply that neither these essences nor what are called eternal truths regarding these essences are fictitious, but that they exist in a certain region (if I may so call it) of ideas, that is to say, in God Himself, the source of all essence and of the existence of other things" (ibid.). This for Leslie is a clear mistake; and it will initially distance him from Ward and Whitehead. Instead of "inquiring why mere possibilities could not have both ethical and creative importance," Leibniz "transfers the war among them to God's mind," Leslie states (ibid). Moreover, Leslie thinks that this may have been due to the strong pressure of a time when denying God "the ultimate foundation of all explanations" could bring rather severe consequences. "It is therefore no surprise," he writes, "that Leibniz hurries to assure us that the struggle between possible things really took place in God's mind when God considered what best to create—instead of saying that God Himself, even when infinitely sure to succeed in any struggle between possibilities, had actually been compelled to take part in such a struggle, a creative process occurring *independently* of His will" (ibid., 106; emphasis his). Despite what Leslie considers a strong oversite here, Leibniz nevertheless remains for him an exemplary figure of axiarchism. On his interpretation, Leibniz's God is a person who is "far the best member of a cosmos" which exists solely because of its "ethically requiredness" (IM, 181).

In turning to Spinoza, Leslie encounters yet another axiarchist he greatly admires. He not only incorporates much of Spinoza into his own thought but also goes far beyond him on behalf of what the "best" determines. For Spinoza, the divinely Self-Caused Substance is "that of which the essence involves existence" and "that which is in itself and is conceived through itself" (quoted VE, 211). How can this be so? Spinoza assures us that the essence of God is "absolutely infinite and supremely perfect," such that the "welfare and perfection of all" is desired. As *perfect*, God must be necessarily existent and utterly unchanging; and as *infinite*, God must be One all-inclusive reality. "Whatever is, is in God" and "outside God there is nothing," Spinoza insists (quoted IM, 184; VE, 212). The universe therefore is among the infinite modes of God, a divine Mind whose own intellectual activity (*natura naturata*) is constituted in and as the World itself. Why does God-or-Nature exist? For Leslie, Spinoza's answer exposes his axiarchism. "God has from himself an absolutely infinite power of existence," and this power flows from the fact that "perfection does not prevent the existence of a thing but establishes it" (quoted IM, 185). "Perfection," Spinoza states, "must give a thing its existence" (quoted VE, 212).

Leslie praises Spinoza's view that the whole complex of things, "God-or-Nature," exists because it is ethically required to do so. "Spinoza's God is an all-inclusive divine mind existing because this is best" (IM, 185). As much as Leslie admires Spinoza's pantheist axiarchism, however, he can find no coherent reason to suppose that there would only be *one* divine Mind if Value or Goodness reigned supreme in the nature of things. Leslie is confident in fact that if there were a "scheme of things which existed because of its ethical requiredness," things would actually "be far richer than the one

Spinoza describes" (ibid.). Spinoza's cosmic mind only contemplates one universe; but for Leslie this is "a preposterous restriction to place on the divine thoughts" (ME, 139). He rather insists there would have to be "infinitely many immensely knowledgeable minds, each contemplating the details of innumerable universes" (ibid.). This manifold of divine Minds, Leslie thinks, is nothing short of what necessarily follows from asserting the creative supremacy of Value. If Value were truly "in control," then "there would exist innumerable further minds of the same supremely good type." In fact, he likens this divine council to an "infinite ocean." Just as a constellation of islands is still referred to in the singular as "Island," so too might this oceanic plenitude of divine Minds be termed "God" (ME, 109).[5] We will find Ward taking particular issue with this notion of "infinite Gods" in the next chapter.

In a way deeply resonant to that of Spinoza, Leslie finds in Hegel a vision of all things "present inside a single, fully unified existent which can be called God" (ME, 106). As "Absolute Reality" or the "Idea," Hegel tells us that God "embraces all characteristics in its unity," and is entirely mental: the very "Idea that thinks itself." This divine Idea, however, is "not so impotent as merely to have a right or an obligation to exist without actually existing" (quoted ibid.) At the foundation of this "right" or "obligation," Leslie pinpoints Hegel's extreme axiarchism—God's ethical or axiological "requiredness" to exist. Indeed, Hegel states that the "Idea" stripped of its limitations would appear as "universality moulded by Reason," the "absolute and final end or the Good" as "realized in the world." The very impulse of the Good is that of "self-realization" in the creative molding of God-and-World. Hegel does suggest that the reason or explanation for this God-World complex is found in a kind of ethical requirement that "the Good is really achieved" (ibid.; VE, 214). One wishes, however, that Leslie would speak further to the relationship this required "Good" has to the fact that the Idea "thinks itself." This relationship seems to bear a kind of internal reciprocity: the "Good" that necessitates divine Existence is precisely what is divinely "Thought." This suggests not *unilaterality* from Value *to* Mind, but rather *mutuality* between Value *and* Mind.

In briefly treating Whitehead, Leslie finds that he is reflective of Hegel, deeply indebted to Plato, and positively dismissive of Leibniz's "audacious fudge" to "save the face of the Creator" with his theory of the "best of possible worlds" (PR, 47; quoted VE, 214). Nevertheless, Leslie insists that Whitehead still "supports axiarchism with vigor" (VE, 214). This is not an overstatement. We have already seen that the place of aesthetic Value in Whitehead's philosophy is utterly central, such that the very existence of the world presupposes a more fundamental aesthetic drive. "The teleology of the universe is direction to the production of Beauty," Whitehead insists (AI, 265).

Leslie looks briefly to quotations from Whitehead's principal works, mainly in *Modes of Thought, Religion in the Making, Science and the Modern World*, and *Process and Reality*, to further justify his claims. In *Modes of Thought*, Whitehead insisted that the "Hume-Newton" approach had rejected the need for explanation of causal regularities, and presented a "dead" and "meaningless" world, where neither "physical nature nor life can be understood" (quoted VE, 214). This is clearly inadequate, and its remedy would include the fact that value is *inherent* in actuality and the very telos of existence itself. Leslie combines together Whitehead's scattered statements that communicate precisely this: "All ultimate reasons are in terms of an aim at value. Life exists for its own sake, as the intrinsic reaping of value. Existence is the upholding of value-intensity. The drive toward aesthetic worth constitutes the drive of the universe" (ibid.).

In quest for how Value gains "its influence," Leslie finds Whitehead discussing those "elements which go to the world's formation" in *Religion in the Making*. According to Leslie, these are (quoting Whitehead) "the realm of ideal entities, or forms, which are not actual but are exemplified in everything actual." Whitehead tells us, moreover, that the "actual world is the outcome of the aesthetic order" and that the "aesthetic order is derived from the immanence of God" as the all-inclusive "non-temporal entity." Leslie is confident in fact that this divine entity performs "much the tasks of The Good of Plato" (ibid., 215).

In commenting on Whitehead in his later work, Leslie evidently thinks that his God is on par with "the realm of ideal entities" in terms of *not being actual*.[6] This claim, in fact, is misleading. In contrast to his earlier vision of God in *Science and the Modern World*, where God is conceived as "not concrete," a nonactual limiting factor among formative realities, and a "principle" or "mode" of "eternal activity" (in resonance with Spinoza's "one infinite substance"), Whitehead is repeatedly clear in *Religion in the Making* that God *is* an *actual entity* different from—not just a mode or attribute of—eternal activity (now termed "creativity") (SMW, 177).[7] Leslie quotes *Science and the Modern World* when Whitehead assures us that "it stands in [God's] very nature to divide the Good from the Evil," but it is precisely the difficulty of grasping how *abstractions* or *principles* alone can perform any functions, let alone "division" or "envisionment," which led Whitehead to embed them in the integrative actuality of God.[8] The provision of this divine Actuality undergirds the entire process of the Universe; it is Mentality or divine Conceptual Activity, which is essential to the fountain of Becoming. Although Leslie quotes Whitehead's *Process and Reality* where, in consonance with the ontological principle, things temporal and eternal are mediated by the actuality of the "divine element," Leslie does not include Whitehead's designation of this "element" as the "primordial mind of God" (VE, 215;

PR, 46). Nonetheless, Leslie's emphasis on the preeminence of Value in Whitehead is correct—even if abstractly so. We can even state the case more strongly, as Whitehead himself does in his latter essays. We will come to a few of these statements regarding "the world of value" and the permanence of divine Mentality in chapter 5.

Despite some important differences between them, Leslie consistently refers to the work of Keith Ward in positive resonance to his own.[9] In saying that there "is no conceptual absurdity in the Platonic theme that an ethical need, alias an ethical requirement, might *by itself* be responsible for a things existence," Leslie quotes Ward commenting that "something being desirable does not entail its existence," if "entail" must mean "*make demonstrable by logicians.*" However, if per Aristotle, something "cannot exist otherwise than it does, the best reason for its existence," Ward states, "would lie in its supreme goodness" (IM, 162; quoting RC, 196). Although Leslie and Kuhn position Ward in the "Value/Perfection as Ultimate" section of *The Mystery of Existence*, Ward has consistently advocated the ultimacy of Mind and, indeed, its *priority* and *primacy* in the nature of things.[10] Nevertheless, Ward has also linked the necessity of Mind directly to its Value holding that "a good reason" for Mind's existence "is that it is intrinsically valuable that it should exist." This Mind's existence, Ward states, would be "supremely desirable, not least to itself" (RC, 195; quoted ME, 125. Cf. IM, 184). Here, Ward recognizes a kind of *reciprocity* between Ultimate Mind and its Supreme Value, somewhat akin perhaps to that of Aristotle and Hegel above. This is not so clear in Leslie, however, where Value or Goodness appears to reign supreme in a unilateral fashion. Nevertheless, that a divine Mind alone owes its existence to ethical requirements is "fully compatible" with a Platonic creation as Leslie has repeatedly insisted. As shown above, this too can find a place under "extreme axiarchism." Ward along with thinkers like A. C. Ewing and John Polkinghorne do affirm this position, but in contrast to Leslie, they hold that whatever else exists is "thanks to that divine mind's creative activity" (ME, 136). Although Leslie himself does not hold to this, he does see it as an interesting and defensible "variant of the idea" that things owe their existence to their ethical requiredness. Ward thus belongs in Leslie's axiarchic tradition, but courtesy is again paid to Value more so than Mind.

THE CREATIVE SUPREMACY OF VALUE

In this selective overview of Leslie's reading of the tradition, I've sought to highlight some of the ways in which the Creative Supremacy of Value has been his upmost concern. While not wrong, the place of Mind does tend to be subjugated to that of Ethical Requirements. My concern is that he (along perhaps with certain dimensions of the tradition) risks speaking of Value in *abstraction* from Mind such that Value effects a *unidirectional* determination of Mind. Although he recognizes an essential place for Mind in the tradition, and especially in his own contribution to it, his emphasis remains thoroughly axiarchic such that Mind appears to add nothing at all to Value. In moving now to Ward's reading of the tradition, we will see that his philosophical idealism tends to emphasize the concrete Primordiality of Mind as the context in which abstract Value can actually be rendered coherent.

NOTES

1. Leslie first introduced this term in "The Theory That the World Exists Because It Should," *American Philosophical Quarterly* 7 (1970): 286–98.

2. Leslie has at times made comments that might suggest "a time when the divine Mind was not" (to hark back to Arius). For example, he has said that "the very *first thing* the Platonic Principle generated might be God as a Being" (ME, 8, my emphasis). Nevertheless, his clarifications through personal correspondence are noteworthy: "A philosopher might well think that God as a Being was the thing most to be expected as a product of Platonic creation, the thing 'first to be created' in the sense only of having priority over all else, with the word 'priority' NOT meaning 'temporal priority.' I would never take seriously the idea that, in a temporal sense, there was FIRST a Platonic need for a divine mind to exist, and THEN (i.e., LATER ON) this Platonic need succeeded in generating a divine mind. I myself don't take seriously even the idea (which Augustine rejected) that a divine mind existed for a while before creating any other things. I picture the entire cosmos as existing in eternal satisfaction of the Platonic need for it to exist." E-mail correspondence, May 8, 2019.

3. See, for example, Charles Hartshorne, *Anselm's Discovery: A Re-Examination of the Ontological Proof of God's Existence* (Chicago: Open Court, 1991); *The Logic of Perfection* (Chicago: Open Court, 1991); Alvin Plantinga (ed.), *The Ontological Argument: From St. Anselm to Contemporary Philosophers* (New York: Doubleday Anchor, 1965); Daniel A. Dombrowski, *Rethinking the Ontological Argument: A Neoclassical Theistic Response* (New York: Cambridge University Press, 2006).

4. *Summa Theologica*, "On Ideas," Q 15.

5. See Leslie's recent article, "What God Might Be," *International Journal for Philosophy of Religion* 85 (2019): 63–75.

6. "In Whitehead's *Religion in the Making*, God is part of the 'realm of ideal entities, or forms, which are *not actual* but are exemplified in everything actual'" (IM, 181, emphasis mine).

7. John B. Cobb Jr. highlights this important change in *Religion in the Making*: "In *Religion in the Making* . . . a remarkable change has occurred without explanation. God is consistently referred to as an actual entity. This is not a rejection of the view that God is the principle of concretion (or limitation) but the affirmation that it is an actual entity that performs the function of providing limitations that make concretion possible. Hence envisagement can be understood as a way in which an actual

entity is conceptually related to ideal possibilities." John B. Cobb Jr., *A Christian Natural Theology: Based on the Thought of Alfred North Whitehead*, second edition (Louisville: Westminster John Knox Press, 2007), 89.

8. According to Faber, "Not only does 'God' appear as one of the three formative elements, but their whole setting . . . 'God' really became the integrating element of the cosmological triad of principles Whitehead developed in *Religion in the Making* [between actual entities, abstract forms, and creativity]. . . . [I]n *Religion in the Making* over and against *Science and the Modern World*, Whitehead for the first time realized that, if a principle really has to *decide* amidst activity and possibility in order to create temporal concreteness, it *must* be understood as an 'entity.' Hence this cosmological structure tended to integrate all other principles as abstractions of this one non-temporal actuality, named 'God.'" Faber, *Depths As Yet Unspoken*, 258. That God *provides* and not *is* the "principle of concretion" is confirmed by A. H. Johnson in his conversation with Whitehead. See A.H. Johnson, "Some Conversations with Whitehead Concerning God and Creativity," in Lewis S. Ford and George L. Kline (Eds.) *Explorations in Whitehead's Philosophy* (New York: Fordham University Press, 1983), 5.

9. Pointing to Ward's work in *Pascal's Fire* (PF) in particular, Leslie insists that "Keith Ward develops ideas markedly similar to mine. However, he argues for just a single infinite mind" (ID, 15).

10. Kuhn in fact recognizes this clearly. In describing "Ultimate Mind" as a nonphysical cause of the universe, he rightly includes reference to Ward: "A Supreme Consciousness that hovers between a personal theistic God and an impersonal deistic first cause, a nonpareil artist who contemplates limitless possibilities; a quasi Being with real thoughts who determines to actualize certain worlds (Keith Ward). Understanding this kind of God does not begin with an all-powerful 'person' but rather with an unfathomable reservoir of potentialities expressed in all possible universes, for which Ultimate Mind is the only and necessary basis" (ME, 255).

Chapter 4

Idealism

The Primordiality of Mind

For decades Keith Ward has advocated an "idealist view of life" over and against "materialism and its discontents" (MM, 182; GP, 130). Having had his own philosophical training in the British Empiricist tradition (Locke, Berkley, and Hume), Ward prioritizes experience and consciousness and strongly opposes reductive materialistic explanations of human beings and the cosmos at large. In general, philosophical idealism "holds that mind is the only primordial reality and that the whole material universe is a product of mind." The physical universe, Ward states, "would not exist without mind, and the true nature of the universe is that it is an expression or appearance of a basically mental reality" (CIG, 9). Ward's advocacy of "personal Idealism" in particular holds that this one supreme Mentality is "personal" in the sense that it knows, thinks, feels, and intends (ibid., 1).[1]

In holding to the primordiality of Mind, Ward can assert not simply a *nomological* explanation of the universe in terms of the physical or law-like domains of natural science but also an *axiological* explanation in which intentional, purposive, and evaluative dimensions of the universe actually have a place. Indeed, for Ward, such a "principle of axiology" could apply to the entire universe such that a purposeful explanation in terms of value "would provide an explanation of why [the universe] exits in the way it does" (EG, 72, 51). Supposing there is a necessary "array of possible states, with the values they necessarily have," then "there would be an intrinsic reason for the existence of any universe—namely, the goodness that it would exhibit." Its intrinsic worth would give it a "wholly satisfactory" axiological explanation (CIG, 97).

WARD'S IDEALISTIC PRIORITY

For Ward, an objective framework of Value in the universe requires embedding within some kind of Primordial Mentality or Consciousness.[2] Indeed, the "addition of Mind to the Good," he states, "provides a principle for selecting actual goods (that is, for creating a cosmos) . . . that a purely conceptual 'Ideal' cannot" (MAG, xiii). This divine Mind, moreover, would *know* itself such that its own existence is explained not only in terms of its *Goodness alone* but also in terms of its *Knowledge of its Goodness*. A necessary Mind, supreme in Goodness, would be ultimately explanatory, Ward states, "in that it necessarily desires its own existence as that which is most worthy of existence, and does not derive it from any other being" (RC, 196). This view for Ward, moreover, is not at all foreign, but has been expounded by the "best-known philosophers" of the tradition (GP, 1). Plato, Aristotle, Anselm, Aquinas, Descartes, Leibniz, Spinoza, Locke, Berkeley, Kant, Hegel, and many others all shared the "general view" that "ultimate reality has the nature of mind or consciousness, and that the material universe is the appearance or creation of that ultimate mind" (ibid., 130). As such, they saw philosophy "as an inquiry into the nature and purpose of the intelligible mind which underlies the physical universe." Although their views were by no means identical, Ward nevertheless insists that they "all thought that the most acute human enquiry would show that the heart of reality lay in something akin to intelligence and intellectual beauty—something hard to define and describe, but hard only because it was greater than, not less than, the human mind and the limits of human language" (CIG, 8). In this chapter, we look to some of the ways in which Ward reads the same Greek, Medieval, and Modern figures, including Whitehead and Leslie, in ways that aim toward the ultimacy of Mind.

The Greek Idealistic Lineage

While Plato hardly left a "rational theology" in any kind of systematic form, Ward does hold that he defined "the intellectual terms in which rational theism has ever since been developed in the west" (RCG, 211). In famously distinguishing the world of the "forms" from the sense-experienced material world, Plato set at the apex of reality a mysterious "thing that every soul pursues as the end of all her action, dimly divining its existence, but perplexed and unable to grasp its nature." This is the form of The Good and the "highest object of knowledge"; it is "beyond being" but that through which "everything that is good and right derives its value" (ibid). For Ward this is an "unmistakable adumbration of the God of the philosophers," but he reminds us that Plato says nothing more of this "ultimate cause and object of intellectual knowledge" and how it might coherently relate to the other Forms, and to the obscure independent existence of matter. Plato's Demiurge is pictured as using the Forms in making the best world, but "where he comes from, or why he should have the nature he does," Ward states, "is again left tantalizingly without explanation" (ibid., 211–12). Ward thus states that at the origins of Western philosophy, we have a "hint," or at least an "obscure sketch" that "material reality has a conceptual basis, and that the truly real is the changeless, the good and the immaterial, hidden from the senses but knowable by the intellect" (ibid., 212). These idealistic sketches would evolve, but never entirely leave the Western philosophical and theological tradition.

Although Plato's conceptual world, in contrast to the finite grasping of human minds, is not envisioned as "conscious and aware of its own content," Ward has held that it is not absurd to conceive the Intellect (*Nous*) as at least conscious and "possessed of conceptual objects and awareness"—as did later Middle Platonist thinkers (MAG, 98). This would be a means of integrating the Platonic picture of reality so that unconscious Value is wedded to conscious Mind. For Ward, a reason for the existence of something in terms of Value seems to commit one to a framework of knowledge, awareness, and Mind. This is not obvious in Plato, but its hints are present such that it is a reasonable trajectory of his thought, even if not explicitly expressed. Ward remains confident that if "something is to operate as a reason for existing, it must be understood as a reason, and deployed as a reason, by an Intellect that is capable of understanding and acting in accordance with that understanding." What is more, he insists that "value can only be experienced as an actual value by an Intellect that is aware of its value." The main difference in this perspective from the Platonic view—but arguably necessitated by it—is "the attribution of some form of consciousness to the Good" (ibid., 98–99). Value in this sense *needs* Mind.

In Aristotle, Ward finds this much more explicitly. Having argued that "it is necessary that there should be an eternal unchanging substance," Aristotle insists that this "substance" is best conceived as an Intelligence which, although imparting change to all else, does not itself change (quoted GGP, 119). This Mind ceaselessly contemplates what is best and "since the best possible thing is the Divine intellect itself," Ward states, "its object of thought must be itself." Aristotle tells us that the activity of the Divine is *noesis noeseos*, "a thinking of thinking" such that "the object of thought and the act of thinking do not differ" (RCG, 212). Contemplating its own essence, Ward remarks that Aristotle conceives divine Knowing as an "actual uniting with the Form of its object" so that if "God knows himself, then his knowledge and its objects, being pure Forms, are one" (ibid., 213). By integrating Value with Mind, Aristotle is closing "the gap" between Plato's "Demiurge and the Good by making the best of all beings itself the cause of change in the cosmos" (GGP, 119). For Aristotle, it is good that there exist a supreme state of pure contemplation of goodness and beauty. These brief comments add substance to the mystery of the relation between Mind and Value. Ward agrees with Aristotle: the most coherent reason for the existence of a divine being of supreme goodness is that it is supremely valuable, especially to itself. There is then something like a *noesis noeseos* at the base of things wherein *both* Value and Mind coincide.

In Plotinus, Ward finds the "Divine Being" expressed through the hypostatic triad of the ineffable One, the Intellect or world of Forms, and the World-Soul, as author and shaper of the world. Matter is understood to necessarily emanate from God until it eventually evaporates in entropic nothingness. For Ward, Plotinus offers an ingenious synthesis of disparate elements in Plato. The notion of *emanation* is central and integrative in this regard and has had a significant impact on the Western theological tradition (RCG, 61). Plotinus, Ward states, "unites the concepts of matter, a world-designer, Plato's ineffable form of the Good and the eternal world of Forms in one intelligible system, with the aid of the uniting idea of emanation" (ibid.). Here the One, as development of Plato's Good, is at the apex of the "metaphysical hierarchy" and naturally overflows into the Intellect as "the eternal Mind" in which the Forms subsist. This gives rise to the "Cosmic Soul," what Ward calls the "creative mind of the universe"; the Demiurge and shaper of the world; and Matter is the "last necessary outflowing of the Divine." In contrast to Aristotle, however, the Plotinian God does not ignore finite reality but produces it by necessity and includes all things within itself (ibid.).

In Plotinus, Value reigns supreme, but it is still necessarily related to Mind such that they appear unable to be abstracted from one another. Ward cites Plotinus saying, "In turning towards itself the One sees. It is this seeing which is Intellect" (quoted ibid., 59). This statement itself might suggest something unique about the relationship between the ineffable Value which is beyond being and the Mind which is the means by which Value "sees," and even "acts" and "does." Intellect, Plotinus tells us, is both "word and deed" of the One. Ward's comments here are directed more toward the inconsistency involved in saying an immutable One in fact "turns towards itself," but he also expresses trouble in conceiving how it can be that an abstract and "indescribable" One can be said "to act, to see or to be the cause of all" (ibid.). A possible way this could be rendered intelligible is through conceiving the One (as "the Good") through its necessary relationship to the actuality of Mind. Ward does not explicitly say this of Plotinus, but it is not contrary to his fundamental idealistic intuitions in reading the tradition. The indispensable role of the Mind, at the very least, seems apparent in Plotinus's system such that one might conceivably make this case. The question again would surround the relationship between Value and Mind.

Medieval Expressions

For Ward, one of best expressions of the notion of God's necessary existence comes from the pen of Anselm. By defining God as the "best conceivable being" and by including "necessary existence" as a property clearly better than not, Anselm birthed the ontological argument which has "infuriated philosophers ever since" (GGP, 127). One version Ward offers as an example runs thus: "If it is possible for there to be something that, if it is possible is actual, then it is actual. God is such a thing, by definition. Therefore, if God is possible then God is actual. But God is obviously possible. Therefore God exists" (ibid.). At a minimum what such an argument shows is that there is something utterly unique about the idea of God. If God exists, God does not just "happen to exist" when God might not otherwise have; this would be a God existing in *some* possible worlds, but not *all* possible worlds. While some thinkers have insisted that they can in fact imagine a world *without* God, much of the tradition, following Anselm's intuitions, have insisted that if God exists, God does so in *every possible world*. Put differently, Ward asks us to consider an array of possibilities, those which take account of everything that could ever be. He insists, however, that we cannot just have "possible worlds" existing as "merely possible, and not actual." Possible worlds—should they exist at all—must exist in something *actual*, a real existent. What could this something be? "The nearest we can come to imagining this is to think of an actual mind or awareness," Ward concludes, "in which all possible worlds exist as ideas. That mind is God, and the possible worlds are ideas in the mind of God" (ibid., 128). This is no easy "proof," but it does appear a coherent thought experiment in approaching necessity.

At the foundations of these considerations is Anselm's "infuriating" influence. "Necessary existence," however, is not all that an imagined being of supreme Value would have. Ward cites Anselm also including both *metaphysical* and *personal* properties in a best possible being: life, wisdom, power, truth, justice, beatitude, being, reason, beauty, incorruptibility, unity, immutability, and eternity. Like other Platonists, Anselm mistakenly thinks the abstract is "more real" than the concrete or particular, such that "every created substance exists more truly in . . . the intelligence of the Creator, than it does in itself" (quoted RCG, 135–36; RC, 245). Being perfect and self-sufficient, whatever "God contemplates must be part of [God's self]" so that God is "the beautiful as well as its contemplator." Alternatively, we might say that in God coincide abstract metaphysical Value and concrete personal Mind. Following Anselm, Ward states that when "seeking an idea of perfection," one is looking for the "highest degree" of values a "rational being" would find worthy of choosing. In subtracting any shortcoming arising from "dependence on other realties," we arrive at a "self-existent rational agent" whose own "rationality is what gives the self-existent whatever positive value it has" (RCG, 135). In this way, Ward finds that Positive Value depends upon Rational Mind.

In dialogue with the monumental influence of Thomas Aquinas, Ward has consistently pushed against his commitment to divine simplicity and its direct link to God as "pure actuality" (*actus purus*), devoid of all potentiality.[3] The repudiation of potentiality in God, Ward states, allows Thomas to assert "that God is not a thing with a nature but is a pure existing nature or Form, indeed the Form of 'existence itself.'" Such a view, however, is not unproblematic. For Ward, it is not clear that an independently existing nature without any *instantiation* is even coherent at all. It is not clear that "existence itself" is anything more than the elevation of abstraction, and it is "not helpful to say that 'existence exists'" (CC, 25, emphasis mine). Abstractions require wider referent to some mode of *relationality:* to *that from which they have been abstracted*. On a different level, Ward stresses that Aquinas fully recognizes, as Aristotle did, that Platonic forms, "while they are necessary and eternal, do not just exist on their own." Rather, "they exist as all concepts do, in minds"—in this case, "a cosmic mind or cosmic consciousness whose thoughts they are" (GP, 23). Once a cosmic mind is admitted, Ward states that "Aquinas clearly sees, you have a consciousness that can be aware of, evaluate, and discriminate" among the infinitude of Platonic realities. Ward stresses this in Aquinas far more so than Leslie.

In Value or Goodness, Aquinas does recognize a Platonic axiological basis to the necessity of God and a coherent means of explaining the universe as a whole. But Mind remains utterly central, and in Ward's reading, it is primary. "Aquinas' explanation of the universe appeals to explanation in terms of both necessity and goodness," he states, and God is conceived as "that mind that necessarily conceives all possible states . . . and sees some of them to be good." This Mind "causes temporal and changing things to be, because they express and imitate the perfect goodness of that [Mind] which necessarily contains all perfections." For Ward, both Aristotle and Aquinas believed in the *uniting ability* of Mind with respect to Platonic Value. For them "the ultimate reality, in which alone a complete explanation of the universe can be found, must be mind, a mind uniting necessity and goodness in itself." The uniting of necessity and goodness *through* this Mind is not only a clue into its very *reason* but also to that of the intelligible universe as such. It is a universe, Ward states, which is "founded on the eternal and changeless reality of perfect mind" (ibid., 27).

Modern Voices

In turning to Ward's treatment of key thinkers of modern philosophy, we find him continually speaking to the primacy of Mind. This is not only the case with Descartes, Leibniz, Hegel, and Spinoza but also with Whitehead and Leslie—both of whom find a valuable place among his idealistic reading of the tradition.

Ward has continually sought to defend Descartes from modern philosophical disdain. Although many continue to insist that "dualism" was Descartes's "original sin," Ward has sought to retrieve his reputation against caricatured versions of "dualism" (Ryle's "ghost in the machine," for example), which in fact do not adequately represent his view (GP, Ch. 3; MM, 112). For Descartes, while mind and matter are two *distinct* kinds of thing, human beings are nevertheless a unified mixture of both. "I am not present in my body merely as a pilot is present in a ship," Descartes states, "I am most tightly bound to it, and as it were mixed up with it, so that I and it form a unit" (quoted GP, 30). Indeed, consciousness and extension are distinct aspects of the soul, which is not an utterly different substance from that of the body but wedded to it in "psycho-physical unity" (ibid., 30–31). When all else is considered dispensable or unknowable, mind holds an essential primacy for Descartes. With his famous utterance "I think therefore I am" (*Cogito ergo sum*), Ward stresses that Descartes was defending the one thing of which we can be certain against the radical skepticism of Montaigne (ibid., 29). This famous statement, however, might also be of some insight when considering the place of God as a divine Mind of Supreme Value in Descartes.

After affirming the reality of a continuous thinking agent and essential distinctions between the extensionless character of thoughts and those of public physical space, Descartes asks whether such thoughts might exist *without* extension. In Ward's words, "Can there be conscious states occurring without any physical states?" Descartes answers in the affirmative and insists God is the paradigmatic example of consciousness without extension. If indeed thoughts could exist without matter, then, Ward states, "a mental and immaterial agent could logically exist also" (ibid., 37). For Descartes, however, God as an unembodied Mind is not just logically possible but also *axiologically necessary*. In commenting on Anselm's second version of the ontological argument, the greatest conceivable being must exist of necessity, for this existence is necessarily linked to the essence of this Being as Supreme Perfection or Value. "Existence can no more be separated from the essence of God," Descartes states, "than the fact that three angles of a triangle are together equal to two right angles can be separated from it" (quoted RCG, 26–27). For Descartes, then, Mind and Value enter into a proper understanding of the existence and nature of God. We might say that it is not just the case that *we think, therefore we are*, but also, on a higher metaphysical level, that *the divine Mind thinks, therefore we are*. On a still higher intra-divine level, the divine Mind is aware of the divine Value such that we might even say that *the divine Mind thinks, therefore the divine Mind is*. For Ward,

Descartes holds an important place among "classical rationalists," not only in viewing "value, purpose and consciousness" as "closely connected and of fundamental and irreducible importance" but also in holding that "the ultimate basis of reality" lies "in a supreme consciousness which unites in itself necessity and value" (GP, 39).

Leibniz too is to be included among those classical rationalists Ward analyzes in terms of the primacy of Mind. For Leibniz, reason leads to an affirmation of the ultimate reality of God as the "one and only necessary and perfect Mind" (ibid., 34). In knowing God's "own eternal being," God "sees" the totality of all possible worlds and chooses the Best "in accordance with the principle of perfection," Ward states (RCG, 74). The Supreme Value or Perfection of God means that God must select the *best possible* world and "cannot fail to bring it about." God is thus free in the sense of "acting in accordance with his own intellectual perception," but God cannot help but bring about the best possible world. Possibilities are dependent upon the perception of the divine Mind and, like this Mind, they necessarily have the Values they do. This even includes negative values associated with possibilities of suffering. "If suffering is a possibility which exists by necessity," Ward states, "then even God cannot exclude it as a possibility," although "God could exclude it as an actuality that God wills." This for Ward is what Leibniz implies when he states that "evil springs . . . from the ideas that God has not produced by an act of his will . . . in the ideal region of the possible, that is, in the divine understanding" (quoted, GC, 175). Note that for Ward, in contrast to Leslie, Leibniz has not obviously erred by locating possibility *in* the divine Mind. Still, "there is in things that are possible . . . a certain need for existence, or . . . a claim to exist," Ward states, such that "the world, as it were, presses into existence" actualizing the greatest possible amount of possibility. The world, while not being "metaphysically necessary," is "morally necessary" such that its nonexistence—just like that of the divine Mind—would constitute moral absurdity and imperfection (RCG, 74). If then by the dictates of Perfection, God must be what God necessarily is, then the world too must necessarily be what it is. The divine Mind exists because of its supreme Value and the world exists because it is *best*.

Ward is no great fan of the "rationalists necessitarianism" of Leibniz, nor of his notion that ours is "best possible world" (ibid.). Here, he agrees with Aquinas in strongly doubting that there is "just one 'best possible' world"; rather, Ward thinks we should opt for the likelihood that "there are many possible worlds that are good in different respects" without any one of them being "absolutely the best" (PF, 134). We will see below that these intuitions put Ward at odds with Leslie on similar points. Nevertheless, Leibniz remains admirable in his explanation of the reality of God and also that of the world. While Ward will not follow him into assertions surrounding a best possible world, he does agree with him that "the best ultimate explanation of the universe is an actual being that contains in itself, and is aware of, all possible states and that chooses to actualize some of them because it finds them to be of intrinsic value" (ibid., 135).

In Spinoza, Ward finds perhaps the "only consistent rationalist philosopher" (RCG, 56). This is because his system is grounded in the idea of an all-inclusive and self-subsistent being, which "in itself is conceived through itself" and which possesses all *possible properties* as *actual properties*, such that it is identical with the Universe itself ("God or Nature") (quoted ibid., 57, 56). Sheer plentitudinous necessity unfolds from the metaphysical Perfection of God as the One Infinite Substance. "All things are in God," Spinoza insists, "and everything which takes place takes place by the laws alone of the infinite nature of God and follows ... from the necessity of his essence" (ibid., 56). Despite the difficulty of holding that a "simple being" includes an infinitude of properties, or that an immutable *Deus* is somehow identifiable with a mutable *Natura*, the necessity at the heart of Spinoza's vision, Ward states, may in fact come "nearest to the dreams of modern cosmology" (GP, 32).

Spinoza imagines the "realm of the ultimate" as beyond either "intellect" or "will" with finite intellects and wills only comprising a small portion of its infinite modes. Knowing, thinking, and choosing in the way humans do is not applicable to the "necessary basis of infinite worlds," which necessarily actualizes all possible worlds. Ward points out, however, that despite Spinoza's denial of "intellect and will of the primary substance," the "intellectual love of God" is at the heart his *Ethics*—and not just by human beings. Spinoza states that "God is absolutely infinite," such that the "nature of God delights in infinite perfection ... accompanied with the idea of Himself as cause, and this is what we have called intellectual love." Put differently, he states that "the intellectual love of the mind toward God is part of the infinite love with which God loves Himself" (quoted ibid., 32–33). The cause of all things retains infinite perfection and "delights" in such perfection. For Ward, it remains "impossible to frame this conception without thinking of the ultimate Substance as conscious and capable of delight ... as an intellectual being." It is Mind that "delights" and Value which is worthy of delight. Despite various simplistic claims that Spinoza was an "atheist," "materialist," or "pantheist," Ward stresses that he saw God as "ultimate, perfect and immaterial Mind." It is this, rather than "some sort of matter or blind energy," that is the actual "cause of the universe" as well as "its ultimate nature" (ibid., 35).

For Ward, Hegel follows the "inclusivist" tradition of Plotinus and Spinoza. The existence of God as "perfect being" entails and includes the existence of the world such that the entire unfolding of history *is* the dialectical self-manifestation of Absolute Spirit (*Geist*). In Hegel, time is interior to divinity. He offers a radically related and temporal renewal of Aristotle's *noesis noeseos*, but now "the self which God thinks" is "the whole history of the world," with the world being "the necessary thought of God" (ibid., 224–25). At the heart of Hegel's dialectical vision are three distinguishable moments in God: "essential Being, explicit, Self-existence, which is the otherness of essential Being, and for which that Being is an object; and Self-existence or Self-knowledge in the other" (quoted GGP, 149; cf. RMW, Ch. 20). In Ward's reading, the first moment, "Essential Being," or "Being-in-itself" is the "complete array of all possible ideas in the mind of God." Hegel in contrast to Augustine and Aquinas sees the ideas in the divine Mind as *only potential*, and not fully real. In order to truly actualize their ideational reality, which is the Divine Being Itself, God *needs* the world. The universe as such is a necessarily a part of divine self-realization; in God there is a "necessity compelling Spirit to . . . make manifest what is inherent," Hegel insists. In manifesting an actual universe, Ward states that the universe "objectifies some of the ideas in the mind of God" so that "God can know them as objects" alienated from the divine nature. This is the objectification of being, the "otherness of essential Being," the second moment in the life of God (quoted ibid., 150).

The third moment concerns the reconciliation and unification of the entire "fallen" universe to God. Here, Being exists "in-and-for itself" when all imperfections are reconciled into a higher divine harmony and "integrated into the finally achieved consciousness of Absolute Spirit." Ward stresses that Spirit is again similar to Aristotle's "Prime Mover" in its blissful contemplation of its own perfection. This state for Hegel, however, only comes at the end of history when all struggles are thwarted and harmonized in the life of Spirit, now existing as fully actualized reality (ibid.). Ward insists, however, that we should not imagine this as a "time-bound process," as if God literally moves from unconsciousness and pure potentiality to the actuality of a "perfect conscious Mind" at the end of the universe. In fact, Hegel holds that the "essential Being is inherently and from the start reconciled with itself"—the Idea which Thinks Itself. Time is essential to the divine Mind's self-realization in a way it has not been in the history of philosophical theology, but this Mind also transcends time and is "perfectly conscious Absolute Spirit, even at the beginning of the temporal process" (ibid., 151). In Hegel's idealism, therefore, divine Mind and Value are necessarily "other-ized" in the temporal unfolding of the universe, but they will also be harmonized in a total Unity of the divine Nature, something far beyond what finite human minds can conceive.

As with Hegel, it is clear that Ward greatly appreciates Whitehead's "process philosophy" as a form of "pluralistic idealism" (MM, 105; PF, 162–64).[4] He does not object to counting himself as a "process thinker," albeit not without expressing key philosophical reservations and theological qualifications.[5] Ward finds in Whitehead's "philosophy of organism" a repetition of

Hegelian intuitions of the universe as "an organic unity, with all its parts constituting an organic whole, and contributing to an all-including cosmic consciousness." Whitehead differs from Hegel, however, by assigning causal priority not to one Spirit, but to the many "actual events that form an infinite series without beginning or end" (GP, 97–98). In transforming long-standing static notions of enduring "substance" into those of creative "process," Ward praises Whitehead, saying, "for the first time in the history of philosophy, a major theistic philosopher not only stresses the reality of the finite, material world unequivocally, but also makes temporality a thing of positive value, the condition of real creativity" (RCG, 227). In contrast to classical theism, this creative temporality is exemplified in God not as defect, but as a mode of divine perfection. This temporal creativity is also embodied in all events which constitute the becoming world. More than any other philosopher, Ward states that Whitehead has "stressed the primary value and importance of creativity, in the sense of bringing into being something radically new" (CIG, 147). Ward confidently states, moreover, that Whitehead's vision of the "temporality and dipolarity of God" provides "the logical key" to reconciling ancient problems of creation and necessity. "Only if God is temporal, can he be a free creator of a universe of free creatures; only if he is eternal, can he possess that necessity which is the foundation of the intelligibility of the world; only if he is dipolar, can he be both." In this way, God is necessary in the divine "eternal nature" and also contingent in the "everlasting temporal acts" in which this nature is expressed (RCG, 230).[6]

Ward is making positive reference here to what Whitehead calls the "primordial nature" of God as the necessary and abstract "Place of Forms," or the "conceptual array of all possibilities." He is also referencing Whitehead's "consequent nature" of God as the receptive inclusion of "all temporal process in the 'perfected actuality' of the divine consciousness." God also has a "superjective nature" for Whitehead, wherein, as Ward states, "the contents of the divine consciousness *pass back* into the temporal world" (ibid., 228; CC, 258–59, emphasis mine). On the whole, Ward strongly supports this relational theological vision. He highlights the "deep influence" process philosophy has had on protestant theology by situating Mind and Value in an evolutionary context where freedom, creativity, temporality, and purpose relationally interact, from the finite constituents comprising nature to the infinite consciousness of God. Ward is in fundamental agreement with what he sees as the core convictions of this vision.

> It is an attempt to work out what the universe must be like if consciousness and value (and the purposes that seek to realise value) are primary elements of reality, rather than unexpected and causally sterile side-effects of unconscious and directionless material forces. It takes evolutionary theory and post-relativity

physics seriously. It insists that change and radical creativity are not imperfections, but positive values that must somehow be included in any idea of God as supreme perfection. It affirms that human history and development affect the being of God in important ways, so that the divine truly shares in the travails of creation. It affirms that humans are free to determine their own destinies, without being determined by eternal divine decrees. And it sees the whole of history of the cosmos as integrated forever in the consciousness of God, and so as contributing to a full realisation of consciously apprehended value that could in principle be shared by infinite numbers of different conscious beings. (GP, 98–99)

Although Ward has not written extensively on John Leslie, he is certainly familiar with his work, having made positive reference to and also some strong critiques of his contributions in several of his own publications. Ward agrees strongly with Leslie that if scientists do "press their questions to the ultimate degree," asking, "Why are the ultimate laws of nature as they are, and why is the initial state of nature as it is?"—then an "obvious" reason to offer is "precisely a teleological reason." In positive nod to Leslie, Ward states that a teleological reason "would state how the initial state and the laws together are well formed to actualize states of value. As John Leslie says, the ultimate reason why things are the way they are is likely to be: because they actualise great and distinctive values." The world could then exist "as a result of an ethical need" (GCN, 22, 33).

Ward also agrees with Leslie that a fundamental axiological reason can be given for a "being of supreme goodness," whose own existence might be "supremely desirable, not least to itself" (RC, 196). In this way, God would not have to "first think about what is good and then choose to be good"—as if this was something God might *not* have done; rather, the "choice" that a supremely good being should exist is a "selection that follows immediately from the nature of the set of all possible states." In this way, Ward states, the "supremely good follows from its own possibility just because it has, as John Leslie has put it, an "intrinsic ethical requiredness" such that the "supreme good is necessarily actualized, in the perfection of the Divine Being itself" (QSR, 26).

In contrast to Leslie, however, there are for Ward "other factors" that will not have this "element of necessity." Should love and cooperation be "great goods," for example, then a "Cosmic Consciousness" would have good reason to "actualize other conscious beings whom it can love and cooperate with"; this reason might not be utterly compelling, however (ibid.). A universe that is truly "other" to God, moreover, might be an object of "further appreciation" and "fuller creativity," for Ward. While there may or may not be "a requirement that some such universe should exist," Ward insists that creative divine choice not only in terms of which universes to actualize but also in terms of how to creatively relate to them would be a great good for a divine Mind (ibid.). We will come back to this point in Part IV specifically.

While Leslie's own Platonic vision resonates with that of Ward's, Ward strongly pushes back against the notion of "Infinite Gods," "best possible worlds," and an essentially domineering "ethical requirement" that is *not* creatively rooted and channeled through a divine Mind, which is, in some real sense, "other" to creation (CIG, 98; CC, 188). In Leslie, Ward finds an "interesting and powerful *reductio ad absurdum*" that there "must be an infinite number of perfect Minds, since the more Minds there are, the more experiences of Good there are." While tempted to agree in part, Ward nevertheless insists that many "instinctively feel" averse to this conclusion. Indeed, on Ward's reading, the axiom that "the more good things there are the better" condemns Leslie to the "Leibnizian Rule" that God *must* produce the "best of all possible worlds" and an "infinite number of good things," including "an infinite number of other Gods." "God" then is really just "a member of an infinitely large class of Gods"—Leslie's infinite divine Ocean (CC, 188).

Ward readily grants the validity of Leslie's argument, but only as it is attached to the Leibnizian Rule. Ward himself rejects this rule, saying, "There may not be such a thing as 'the best possible world." First, it may be that there are an "infinite number of different forms of goodness," but "no such thing as an actually infinite number of things" so that it would be "logically impossible for God to create all those goods." What then of a "best possible world?" Second, Ward says one could simply deny that God is "obligated" to create *anything at all*, let alone a *maximum number of things*. "If God creates good things," he states, "that is good. If God creates more good things, that is better. But there is no "best," and there is no obligation on God to create any good things at all, since God in the divine being is perfect anyway and it may be better to leave well alone" (ibid., 189). Ward's point here is clear, but his words might be seen as a bit flippant (even by Leslie). We will see in another chapter that his own proposal actually cast much doubt on these statements. It remains questionable whether or not he is taking the heart of Leslie's arguments seriously.[7]

Nevertheless, for Ward, Leslie has introduced a "new principle" that "possible goodness is, in and of itself, 'a creative ethical requirement.'" But this is not without its problems. To move from saying it is *good* that something exist, to that it *ought* to exist, to that it *will* exist, is precisely what many people "rightly find unconvincing" for Ward. While he admits that his own vision of God as infallibly knowing what is good and acting for its sake is "a sort of creative ethical requirement," he is unconvinced that there is a *domineering* requirement "that every good thing should exist." What is more, Ward insists that "there is *no requirement at all* unless there is an actual being in whom that requirement can exist as a possible reason for acting" (ibid., emphasis mine). In the next chapter, we will see that Ward shares this critique with other interpreters of Leslie, at least in part. Ward, therefore, believes that Leslie's argument "stands in need of a theistic amendment." This would not only give creative priority to the divine Mind over the Value which ground its inner necessity, but would also recognize a *relational otherness* between God and creation, which is arguably lacking in Leslie's proposal (ibid.). We will explicitly consider the status of the world in Leslie, Ward, and Whitehead in our last two chapters.

THE PRIMORDIALITY OF MIND

In focusing on Ward's idealistic interpretation of the tradition, I have attempted to show the ways in which his reading, despite recognizing an essential place for Value, has sought to emphasize the primordiality of Mind. In many places, however, Ward does seem to recognize a kind of *internal relationality* between Mind and Value in God, and perhaps also in the tradition. He seems to recognize this in a way that is not so obvious in Leslie. Although it is perhaps implicit in their contributions, explicit treatment of this relationality in both thinkers is lacking. While Leslie stresses the abstractness of "ethical requirements" for the existence of the divine Mind, Ward stresses the actuality of Mind as the proper context in which Creative Value can be rendered cogent. Some clear differences between them notwithstanding, they have nevertheless arrived at very similar conclusions from their respective axiarchic and idealistic priorities. Both these "readings" of the tradition, I want to emphasize, are valid. My own reference to this tradition as *axianoetic* aims to recognize this *more explicitly*. Still, I think more can and should be said about the *relationship* between Mind and Value *in* God that does justice not only to fundamental insights of Leslie and Ward but also illuminates ambiguities of the axianoetic tradition in a fresh way. To this end, we turn to the relational insights of Whitehead, which I believe offer much when considering this question. We will then show how the essential relationality of Mind and Value lies just below the surface of key comments and contributions others have made in relation to Leslie's extreme axiarchism.

NOTES

1. For Ward's discussion of distinctions between Absolute and Personal Idealism, refer to *Morality, Autonomy and God* (MAG), Ch. 14.

2. "It is plausible view," he states, "that the existence of any good depends upon the existence of some consciousness which values it as good. It is not very plausible to think that one state of the universe would be better than another if no being was conscious of the difference. It is hard to see what 'betterness' would come to in such a case. The philosopher G. E. Moor once held that a beautiful universe, unseen by anyone, was better than an ugly universe. But it seems to me that without being appreciated or disliked, no state of the universe would really be of greater value than any other. If that is so, value must consist in appreciation by some consciousness" (RC, 183).

3. See for example, Keith Ward, *Religion and Creation* (RC), 209–14; *Christ and the Cosmos* (CC, Ch. 5), and his recent text, *Sharing in the Divine Nature* (SDN).

4. "Whitehead's form of pluralistic idealism presents a philosophical hypothesis that takes account of the continuity and emergent development of the natural world and stresses the value of creativity, individuality, and freedom in nature that can be overlooked in some forms of absolute idealism" (MM, 62). "I call [Whitehead's view] a form of idealism because the engine of the process is not the mechanical movement of non-purposive physical entities, but the potentially mind-like reality or realities that are creatively and progressively expressed in the physical cosmos, and in the gradual unfolding values that where implicit from the first in that cosmos" (ibid., 102). For Ward, the "pluralistic" nature of Whitehead's idealism is based in the fact that "there are many mental realities, rather than just one dominating Absolute Mind" (ibid., 52).

5. "The system of process philosophy—with its apparent denial that God is the originating cause of all things, that there is a completion and fulfilment of the cosmic process, and that there exists substantial persons and things—is only one form of idealism, and it may be misleading to call my view a 'process' view. On the other hand, I would not cavil at that terminology, as long as the ultimate sovereignty of God, the ultimate triumph of goodness, and the ultimate reality of finite persons is affirmed" (CIG, 137, n. 3). In personal correspondence, Ward details some of these qualifications further, saying, "I just don't like 'actual occasions.' They are too small for my liking, and I do think the idea of an enduring (spiritual) subject is necessary to hold streams of experiences together as 'mine' or 'yours.' Also, I find it misleading to speak of electrons as having 'feelings,' even unconscious ones. I [am] wholly unconvinced by the arguments [saying] that it is easier to speak of intelligent consciousness emerging from unconscious feelings than it is to speak of it as emerging from unconscious material things. Though I like the analysis of personal experience, I don't see the need to extend this sort of analysis to everything; and what is wrong with ex nihilo creation? . . . I have not written very fully about this, I am afraid, so those are just random prejudices." E-mail correspondence, October 16, 2017. In a variety of publications, Ward's has nonetheless propounded the "basic" philosophical and theological insights of Whitehead, making it clear, however, that one can appreciate these insights without following Whitehead all the way. "As with many philosophical systems, it may be wise to accept some general insights [of process philosophy] while resisting the intricacies of detail that seem to go with devising a grand philosophical system. Whitehead himself is alleged to have said, as he was dying, 'I want no

disciples'—to which of course those around him said 'Yes Master.' Process thought is not a final dogmatic system. It is more a spur to thinking in new ways about our complex universe" (MM, 61).

6. Ward qualifies these comments, however, saying, "But if one rejects Whitehead's view that 'the ultimate metaphysical truth is atomism,' and if one is not convinced that substances can be reduced to processes, there is no reason why one should not see God himself as the uniquely self-existent being, who freely decides to create beings other than himself" (ibid.).

7. In suggesting that "God had no duty to create anything," Leslie finds Ward's words "hard to accept." In response, Leslie again pushes for infinite minds: "God is fairly standardly described as omnipotent. Why then, no duty to create infinitely many minds that were like God in knowing immensely much that was worth knowing? Why do we see a world which, besides having the plagues and earthquakes which are grist to the usual Problem of Evil mills, can seem severely unsatisfactory through not containing minds of that type?" John Leslie, "Infinity and the Problem of Evil," *European Journal of Philosophy* 11, no. 2 (2019): 1–2. We will consider the problem of evil with respect to Ward and Leslie's proposals in chapter 9.

Chapter 5

The Mutual Immanence of Mind and Value

Whitehead's affirmation of the ultimate status of Mind and Value is grounded in his broad agreement with the philosophical tradition. Although stated variously, the wisdom of this tradition holds firmly to their indispensability in approaching ultimate matters. At the foundations of this tradition stand Plato and Aristotle as pillars of metaphysical genius. Despite being the "poorest systematic thinker," Plato was the "greatest metaphysician" (AI, 166).[1] He is to be praised for his "wealth of general ideas" and "philosophic depth" in producing lasting writings that are an "inexhaustible mine of suggestion." In saying famously that the European philosophical tradition is best conceived as a series of Platonic "footnotes," Whitehead is including his own "philosophy of organism" as a refashioned expression of an essentially Platonic vision of things (PR, 39, 93).[2] Whitehead reaffirms and reconceives Plato's vision of a "basic Psyche whose active grasp of ideas conditions impartially the whole process of the Universe." This Psyche is the "Supreme Craftsman, on whom depends that degree of orderliness which the world exhibits." What is more, "there is a perfection in the Psyche," which, for Whitehead, "Plato finds out of his power to explain" (AI, 147). Of utmost importance, however, is Plato's conviction—if at times wavering—that the "divine element in the world is to be conceived as a persuasive agency and not a coercive agency." For Whitehead, this remains "one of the greatest "intellectual discoveries" in the history of philosophy and religion (AI, 167).[3]

In like manner, Aristotle stands next to Plato. In commenting that "Aristotle found it necessary to complete his metaphysics by the introduction of a Prime Mover—God," Whitehead states that this was an "important fact in the history of metaphysics." In the first place, Whitehead insists that "if we are to accord to anyone the position of the greatest metaphysician, having regard to genius of insight, to general equipment in knowledge, and to the stimulus of his metaphysical ancestry, we must choose Aristotle." Second, in his consideration of the "metaphysical question" of God, Aristotle was "entirely dispassionate," being "last European metaphysician of first-rate importance for whom this claim can be made." Despite not being obviously amenable to religious interests, Whitehead is confident that Aristotle's affirmative conclusion of "God" represents "a first step without which no [religious] evidence on a narrower experimental basis can be of much avail in shaping the conception [of God]" (SMW, 173).

Although undeveloped, Whitehead early on finds his own philosophy *requiring* a similar theological need for coherence. As it developed, however, it would not simply reproduce that of Aristotle (ibid., PR, 342–43). Still, Aristotle merits much praise for his repudiation of Platonic dualism and Whitehead would come to affirm his general insistence that the "divine element" must be understood in terms of "actuality" in order for facts and reasons to hold any efficacious explanatory appeal. "By this recognition of the divine element the general Aristotelian principal is maintained that, apart from things that are actual, there is nothing—nothing either in fact or in efficacy" (PR, 40). This "ontological principal" for Whitehead insists that "everything is positively somewhere in actuality, and in potency everywhere." As in Aristotle and much of the tradition, application of this principle "issues in the doctrine of conceptualism" such that the "reasons for things are always to be found in the composite nature of definite actual entities—in the nature of God for reasons of the highest absoluteness, and in the nature of definite temporal actual entities for reasons which refer to a particular environment." Defined as such, the ontological principle "constitutes the first step in the description of the universe as a solidarity of many actual entities" (ibid., 40, 18).

MIND, VALUE, AND GOD

Our aim in bringing in Whitehead's affirmation of Plato and Aristotle is *solely theological*. They form the metaphysical foundations of Western philosophy and theology. We are again interested in how Mind and Value might relate *in* God in a way that coherently sustains divine existence as *Necessary*. Much more of course can be said of Whitehead's relationship to the tradition; it is manifold and layered in a host of intricate ways.[4] My intention here, however, is *not* to offer a systematic treatment of his theological reading of this tradition in terms of Mind and Value. This is not even possible. In contrast to Leslie and Ward, Whitehead does not offer such a narrowly focused reading of the select figures. His dialogical aims with the tradition are many, and certainly far *less* theologically concerned than those of Leslie and Ward. Even so, his appeal to the theological contributions of Plato and Aristotle is also an implicit appeal to the fundamental place of Mind and Value in the nature of things. Despite recoil from many of his peers, Whitehead himself would hold firmly to the fundamental place of "God" in his philosophy conceived in these terms.[5]

In reference to Aristotle, not only did Whitehead insist in his first ever chapter on "God" that "nothing, within any limited type of experience, can give intelligence to shape our ideas of an entity at the base of things, unless the general character of things *requires* that there be such an entity," he also reflects upon his mature metaphysics saying, although the necessary "primordial nature" of God was *not* included in his "categoreal notions . . . it should have been" (SMW, 173–74, emphasis mine).[6] For Whitehead, to speak of a "requirement" for God is to speak of God's *necessary existence* in and for the nature of things; and to say that God *belongs* among the "categoreal notions" is to affirm the necessity of God for *his* metaphysics. With Leslie and Ward, we can ask after the nature of this "requirement" for God and how Whitehead conceives the divine nature, particularly as it relates to the relationship between Mind and Value. These are not questions Whitehead himself explicitly treats, but he does offer much for us in approaching an answer that is consistent with his relational scheme of thought.

Mutual Immanence as a Relationship within God

For Whitehead, God is best conceived as a divine Mind with *both* a "primordial" and "consequent" nature. Taken in abstraction, God's "primordial nature" is permanent conceptual Mentality; it is the eternal and necessary foundation of Divinity (and the World) understood as unconscious, nonactual, and complete within itself. Here, God is the "unlimited conceptual realization of the absolute wealth of potentiality" (PR, 343).[7] By contrast, the consequent nature of God is fully aware Intellect, actual, and in receptive relationality with the world process. Here, God is the conscious and everlasting "realization of the actual world in the unity of [the divine] nature, and through the transformation of [divine] wisdom" (ibid., 46, 345). God as a divine Mind, therefore, is a *relational* and *dipolar fusion* of abstract and concrete, independent and related, permanent and transient domains. "I think the universe has a side which is mental and permanent," Whitehead states. "This side is that prime conceptual drive which I call the primordial nature of God." On the other hand, Whitehead holds that "this permanent actuality *passes into* and is *immanent* in the transient side"—the consequent nature of God (PR, 126, emphasis mine). For Whitehead, moreover, it is essential to grasp that "God as primordial is *not* a distinct actuality; only the *union* of primordial and consequent natures forms a distinct actuality."[8] This relational "union"

Whitehead calls "mutual immanence"; it is a relationship *in* God that understands "each side lending to the other a factor necessary for its reality" (PR, 126). "The primordial nature is conceptual," while "the consequent nature is the weaving of God's physical feeling [derived from the world] upon his primordial concepts" (PR, 345).

It remains difficult to consider God in abstraction from the World in Whitehead's scheme of thought. For now, however, it is important to state briefly what we will consider much more deeply in chapter 10, namely that mutual immanence for Whitehead is not only an *intra-divine* mode of relationality but also the proper mode of relationality between God and the World as such. "It is as true to say that the World is immanent in God, as that God is immanent in the World," Whitehead tells us; the World is to be understood "as requiring its union with God, and God as requiring his union with the World" (PR, 348; AI, 168).

Whitehead traces the origins of mutual immanence to the "metaphysical discovery" of Christian theology in its struggle to clarify multiplicity in the divine nature and in God's relationship to the world more generally (AI, 168–69).[9] In the development of the tradition, however, it was largely forgotten that "every entity"—including God—"is to be understood in terms of the way in which it is interwoven with the rest of the Universe" (Imm., 91). Whitehead makes strong claims for mutual immanence. This mode of Relationality is "the key to metaphysics" and indeed a "fundamental philosophical doctrine" not only with respect to God *in se* but also in terms of God's relationship with the World (PR, 126; Imm., 91). It is in this sense that Roland Faber is fully justified in saying that over and above all formative elements in Whitehead's metaphysics, "mutual immanence" as the fundamental *way* in which things are *entangled* and *reciprocally supportive* is *"the* ultimate reality in Whitehead's thought" (TBG, 97). In abstraction from the World then, God is conceived as Permanent Mentality with unconscious and conscious domains, those *abstract* and *axiological* on the one hand and those *concrete* and *evaluational* on the other. Only in the mutually immanent union of these domains can one speak of God as fully actual Mind.

Value as Reason, Purpose, and Foundation of Divine Mind

That the "reason," "purpose," or "foundation" of God is to be found in the Supremacy of divine Value is at the heart of Whitehead's philosophy. In his early statements about God, he provocatively spoke of God's "existence" as the "ultimate irrationality," saying that "no reason can be given for the nature of God, because that nature is the ground of rationality." The limits of rationality are reached; there must be a divine "categorical limitation" operative in the nature of things "which does not spring from any metaphysical reason." While there is a "metaphysical need" for a divine "principle of determination," Whitehead insists that "no metaphysical reason" can be given "for what is determined" (SMW, 178). Although one might hark back to Leslie's critique and perhaps interpret these statements as an appeal to God's "brute" or "reasonless" existence, or indeed, as a nod to divine existence as "logically" necessary, this would be a mistake. Whitehead already insists that "limitation" or "determination" in the "envisaging mode of [divine] activity" is the "price of value" and that there "cannot be value without antecedent standards of value." From where, however, do these *antecedent standards* of value derive? Whitehead states that it must stand in "God's nature to divide the Good from the Evil" (ibid., 179). Here, according to Stephen Lee Ely, is Whitehead's early assertion "without explanation, that God is good."[10] Indeed, this is a clear association of Goodness with the divine Nature, suggesting that the foundations—perhaps even the "reason"—of divinity has direct recourse to the creative efficacy of Value or Goodness.

This becomes far more explicit as Whitehead's thought on God develops. God becomes an "actual entity" whose "conceptual" or "perceptual" activity axiological conditions the process of the world. It is "God" who is "the measure of the aesthetic consistency of the world," Whitehead insists, and whose creative purpose is "the attainment of value in the temporal world" (RM, 86–87, 90). This value derives from God as the limiting "ground antecedent to transition" who includes "all possibilities of value conceptually." "The limitation of God is his goodness," Whitehead states, and God as divine Mind "gains his depth of actuality by his harmony of valuation" such that the "transmutation of evil into good enters into the actual world by reason of the inclusion of the nature of God." Indeed the "power by which God sustains the world is the power of himself as the ideal," such that the very world lives through its incarnation of divine Value (ibid., 137–40). These statements seem clear: the divine "purpose" and "the depth of actuality," which is the divine existence, are axiologically grounded. Not only does Value sustain the existence and reason for the world, God *in se* is sustained and reasoned by the necessity of the Divine Value.

If one should be skeptical of this reading, Whitehead makes even stronger statements to this end in his mature works. In discussing the interplay of the primordial and consequent natures in God, he insists that "the necessary goodness" of the primordial nature "expresses the determination of his consequent nature" (PR, 345). He associates God directly with "the World of Value" where Value represents the infinity of values in their timeless infinity. The "concept of God" in terms of the "World of Value" concerns "the essential unification of the Universe," he states (Imm., 97).[11] What is more, the necessity of the divine existence itself is fundamentally axiological such that Whitehead insists unambiguously that God's existence "is founded in Value" and is to be conceived as persuasive toward "ideal co-ordination." The "nature of God" is "founded on ideals of perfection, moral and aesthetic"; God receives into the unity of the divine nature "the scattered effectiveness of realized activities," but they are "transformed by the supremacy of [divine] ideals." What results, Whitehead imagines, is *tragedy* in God, which takes realistic precedence over "profane" ascriptions of "mere happiness," let alone visions of blissful perfection (Imm., 98, 101–2). Elsewhere in fact, Whitehead's insists that "God is tragic and noble, not perfect." In contrast to "Absolute Idealism," evil is not "ultimately a neutral element in an all-inclusive perfection," but is rather experienced as tragic in comparison to the ideals of the divine nature.[12] Nevertheless, a mode of perfection *does* remain in "God's subjective aim," for Whitehead. This aim is derived from the axiological completeness of the primordial nature and issues forth into the character of the consequent nature (PR, 345–46).

Whitehead has insisted clearly that *Value* conditions all ultimate explanations—that "all ultimate reasons are in terms of an aim at value" (MT, 135). According to the ontological principle, all reasons are *also* in terms of *Actuality*. Value and Actuality come together in Mental Activity—the conceptual workings of Mind as the "organ of novelty" and the "urge of appetition." This is the case both for finite worldly entities (to limited degrees) and for the eternal and everlasting Actual Entity, which is God (to upmost degrees).[13] As Actual Entity, God grounds order, value, and novelty by virtue of God's primordial Mental Appetition.[14] In quest for a *reason* or *explanation* of God, therefore, we find these two insights wedding abstract Value and actual Mind together. At the base of the Primordial Actuality of Mind is the Creative Supremacy of Value, each offering to the other what in isolated abstraction each would lack. Although Whitehead does not explicitly put it this way, I believe it is consistent with his, and also Ward and Leslie's thought, to say that it is *Value* which gives God God's ultimate reason or explanation, and *Mind* which is the *proper context* in which any axiological reason *can actually be given*. In God, both coincide in that *kind of relationality* Whitehead calls mutual immanence. The divine Mind therefore *requires* Value just as Value *requires* the divine Mind; each reciprocally procures the existence of the other. In doing so, each also transcends the other in providing what the other cannot provide for itself. Taken as a whole, the mystery of divine necessity, therefore, is the mystery of the mutual immanence and transcendence of Mind and Value—the irreducible way in which each is *requiring* of the other. It is this relational Whiteheadian vision that may silently undergird not only Leslie and Ward's contributions but also those of other voices who have entered the discussion.

THE UNSPOKEN MUTUAL IMMANENCE
OF MIND AND VALUE

John Leslie's contributions as to a creative "ethical requirement" for the existence of a divine Mind, and a Universe of things, have bloomed a variety of responses in the current discussion. In addition to being positive and complimentary, these responses have also been critical on key points of concern. My goal in the rest of this chapter is to show the ways in which some responses have both critiqued and agreed with his extreme emphasis on the creative determinations of abstract "Goodness" and opened strongly suggestive (albeit unstated) spaces for the mutual immanence of Mind and Value. In part, Leslie has anticipated, and even affirmed, these responses as they come from John Polkinghorne, Mark Wynn, Hugh Rice, Peter Forrest, and A. C. Ewing. On his account, they are viable forms of "axiarchism." Although under the surface, each of these figures assumes or stands in need of a kind of relationship between Mind and Value best conceived in terms of mutual immanence. This is vague in some of their expressions and rather explicit in others. Leslie positively cites each of them in reference to his work, but he does not fully recognize the wider undercurrent of *relationality between Mind and Value* that lies beneath their commentary. Leslie himself, we remember, has repeatedly granted that there could be an eternally creative ethical requiredness for a divine Mind, such that this requirement "would have its sources *in* that mind's own tremendously rich nature," but he too has not properly grasped the *necessity for relationality* between Mind and Value (IM, 156, emphasis mine). Among each of these figures, therefore, I seek to show how intriguing spaces are opened for affirming the kind of mutually immanent relationality Whitehead imagines.

John Polkinghorne: Goodness and Its Instantiation

For John Polkinghorne to say "God is good" is not simply to utter a tautology. This would risk making God a "kind of celestial dictator whose will is 'good' by mere definition." Neither should God be "adjudged perfect on some independently existing scale of goodness." This would seem to make goodness "prior" or "superior" to God. Rather, the answer must lie in a "refusal to refrain from making differentiated statements about God" and an "insistence upon the *self-sustaining integrity of the divine nature*, so that God and his goodness are *neither arbitrarily identical nor absolutely separable*." For Polkinghorne, this is what the tradition of philosophical theology suggests in their celebrated "equation of divine essence and divine existence." In God, "self-subsistent perfection" is the identification within the divine nature, not only of "cause and effect" but also of "*supreme goodness and its instantiation* in a divine bootstrap of virtue" (FP, 58, emphasis mine). Polkinghorne cites Ward approvingly when he states that divine goodness is "a necessary part of the being of God and could not exist as necessary in isolation from the totality of the Divine nature" (ibid., quoting RCG, 177). "If all that is right," Polkinghorne concludes, then "John Leslie's extreme axiarchism (the creative effectiveness of supreme ethical requiredness) is not a Neoplatonic 'Originating Principle' which might have as a consequence, in some emanating and descending chain of being, that there was 'an all-powerful person, an omniscient Designer,' but it is properly to be understood, purely and simply, as an *insight into the divine nature itself*" (ibid., quoting U, 166, emphasis mine; cf., IM, 163, n. 3).

Polkinghorne's comments refuse to separate or identify Value and God; rather, he points to, but does not name the fact that Goodness and God are *related* in such a way that "essence and existence," "cause and effect," and "goodness and its instantiation" are rendered coherent in a "divine bootstrap of virtue." This is rather vague, however. What is missing from Polkinghorne's comments, and arguably assumed by them, is recourse to the *kind of relationship* that obtains in God. In God, Essence is essential to Existence as Existence is essential to Essence, Cause is essential to Effect as Effect is essential to Cause, and Goodness is essential to its Instantiation as its Instantiation is essential to the fact that it is Good. The "divine bootstrap of virtue" is founded in the *relationality* between these domains of divinity and what they each reciprocally grant each other. Put differently, the "self-sustaining integrity of the divine nature" is founded upon the relationship of mutual immanence where Essence and Existence, Cause and Effect, Value and Mind mutually sustain the other. Value *eternally procures* the existence of Mind and Mind *eternally conditions* the creative efficacy of Value. Polkinghorne rightly sees Leslie's axiarchic emphasis as an "insight into the divine nature itself," but Value is *relativized* on behalf of a wider context of relationality in God. This relational undercurrent is underdeveloped in both thinkers, but it is just beneath the surface of their thought.

Mark Wynn: Both Mind and Value Have a Claim

Mark Wynn admits to having no "deep seated objection" to Leslie's contributions. In fact, the approach he himself commends is "closely aligned with the spirit of Leslie's account" (GG, 66). Wynn thinks, however, that "in practice" Leslie's insights "will tend to converge with personalistic theism." His explanation weds Value and Mind together in ways that please Leslie (at least in part): "After all, if we grant that consciousness is a profound value, then we are likely to suppose that there is an ethical requirement that there be a supreme consciousness. So the question of whether Leslie's approach is right is perhaps more a matter of religious sensibility than a matter of ontology, since his ontology is likely to include *both* a set of causally efficacious ethical requirements *and* a transcendent intelligence" (ibid.). Indeed, Leslie does hold that the eternal procurement of Mind by Value is a robust and viable form of axiarchism. Wynn then oddly states that the question "Is there a God" might very well become "a question about which of these realities is appropriately considered divine." Would it not be an odd exercise, however, to attempt to name which of these *inseparable* domains *in* God are "divine"? Wynn admits after all that "it may be that *both have a claim to this title*" (ibid., emphasis mine; cf. IM, 187). If so, adjudicating which is "appropriately considered divine"—presumably over and against the other—hardly makes sense. If *both* Value and Mind have a claim, they both have a claim *for and to the other*, and the question of God's existence must seek that mode of *relationality* that obtains between these divine axianoetic "claims." Space here is again opened for a vision of the mutually immanent "claims" of Value and Mind for each other. While Value concerns the ethical requiredness *for* Mind, Mind contextually reinforces this ethical requiredness *as* creatively effective. The existence of God is founded in the mutually immanent *coincidentia* of both.

Hugh Rice: Goodness without Mind's Mediation

Although his arguments are different from those of Leslie, Hugh Rice has followed him in defending the idea that a world such as ours exists because *it is good that it should*. Yet, he claims he differs from Leslie in saying that one should "identify the basic fact that a thing is good with God's willing that there should be such a thing." Put differently, "we should understand God's willing that something should be so as its *being good that that something should be so*" (GG, vii, emphasis mine). Although this should be distinguished from "explanation in terms of a personal God," the notion that the universe can be explained "directly in term of its goodness," nevertheless, amounts to "an explanation in terms of God's will" (ibid., 49, n. 1). Rice's understanding of God, however, is deliberately *abstract* and does not appeal to an overt conception of God as some mediating agent, person, or mind (ibid., 88; IM, 179–80). Nevertheless, he does affirm an *analogical* sense in which language of God "creating," "knowing," "willing," and "loving" is appropriate to describe the fact that "what is good affects the way things are directly" (ibid., 88–89). This may be misleading, however. He certainly does recognize the essential role of God as a mediating Mind in discussions surrounding the objective goodness of things. "Why might one prefer an account which introduces a mediating God?" Rice asks. "Well, the most obvious reason would be that one took the view that the *only* way in which objective value could make a difference was at the level of thought. For then, if one wished to explain the existence of the world by an appeal to goodness, one would be obliged to suppose that the explanation involved an appeal to a mind which apprehended the goodness; so one would naturally be led to the idea of a mediating God" (ibid., 51).

Although Rice grants that the only experience of goodness is indeed in terms of its effect on, or apprehension by minds, he finds greater difficulty in conceiving how a Mind could *create* anything at all, "except possibly thoughts, *ex nihilo.*" This is at least as difficult, he thinks, as conceiving a universe existing as a *direct result of its goodness*. What is more, he insists that an account which includes a mediating Mind "leaves more unexplained than the account which does not: namely the existence of the mediating God" (ibid., 51–52). He thus insists that a mediating God is *not* to be preferred to his alternative proposal that the abstract Goodness of the universe is *explicitly responsible for its existence*. Ockham's razor, Rice claims, supports this approach.

These comments, however, are strange; for Rice had already acknowledged the fact that A. C. Ewing "argued that the existence of *God* should be explained in terms of the fact that it is good that he should exist" (ibid., 49–50, n.1.). We will discover below in fact that attention to Ewing's insights reveal his clear commitment to the *mutual immanence* of Mind and Value, rather than a choice *between* them. More than any other, Ewing has achieved remarkable clarity in this regard, but his affirmation of the *mutuality* between Mind and Value has not been duly acknowledged, either by Rice or Leslie. While Rice does raise an important point we will later consider in Part IV, namely the difficulty of conceiving how the *thoughts* of divine Mind could effectively create laws, let alone a universe, he does not realize the insight of at once *relating* Mind and Value in such a way that Value gives Mind its *explanation* as Mind gives Value its *mediation*.

Peter Forrest: Combining Value and Mind

Peter Forrest has strongly promoted the "Aesthetic" or "Value Principle," which, through *"evaluative* understanding," might explain many of the features of the universe, "including its suitability to life, by appealing to its value, including its aesthetic value" (GWS, 149). Forrest recognizes Leslie's "extreme axiarchism"—that "things are as they are ethically required to be"—as a robust, but not unproblematic version of evaluative understanding. In part, he endorses Mackie's criticism of Leslie, which he thinks might also be "adopted by theists." This criticism focuses on the place of agency with respect to value: "All familiar cases in which things occur because they are ethically required are cases that can be understood in terms of *agency*. It is the belief that *something ought to be the case*, not the fact that it ought to, which brings it about. Moreover, if that belief brings something about, then it does so because *someone has the belief*" (ibid., 151). Forrest agrees that "what is ethically required does tend to get done, but only because there are good people around." Beauty does indeed come to exist, "but only because people seek beauty." At the heart of these claims is the fact that "agents act for reasons." Assuming the whole cosmos is replete with discernable value, one can plausibly appeal to divine agency. Forrest states, "Anything we can understand by pointing to the beauty, goodness, or reasonableness of the universe could also be understood by appealing to the motives God has for creating it" (ibid.).

Forrest thus agrees with the "widespread thesis that, necessarily, there can be no values without consciousness of the value." When he combines this with his own speculative identification of God with "unrestricted consciousness," he finds that the two presumably "rival theories" now "come quite close together." "Anthropic theism now states that things are to be explained as a *result of consciousness of their value* whereas extreme axiarchism states that things are to be explained *as a result of their value*, of which *necessarily there is consciousness*" (ibid., 152, n. 8; emphasis mine). Forrest's statements in fact nicely undergird the respective emphases on Mind and Value exemplified in Ward and Leslie's reading of the tradition in the last two chapters. He himself draws the contrast between his and Leslie's proposal in a similar way: "On my speculation, God creates out of awareness of what is good, whereas on Leslie's account goodness itself brings about the existence of what is good without any awareness" (ibid., 209). Forrest may overstate this with respect to Leslie, however; for Leslie *does* hold that things are to be explained in terms of their Value, of which necessarily there *is* an infinite Awareness or divine Mind (infinite divine Minds).

Forrest does clearly show that he prioritizes Mind while Leslie prioritizes Value. Still, both "rival" theories do "come quite close together." In saying this, he suggests that these theories may not be all that "rival" after all. He confirms this saying, "Perhaps we do not have to choose between fundamental ways of understanding things. In that case we could claim that *both* evaluative and theocentric understanding approximate the truth" (ibid., 153, emphasis mine). To affirm *both*, however, does not yet ask the question of their *relationship* to one another. The question surfaces as to whether one can conceive their "closeness" or "togetherness" in such a way that claims of their supposed *rivalry* are transformed into claims of their *mutuality*. This is precisely what happens when one conceives Mind and Value in terms of their mutual immanence. Forrest vaguely realizes this in saying one can take an "integrated approach" that sees agency as supremely valuable such that "the production of what is good by someone acting for reasons is itself *better* than the spontaneous coming into existence of what is good." On this account, "it is *better* that there be a God who creates this universe than that this universe comes into existence spontaneously." What this would do, Forrest rightly recognizes, is limit the application of the Value Principle so that "it was restricted to an explanation of God." Here he also appeals to the insights of A. C. Ewing. The key result of "retaining both evaluative understanding and personal explanation," he states, "would be to endorse A.C. Ewing's answer to the question, 'Why is there a God?'" namely, "Because it is good that there is a God" (ibid.). While Forrest, like Rice, does not recognize that Ewing pinpoints precisely the *mutually immanent relationality* of Mind and Value, he does come close in his own proposal: "Finally," he states, "we might propose *combining* our fundamental ways of understanding. That results in an endorsement of theocentric understanding with the bonus that we can answer the question, Why is there a God" (ibid., 154, emphasis mine)?

A. C. Ewing: The Mutual Immanence of Mind and Value

Leslie often expresses his admiration and indebtedness to A. C. Ewing "for showing that an expert at philosophical analysis really can defend Platonism's creation story which he applied to explaining God's necessary existence." Ewing, Leslie claims, was "possibly the greatest idealist philosopher of the twentieth century," holding that the "existence of a divine person could be due *directly* to the ethical need for such a person to exist" (IM, viii, 163, emphasis mine). We will see below, however, that this is only *partly true in abstraction* for Ewing. Leslie again wants to *emphasize* the place of Value in Ewing as a premiere axiarchist. This is not false, but it does miss the fact that Value for Ewing is *not* simply unilateral or even "directly" responsible for the existence of God. Rather, Ewing points to a *wider relationality* between Value and Mind, and with a clarity only rivaled by statements Whitehead himself makes about the mutual immanence of God and the World.

Ewing has argued compellingly that God's necessity is *not* to be conceived in terms of logical necessity. In part, he is agreeing with and responding to Kant's "fatal objection" on this point (VR, 147).[15] Need divine necessity be conceived in terms of *logical necessity* after all? "Might not God be necessary in some sense other than that in which his necessity would mean that there was an internal contraction in denying his existence" (ibid., 155)? Providing a plausible "explanation" for God is central to the philosophical task because "an explanation of why something is true by reference to something else *which itself is unexplained* is not a satisfying explanation." Indeed, "without an answer on this point the child's question—What is the cause of God?—is sufficient to make the argument collapse" (ibid., 163, 157, emphasis mine). It is a truism for Ewing that "an affirmative existential proposition cannot be logically necessary," meaning that "an explanation in terms of logical argument is not possible." What ultimate explanation then can be offered for the existence of the world and the existence of God? Ewing arrives at Value as the only plausible alternative.

> If we are to meet the demand of the human intellect that there should be a reason, we seem to need a reason of such a kind as will give an explanation of existence without making the non-existence of anything logically self-contradictory. There remains only one alternative, as far as can be seen, which might do this, namely an explanation in terms of values. In that case, God's existence will be necessary not because there would be any internal self-contradiction in denying it but because it was supremely good that God should exist. It is not indeed evident to us a priori that the best possible being must exist, but a universe determined by values would certainly be rational in a very important sense in which a universe not determined by values would quite fail to be so, and the hypothesis that a complete perfection does constitute an adequate ground for existence does seem to be the only one which could make a universe intelligible and give an ultimate explanation of anything. (Ibid., 157)

These statements are compelling. If indeed the existence of God is axiologically determined, then, Ewing claims, the "existence of everything is." Put differently, "If any being exists on account of its value, the most perfect possible being must," so that "God's existence is not contingent," but "made necessary by his perfection" (ibid., 158). The "determination" by Value, moreover, is not "outside" God; nor is it properly conceived as "prior" or unilateral in nature. Ewing's statements as to the *relationality* of Mind and Value begin to emerge.

> So if the principle that the most perfect being must exist be true a priori—let us call it the value principle for short—since it entails that God exists, this would exclude and not imply the priority to God of the value principle. If essence entails existence, it will be because *essence cannot subsist without being realized in existence.* Somebody who argued, as many have done, that there must be a God because the laws of logic and ethics could not have being *except in a mind* is saying that these laws entail God, but he certainly would not be accused of therefore making them prior to God. One the contrary he would be saying, rightly or wrongly, *not that God could not exist without their being true but that they could not be true without God existing.* . . . A [value] principle is not a foreign existent outside God, and to assert the principle is simply to say that God's nature is such that he is completely self-sufficient and must exist. It is further equally true *that the principle could not be realized in existence and therefore could not be a true principle if God did not exist.* (Ibid., 164–65, emphasis mine)

While these statements clearly assume a kind of internal relationality between Value and Mind in God, Ewing has not yet stated their mutual immanence in full force. He first defends himself against those who might say, "God was created by another being." For him, this would clearly be "incompatible" with divine perfection. To the contrary, he claims that he has simply restated the "well-recognized theological doctrine by no means unorthodox in character," namely, that God is *causa sui*. He does not just say this, however. Ewing in fact goes further by pointing to a *kind of relationality* (albeit, unnamed) that obtains in God as *causa sui* that has arguably *not* been adequately recognized. To recognize this more explicitly is the central aim of this chapter. "To the objection that I am really suggesting that God is dependent on something other than himself, if only a [value] principle, I reply that to say that God depends on a principle for his existence is radically different from saying that God depends for his existence on some other existent being." Rather than existing "before God and creating him" the value principle "must always have been exemplified in the existence of God." As "actualized in the mind of God," the "value principle plus the principles determining the nature of a good life" have an "objective fundamental status" in the universe (ibid., 203).

In God, Ewing now explicitly expresses this relationship in terms of mutual immanence saying, "It would be as true to say that the [value] principle could not be true without God existing as to say that God could not exist without the principle being true" (ibid.). Readers of Whitehead will immediately recognize the resonance of Ewing's language with Whitehead's own when he expresses the mutual immanence and transcendence of God and the World: "It is as true to say that the World is immanent in God, as that God is immanent in the World. It is as true to say that God transcends the World, as that the World transcends God" (PR, 348). While these resemblances are striking, Ewing is focusing on God *in se*, which, as mentioned above, is rather challenging to do in Whitehead. Nevertheless, I think Ewing's statement is consistent with Whitehead's vision of God as a divine Mind whose "existence is founded in Value," on "ideals of perfection, moral and aesthetic."

Perhaps more than any other modern philosopher, Ewing recognizes clearly the *mutuality* between Value and Mind in God such that each *lives through what the other provides*. There is a sense of both immanence and transcendence in this mutuality. What is more, he grants that one could emphasize (as Leslie and Ward have done) one or the other, but that this would in fact only be *abstracting* them from their mutually immanent relationality. "These [value] principles and God would be inseparably linked," he states, "though in some respect or sense one might regard God as prior and in another sense the [value] principles. The latter would be prior in the sense that they gave the *reason* why God existed, and God in that the principles *could only be realized in being, have objectivity through God*" (VR, 203, emphasis mine).

This is a remarkable statement as to the mutually immanent roles Value and Mind play for each other in grounding God's necessary existence. As Whitehead puts it, "Each side lend[s] to the other a factor necessary for its reality." Although it may only be implicit in their proposals, it is this *kind of relationship*, which arguably integrates the respective emphases on Value by Leslie, and on Mind by Ward. It is this *mode of relationality*, which arguable undergirds the comments and critiques of the above thinkers who have entered the discussion; and it is this *presuppositional reciprocity* between Mind and Value in God that might illuminate ambiguities of the axianoetic tradition anew. To conclude, I will comment briefly in these directions.

MUTUAL IMMANENCE AND THE AXIANOETIC TRADITION

My goal in Part II has not only been to acknowledge more readily the *joining* of Value and Mind in some key figures of the tradition, but also to inquire into the *relationship* between Value and Mind as an insight into divine Necessity. Arguably, this question undergirds the entire tradition from Plato to Whitehead, Ward, and Leslie. I've sought to enter this discussion by showing that different emphases or priorities are possible. Despite their clear affinities, Leslie and Ward do retain distinctive *axiarchic* and *idealistic* emphases in approaching the tradition. While Leslie elevates the abstract priority of Value over Mind, Ward elevates the concrete priority of Mind over Value. In part, each has recognized that these need not be at odds with one another. My appeal to this tradition as *axianoetic* has sought to recognize the ultimacy of *both* Value and Mind in a more holistic and relational way.

I've wanted to go a step further, however, in claiming that Whitehead's own relational vision of mutual immanence actually offers a fresh way of illuminating the mystery of divine Necessity. At the heart of this mystery is the *reciprocal coinherence* of Mind and Value, each granting the other something indispensable for its reality. To conclude, I want to briefly comment on the implicit place for mutual immanence in Ward and Leslie's proposals, as well as suggest that mutual immanence may provide a lens for interpreting ambiguous statements of the axianoetic tradition anew.

Although Ward tends to emphasize the concrete priority of Mind, he nevertheless also recognizes some manner of *inherent relationality* between actual Mind and abstract Value. This is seen in his comments agreeing that Supreme Value or Goodness is a defensible axiological reason for God. The best explanation for God is that God is "supremely desirable, not least to [the divine] self." There is an implicit recognition here of a *relationality* between Value and Mind such that God's existence is explained not only in terms of *abstract*

Goodness but also in terms of *actual divine Knowledge or Awareness* of this Goodness. There are two relations here: *from Value to Mind* and *from Mind to Value*; they can be distinguished, but not fully isolated from the other. Ward conceives Goodness as "a necessary part of the being of God" that "could not exist as necessary in isolation from the totality of the Divine nature." From one direction, the "addition of the Mind to the Good" offers the "Good" what it cannot (as "pure conceptual ideal") offer itself—namely, its *creative efficacy* in sustaining Mind and any worlds Mind produces. From the other direction, the Good offers Mind what Mind devoid of the Good would lack—namely, a coherent axiological explanation (or reason) and criterion for adjudicating worlds. The mutual immanence and transcendence of Value and Mind in this regard appears rather straightforward in Ward. Indeed, one could even read it directly into his further claim that "God is the self-existent Ideal—not just an ideal without being, and not just the source of all derived being, without value; but the *congruence of ultimate value and reality in one transcending infinity*" (CG, 151–52, emphasis mine).

This kind of relationality is admittedly less apparent in Leslie, but not wholly absent. On his vision, Value *unilaterally* procures and explains the necessity of infinite Mind(s) as "supremely needful," and with an eternal creative success. He readily grants that such a Mind could have an "ethical side to it," an "ethical requiredness" with sources internal to that mind's own nature. What is arguably *underemphasized* in Leslie's "extreme axiarchism," however, is what Mind *offers* to Value in return. In holding that an abstract ethical requirement *for the existence of this Mind* is not ultimately separable from the *actuality of this Mind really existing*, Leslie does seem to open himself to conceiving a mode of relationality between Value and Mind that is not just unilateral. What does the existence of Mind consist in for Leslie? He insists that the divine Mind contemplates *everything of utmost value*. This is a knowledge of absolutely everything *worth* knowing, one which, of necessity, must contemplate not only *all worthwhile worlds* but also *Itself* as eternally required by Value. If it is "worth knowing that ethical requirements are what are responsible" for the divine Mind's existence, Leslie states, then the divine Mind "automatically knows these things" (IM, 165). It is through the inclusion of this Mind's *own* Value in its *own* Contemplation, I claim, that we arrive at a relationship of mutual immanence. This very *awareness* of divine Value *is* the *creative gift* of Mind to Value. As with Leslie, moreover, the mutual immanence of Value and Mind is arguably the unspoken relational framework beneath both praises and critiques offered by Polkinghorne, Wynn, Rice, and Forrest, some of whom (with Leslie) have admired Ewing's significant contributions. In ways deeply resonant to Whitehead, Ewing's contributions point directly to the mutual immanence of Value and Mind for each other.

The axianoetic tradition is not without deep ambiguity as to the status of, and relationship between, Mind and Value. These divine matters remain utterly shrouded in mystery, and there is scarcely a simple way of uniting such a diverse tradition under a single notion. My claim is far more modest, however. At a minimum, the relationality of Mind and Value in terms of mutual immanence offers a clue into the mystery of divine necessity and might very well illuminate some of the ambiguities of the axianoetic tradition anew. Let me offer a select few examples in closing.

What can it mean when Aristotle expresses something of the relationship between Mind and Value in God as *noesis noeseos*, "a thinking of thinking?" What can it mean when Plotinus ambiguously states that "in turning toward itself" the One or Good "sees," and that this "seeing which is Intellect," is also that through which the One "acts" and "does"—being both "word and deed" of the ineffable One? What can it mean when Anselm speaks of God as "the beautiful as well as its contemplator," or when Hegel speaks of "the Idea that thinks itself?" What can it mean when Pokinghorne refers to "Goodness and its instantiation" or to the mystery of the equation of Essence and Existence, Cause and Effect, the Abstract and the Concrete in the tradition? When considered in light of the mutual immanence of Mind and Value, these statements, blurry as they are, might begin to admit some manner of novel clarity. Still, we must always heed Whitehead's reminder: "We must not expect simple answers to far-reaching questions. However far our gaze penetrates, there are always heights beyond which block our vision" (PR, 342).

In full recognition of such metaphysical heights, we nevertheless seek to deepen our vision of Mind and Value still further. Both Parts I and II have suggested at different points that the universe riddles with possibility. These riddles, and answers to them, uniquely surface in Whitehead, Ward, and Leslie, and other voices of prime influence. The nature of the possible adds yet another axianoetic layer to our investigations into ultimacy and explanation.

NOTES

1. "Plato always failed in his attempts at systematization, and always succeeded in displaying depth of metaphysical intuition—the greatest metaphysician, the poorest systematic thinker" (ibid.).

2. "The safest general characterization of the European tradition is that it consists in a series of footnotes to Plato. I do not mean the systematic scheme of thought which scholars have doubtfully extracted from his writings. I allude to the wealth of general ideas scattered through them. His personal endowments, his wide opportunities for experience at a great period of civilization, his inheritance of an intellectual tradition not yet stiffened by excessive systematization, have made his writings an

inexhaustible mine of suggestion. Thus in one sense by stating my belief that the train of thought in these lectures is Platonic, I am doing no more than expressing the hope that it falls within the European tradition. But I do mean more: I mean that if we had to render Plato's general point of view with the least changes made necessary by the intervening two thousand years of human experience in social organization, in aesthetic attainments, in science and in religion, we should have set about to construction of a philosophy of organism. In such a philosophy the actualities constituting the process of the world are conceived as exemplifying the ingression (or 'participation') of other things which constitute the potentialities of definiteness for any actual existence. The things which are temporal arise by their participation in the things which are eternal. The two sets are mediated by a thing which combines the actuality of what is temporal with the timelessness of what is potential. This final entity is the divine element in the world, by which the barren inefficient disjunction of abstract potentialities obtains primordially the efficient conjunction of ideal realization" (ibid., 39–40).

3. This insight, moreover, was not only Plato's intellectual discovery but also the very heart of Christian revelation. "The essence of Christianity is the appeal to the life of Christ as a revelation of the nature of God and of his agency in the world. The record is fragmentary, inconsistent, and uncertain. . . . But there can be no doubt as to what elements in the record have evoked a response from all that is best in human nature. The Mother, the Child, and the bare manger: the lowly man, homeless and self-forgetful, with his message of peace, love, and sympathy: the suffering, the agony, the tender words as life ebbed, the final despair: and the whole with the authority of supreme victory . . . Can there be any doubt that the power of Christianity lies in its revelation in act of that which Plato divined in theory" (ibid.)? For an engaging treatment of the significance of the Platonic-Whiteheadian appeal to persuasion rather than force, see Daniel A. Dombrowski, *Whitehead's Religious Thought: From Mechanism to Organism, from Force to Persuasion* (New York: SUNY, 2017).

4. For a beginners overview of Whitehead's relation to key figures in the tradition, see Johnson, *Whitehead's Theory of Reality*, Ch. 7 and Donald W. Sherburne (ed.), *A Key to Whitehead's Process and Reality* (Chicago: University of Chicago Press, 1981), Ch. 6.

5. William Ernest Hocking recounts Whitehead's comment on the inclusion of God in his philosophy: "I should have never have included [God] if [God] had not been strictly required for descriptive completeness." William Ernest Hocking, "Whitehead as I Knew Him," in *Alfred North Whitehead: Essays on His Philosophy*, George L. Kline (ed.) (Englewood Cliffs: Prentice-Hall, 1963), 16. Although theology was certainly not Whitehead's *primary* concern, A. H. Johnson recalls Whitehead saying he brought God into his metaphysical system to show that "He belonged." Johnson, "Some Conversations with Whitehead," 4.

6. See Johnson, "Some Conversation with Whitehead," 4.

7. Whitehead positively associates the primordial nature with a passage from Aristotle's *Metaphysics*, which expresses not only analogies but also important differences from him: "And since that which is moved and moves is intermediate, there is something which moves without being moved, being eternal, substance, and actuality. And the object of desire and the object of thought move in this way; they move

without being moved. The primary objects of desire and thought are the same. For the apparent good is the object of appetite, and the real good is the primary object of wish. But desire is consequent on opinion rather than opinion on desire; for thinking is the starting-point. And thought is moved by the object of thought, and one of the two columns of opposites is in itself the object of thought." Whitehead comments, however, that Aristotle neglects to make proper distinction between unconscious and conscious domains in the primordial mover. "Aristotle had not made the distinction between conceptual feelings and the intellectual feelings which alone involve consciousness. But if 'conceptual feeling,' with its subjective form of valuation, be substituted for 'thought,' 'thinking,' and 'opinion,' in the above quotation, the agreement is exact" (PR, 244).

8. Johnson, "Some Conversation with Whitehead," 5–6; emphasis mine.

9. Whitehead's conviction here is drawn from the Trinitarian controversies. "The accepted solution of a multiplicity in the nature of God, each component being unqualifiedly Divine, involves a doctrine of mutual immanence in the divine nature. I am not in any way venturing upon a decision upon the correctness of the original assumption of this multiplicity. The point is the recourse to a doctrine of mutual immanence. Again, the theologians had also to construct a doctrine of Christ. . . . They decided for the direct immanence of God in the one person of Christ. They also decided for some sort of direct immanence of God in the World generally. This was their doctrine of the third person of the Trinity. I am not making any judgment about the details of their theology, for example, about the Trinitarian doctrine. My point is that in place of Plato's solution of secondary images and imitations, they demanded a direct doctrine of immanence. It is in this respect that they made a metaphysical discovery" (ibid.; see Ch. X). Faber clarifies that "Whitehead paints mutual immanence as inevitable breakthrough of the maybe most profound divine truth (given its eminent importance, this is not necessarily a hyperbole), not only in theory, but also as active realization of existence in the face of God, in the history of 'rational' religion, exemplified in the intersection of western philosophy, Plato, and occidental religion, the Christ event and its theological interpretations" (TBG, 122).

10. Stephen Lee Ely, "The Religious Availability of Whitehead's God: A Critical Analysis," in Ford and Kline, *Explorations in Whitehead's Philosophy*, 177.

11. "The World of Value exhibits the essential unification of the Universe. Thus while it exhibits the immortal side of the many persons, it also involves the unification of the personality. This is the concept of God. . . . He is the intangible fact at the base of finite existence" (ibid., 97–98). Faber clarifies that the world of value "contains all the world's potentiality, structurality, and determination of content in its abstract quality as *valuation*; its foundation is God, the occurrence of value as such that provides meaning" (GPW, 142).

12. Johnson, "Some Conversations with Whitehead," 7.

13. Indeed, not only does Whitehead insist that "mental experience is the organ of novelty, the urge beyond" in all finite events as they "vivify the massive physical fact, which is repetitive, with the novelties which become," he also insists that "God is the organ of novelty, aiming at intensification" (FR, 26–27; PR, 67; cf. MT, 26).

14. Hosinski, *Stubborn Fact*, Ch. 7.

15. "Nothing has be done to overcome Kant's strongest objection to the proof of a necessary being, namely that there could not be any contradiction in something not existing, because you must ascribe conflicting attributes to something if you are to contradict yourself, but if you merely deny the existence of something you are not ascribing any attributes to anything, so there are no attributes to conflict. This seems to me a fatal objection to the view that the existence of God is logically necessary" (ibid.).

Part III

GOD AND THE POSSIBLE

Chapter 6

Riddles of the Possible

It seems to me a defensible (if also haunting) claim that the universe stretches in reach of Value and Mind. One can certainly deny this; but they do so at the expense of denying themselves—both their *mental acuity* in considering the claim and the *worth of their existence* in drawing a negative conclusion.[1] Human beings are those startling value-realizations that actually *reach back*; and they do so with awareness, wonder, and concern.[2] It is not unnatural to hold to some manner of continuity between the *kind* of things that exist and the *kind* of universe we inhabit. Indeed, the axianoetic nature of *Homo Quaerens* suggests the deeply axianoetic nature of the universe itself. We not only reach back in quest for origins, understanding, and meaning, however; we also *reach forward* amid a myriad of possibility, of which we, and the universe we inhabit, are particularly acute and layered actualizations. We are forged from the sedimentations of the past, but we have emerged from, and are oriented toward, a fundamental *futurity* in the nature of things. We are creatures of the possible in a universe of anticipation.[3]

We largely take it for granted that the universe in every moment riddles with what seems to be *necessary* and *transcendent* possibility. We recognize in bewilderment that we are *contingent actualizations* of a kind of possibility in the universe that we did not envision. The *possibility* of our existence *transcends* the *actuality* of our existence; our conceptual entertainment of the potentiality of our lives is dependent upon the *more fundamental* possibility of our existence as such. Recognizing the modal distinction here between "possibility" and "potentiality" is paramount. Ingolf Dalferth rightly notes that "the modal distinction between possibility ('it is possible to φ') and capacity or potentiality ('It is possible for me to φ') does not translate to the deep passivity of existence. If I exist, it is possible that I exist, but I do not have a capacity or potential to exist before I actually do."[4] So too in this regard do Rescher's intuitions as to a "turn to metaphysical possibility" ring true. "The nature of contingent existence must be explained not on the basis of existing things or substances," he states, "but rather on the operation of principles that function with respect to the manifold of possibility" (MP, 14).[5]

This is an extraordinary thought. It is one that, in a sense, leads us deeper than the ontological question as to why there should be anything at all—and deeper than the cosmological question as to our particular contingent order. We arguably arrive at a more fundamental question as to why (and how) there can be *possibility* for anything at all. What indeed are the conditions of such possibility? This, I submit, is a fantastic question that is nothing short of primordial in scope. It is far from new, however, and far from simple to adjudicate. This question has undergirded not only historic discussions in philosophy and theology but also current discussions in physics, cosmology, and biology. A few initial comments in this regard will set the stage before we wade into key riddles of possible in the next three chapters.

DISCIPLINARY ENTRY POINTS

Discussions in philosophy and theology in particular have often focused upon the enigmatic question of *priority* between the possible and the actual, both in the world and in God.[6] For example, Aristotle declared metaphysics or "first philosophy" the *science of the actual*—that which "investigates being as being"—or *what is insofar as it is*. Aquinas followed, theologically subordinating the possible to the divine Actuality (*actus purus*). Nevertheless, some two thousand years later, Christian Wolff declared philosophy the *science of the possible insofar as it can be*. Philosophers like Heidegger insisted that "higher than actuality stands possibility," and theologians like Jüngel and Moltmann proposed the ontological "priority of possibility over actuality."[7] What is one to make of these distinctive priorities?

In the world of physics and cosmology, reality at its most fundamental level riddles in possibility. Discussions surrounding the prevalence of the possible run from the microscopic spheres of physics, where shadowy events spark at the base of physical reality, to the macroscopic structures of cosmology, where infinite "possible worlds" comprise cosmological totality. Everywhere in between lay vast arrays of possible biological forms, some of which have been actualized, some of which have not, and some which have been rendered extinct. How truly indispensable possibility seems!

Quantum wave functions describing quantum systems are often understood in terms of a "superposition of states"—as probabilistic mathematical descriptions of all possible states that systems *might* manifest. Live possibilities erect a screen of indeterminacy, where, at best, statistical probabilities predict the likelihood of certainly possibilities being actualized (TMG, 215–16).[8] Probabilities have an inherent relation to possibilities, such that Stuart Kauffman insists that "one cannot assert 'probability' without assuming first 'possibility.'" For him, such possibilities are nothing short of "ontologically real" in the nature of things.[9] Nor can one simply escape the *real* effects of what George Ellis calls "possibility spaces," and insist instead upon only physical causes in the universe. He remains adamant that there "is not only physical input in the universe: there is abstract input as well from these possibility spaces, which are knowable by the human mind, and represent crucial parts of necessity."[10]

In a similar way, Howard J. Van Till speaks of "potentiality spaces" with respect to emerging physical and biological structures. For him, "the unimaginably vast array of potentialities for both physical structures and living forms is an enormously important aspect of the universe's being that needs to be appreciated far more than it has been." Why should we appreciate this? Van Till answers, because "these potentialities were part of its being from 'time zero.'"[11] Nagel too approves: such "possibilities were inherent in the universe long before there was life, and inherent in early life long before the appearance of animals." What is more, he rightly claims that a "satisfying explanation would show that the realization of these possibilities was not vanishing improbable, but a significant likelihood given the laws of nature and the composition of the universe" (MC, 32). There is much agreeable in such a statement to be sure; yet, what is one to do when the very "laws" and "compositions" themselves *already* express what Whitehead described as "matter of fact determinations" or "general limitations at the base of actual things"? Do these not seem utterly "arbitrary in respect to a more abstract possibility" whose determinate limitations undergird the very emergence of such laws and compositions in the first place (SMW, 161)?

SOME INITIAL QUESTIONS

Striking questions truly abound with respect to possibility and too often they have been ignored. Should we not also ask after the manifold of abstract possibilities themselves? Does not possibility too require "satisfying explanation?" Can we really just assume the universe to be utterly rich with potency—not least our own? Our existence no doubt testifies that the womb of nature is oddly pregnant with possibility. Indeed, the history of the universe itself seems to be a vast and wild exploration of these possibilities and one should not miss the variety of serious metaphysical quandaries that arise.[12]

My goal in this and the next two chapters is to engage some of the key riddles of the possible as they differently arise in Whitehead, Ward, and Leslie, as well as other thinkers in the tradition, including those who would seek to essentially *rid us* of the riddles possibilities pose. I seek to do so in ways that deepen our focus on Mind and Value still further, both in human experience and at the foundations of existence—even divine existence. How indeed do we explain the riddles of the possible—the ontological status, whereabouts, and relevance—of the possible to the actual? What does the manifold of possibilities suggest about the nature and character of the universe? The riddles of the possible, I claim, are inherently *axianoetic*; they are entangled with Mind and Value from the finite domains of human experience to the infinite domains of divine Experience. Should the possible lead us deeper into the axianoetic nature of God, however, we must face the unnerving fact that God too must also be Possible. This raises the complex question as to how God relates to God's *own Possibility* and, indeed, whether the Possible or the Actual takes *priority* in God, or whether possibility transcends God, as Leslie affirms, in a truly Platonic sense. With others, Whitehead, Ward, and Leslie converge and diverge on these points, but the mutual immanence of the Possible and the Actual in God may illuminate these questions anew.

HUMAN EXPERIENCE AND THE POSSIBLE

One is not led astray if they look to the persistent dimensions of their own experience as harboring clues into the nature and character of things—even ultimate things. This is not a simple claim, nor is attention to the depths of human experience a simple matter. Whitehead reminds us that we cannot start with some ready-made system, but must first *assemble* different modes of experience in order that we might then seek a coherent metaphysical framework to support and sustain them. In the experiential realm, "philosophy can exclude nothing," he insists; "it should never start from systematization." Rather, "its primary stage can be termed assemblage" (MT, 2).[13] In this regard, human experience with possibility is of upmost importance.

Existential Hauntings of Possibility

The notions of "possibility" and "potentiality" are perhaps some of the most unrelenting in human experience. They are so fundamental, in fact, that we are often oblivious to their ubiquity. The Latin proverb Whitehead uses with regard to the inescapabilty of both "symbolism" and "importance" in human life can equally apply to possibility: "Expel it with a pitchfork and it ever returns" (SY, 6; cf. MT, 9).

Possibilities are elusive, yet they are everywhere presupposed, present and effective; they constitute unseen domains in our experience and they temper our lives with both heights and depths. Consider this: Possibilities are indispensably relevant to everything that happens—everything we have *been*, *could be*, and *are*. In this way, Whitehead states, possibilities involve the fact of "alternative realizations, in the past, in the future, in the present"; and they tell tales of "what may be, and may have been" (MT, 77). Possibilities not only *tempt* human life with the glories of *what may be*, however; they also *torture* them with the tragedies of what *might have been*. In this way, they weigh heavily upon us. We know far too well that possibilities can be realized in achievement and also underrealized in loss. "The future is big with every possibility of achievement and of tragedy," Whitehead states. Human awareness of this truth has long sparked both adventure and anxiety. "Hope and fear, joy and disillusion, obtain their meaning from the potentialities in the nature of things" (ibid., 171, 100).[14]

Value, Mind, and Purpose

Although possibilities condition our thinking about the past and the present, they are primarily concerned with the *future*. "To describe a possible thing is to describe what *might* inhabit the realm of existence, not what *does* inhabit a realm of existence," Leslie states; and it is "the *importance* of those possibilities, the real significance of properties *which might be had by existing things*" (VE, 48, 52). Possibilities, in this sense, are inherently *value-laden*; they concern what is better and worse, and their *essential futurity* from the perspective of the present weighs upon us with feelings of attraction or aversion. Our access to the possibilities of the future involves contemplation and imagination; possibilities thus appear both *mind-dependent* in terms of their *conceptual entertainment* and *value-dependent* in terms of our *evaluative concern* for them—that is, our concern for the *achievement* of some possibilities rather than others.

In human experience, "possibility is that in which there stands achievability, abstracted from achievement," Whitehead states, but what *can be* in terms of achievement is tangled with "grades of importance and types of importance" (SMW, 162; MT, 7). In this way, possibilities, and the values assigned to them, fundamentally undergird the notion of *purpose* in human life. For Ward, it is "that sense of choosing a possible future because of its value that gives rise to the idea of purpose, of acting for the sake of obtaining a future good." Wedded tightly to notions of purpose are also those of *intentionality* and *personal causality*. "Personal causality has to be operative in order to bring about envisaged future states," Ward continues, "and that involves intentionality (envisioning objects that do not actually exist), purpose, and value (valuing states one wishes to bring about)" (CIG, 24, 43). It seems rather straightforward that these are mental activities and not purely physical activities; but they are not just *any* mental activities. They are, in fact, highly evolved mental capacities that, to some large degree, draw *Homo Quaerens* out from the rest of nature.

Evolution and Human Uniqueness

The entanglements of mind, value, and possibility are fundamental elements in human experience and also central to human uniqueness. Ward's statement seems fair in this regard; it is only "intelligent consciousness" that has reasons for bringing about certain states, and these reasons are precisely the "actualization and appreciation of some as yet merely possible value" (ibid., 89). We should be unafraid to speak to the uniqueness of the human situation in this regard. We are uniquely disturbed by ideals—those entertained and those lost—and we discern the infinite (however dimly) with faculties and abilities far exceeding the rest of the (known) animal kingdom.[15] The "life of a human being receives its worth, its importance, from the way in which unrealized ideals shape its purposes and tinge its actions," Whitehead insists; "the distinction between men and animals is in one sense only a difference in degree. But the extent of the degree makes all the difference. The Rubicon has been crossed" (MT, 27).[16] In human beings, he continues, "nature seems to have burst through another of its boundaries" and "the conceptual entertainment of unrealized possibility becomes a major factor in human mentality" (ibid., 26).[17] This "entertainment," moreover, is the ground of "outrageous novelty" in human life. The characterization of this "conceptual feeling is that sense of *what might be* and of *what might have been*," and its functioning on high evolutionary levels grounds the most unique axiological dimensions of human experience.

> In its highest development, this [conceptual feeling] becomes the entertainment of the ideal. It emphasizes the sense of importance. . . . And this sense exhibits itself in various species, such as the sense of morality, the mystic sense of religion, the sense of that delicacy of adjustment which is beauty, the sense of necessity for mutual connection which is understanding, and the sense of discrimination of each factor which is consciousness. (MT, 26, emphasis mine)

In human experience, the tangles of mind, value, and possibility are so fundamental that Whitehead states, "When we enjoy fact as the realization of a specific value, or possibility as an impulse towards realization, we are stressing *the ultimate character of the Universe*" (Imm., 91–92, emphasis mine). Indeed, when we move from human experience to the universe at large, the role of the possible only widens and deepens. It is one thing to speak about possibilities (or potentialities) *for* the world and human experience, and quite another to speak of the very possibility *of* the world and human experience. These are different *levels of possibility*, one dependent and one independent; one immanent and one transcendent. Having realized that we do not ground our own possibility, it is only natural to ask after, and problematize, the nature of the Possible as such. Manifold depths of possibility constitute the presupposed riddles of the world's existence, but what is the ontological status and character of such depths, and how can we approach them?

PLATONIC HAUNTING: THE REALITY AND PROBLEM OF THE POSSIBLE

Leslie, Ward, and Whitehead do not ignore the riddles of possibility. Possibilities are necessary, albeit not unproblematic, features of any serious approach to the nature of things—including divine things. It has not always been clear, however, what ontological problems possibilities actually pose and how they should be addressed in light of our experience of the world. Leslie, Ward, and Whitehead each express these problems at different depths, but not without resonance and overlap. Illuminating the different shades of these expressions in this chapter will help set the stage for combating some problematic dismissals of the possible as they have arisen in some influential modern philosophy. We take up this discussion in the following chapter.

Leslie: Kingdoms of Ethically Required Possibility

Consider this question: How is it that the actual existence of the world is not an utter contradiction—like that of a married bachelor or a triangular circle—something the very grasping of which tangles one in cognitive dissonance and logical contradiction? The universe is clearly possible, and it is logically possible *because it is actual*. This seems uncontroversial. "Our actual existing universe is a possible universe," Leslie states; "all actual things are possible ones *as well*" (IM, 16). Yet, the very fact of the actuality of the universe *means something* about the status of its *possibility*. "The logical possibility of our universe did not depend on the actual existence of this universe or of anything" (ibid., 160). In fact, even if everything suddenly vanished into a void, Leslie is adamant that "apples and butterflies and clouds, together with infinitely many other objects, were possibilities in the technical sense that (unlike round squares) they involved no contradiction" (ID, 1). Here, Leslie insists that we are condemned to affirm, as Plato did, that "countless realities to do with *possible things* are real necessarily and eternally" (ibid., 38, emphasis his). Reality—"The Real"—is "infinitely rich" with "infinitely many possibilities." These are not simply possibilities for one thing or another—this "here," or that "there"—but "infinitely intricate" possibilities inclusive of holistic universal scenarios and all that goes with them—including you and I. "Remember," Leslie implores us, "you're a possibility yourself, but you aren't 'a mere possibility.' You are somebody actual as well as somebody possible" (ibid., 46).

Possibilities then are not just useful fictions for Leslie; they are "no less real, and no less intricate through remaining confined to the land of the possible. The kingdom of possibilities isn't a fiction." In fact, one could affirm the fictitious nature of the possible only if they also affirmed the absurd thesis that there "is no conceivable alternative to whatever actually exists." He is right, however, in saying that this "is a doctrine few would willingly accept"; for we can easily imagine the myriad ways in which things might have been utterly different (IM, 26).[18] Indeed, imagining that there are *no possible alternatives* to what currently exists is almost as difficult as imagining an *utter emptiness* (Absolute Nothingness!) devoid even of possibilities! We have already seen, however, that this is no simple task. As Leslie puts it, we "must not fancy that any emptiness could be so empty that even logical possibilities were banished from it" (ME, 129).

But what are possibilities for Leslie? Are they not complete abstractions and should we not flee the abstract in philosophical preference for the concrete—that which we can see and touch with our senses? While this may seem tempting, the concrete or actual cannot evade the abstract and the possible. "How can such a reality escape being an airy abstraction?" Leslie asks. "Rest assured; that is what it is," he admits. His axiarchic vision, as we have seen already, has no fear of the abstract: "The thoroughgoing axiarchist does not scorn the bodiless and the abstract, the hypothetical, the merely possible, the things which *might come to be*." What is more, Leslie insists that "no axiarchist should let himself be frightened by the news that realities eternal and disembodied are today unfashionable" (VE, 52–53, emphasis mine). They may indeed be "unfashionable," but they also seem inescapable in quest for ultimate things.

Although Leslie repeatedly claims that "all realities are 'to do with' actual or possible existence," he reminds us that this "does not imply that all are themselves *existents* in any ordinary sense" (ibid., 53, emphasis mine). Possibilities are *not actual* in the sense that we are actual (actually existent); but neither is it the case that they are *non-existent* or simply "nothing." "The eternal realm of possibilities and truths about possibilities fails to exist in the way we ourselves do," Leslie states, but "we might hesitate to call it 'nonexistent' since this could sound like saying 'not real at all'" (ME, 53). In speaking of "interacting possibilities" associated with quantum mechanics and the double-slit experiment, for example, he finds that the "existence" of the possible is nothing short of "suspicious." "Possibilities that interact complexly raise a vigorous suspicion that they are actually existent realities as well" (ID, 46). They appear to have a *real* mode of existence *other than* the extremes of Actual Existence or Nothingness. This is a mode of being conceived not in terms of *what is*, or of *what is not*, but rather, of *what can be*.

Possibility considered in terms of *what can be* is, for Leslie, far from Valueless. Even prior to the existence of anything, possibilities for different *kinds* of axiological worthwhile states hold supreme "ethical" weight. The fact that such possibilities are inherently value-laden—having an "ethical requiredness" independent of any actually existing things—might also explain *why* there are existing things at all. "The constitution of mere possibilities," he states, "can possess a significance which is prior (if not in time then at least 'in principle') to the facts of *existence*. They need not depend for their ethical weight on such facts. So might they not carry creative weight as well" (VE, 51)?

Note that for Leslie, it is not only that possibilities, ontologically suspicious that they are, derive whatever mode of existence they have from their *ethical necessity*, but that this very *requiredness* itself is causally sufficient to answer why there is "more than just a Platonic realm of logical possibilities and facts concerning them" (ME, 129). It is important to see in this regard that, in contrast to Ward and Whitehead, as we will see below, abstract possibilities in fact appear *less problematic* for Leslie. He does not overtly ask about *where* they are or *how* they can exist and be *efficacious* on behalf of actuality. Rather, Leslie remains a thoroughgoing Platonist: the primeval realm of Platonic Possibility carries a necessary ethical preeminence beyond which one cannot question. Its very *requiredness is* its necessity. Thus, despite acknowledging the suspicious reality of the possible, he never forcefully problematizes the ontological status or locus of possibility, as do Ward and Whitehead. Possibility is a Platonic given and the fact that Possibility procures worthwhile Actuality is a result of Possibility being *ethically filtered* through the creative dictates of Value. What is involved here, Leslie states, is "the fully real significance of how such a world is *possible*, and is a possibility with a requiredness independent of an outside thing." This unconditioned "significance" is what allows Leslie to "speak of an eternal or timeless requirement; it is a significance that is real without being a material object, or in space. The importance of possible goods is a reality precisely as their *un*importance would be" (VE, 52, emphasis his). On Leslie's account, then, we must face the necessary reality of the "Kingdom of Possibilities" and the necessary Values that reign over them. These infinite possibilities are neither fictitious nor nonexistent, but they do remain ontologically suspicious in terms of their necessity. Moreover, we will see later that the place of divine Mind(s) in this complex is integral in bringing both Value and Possibility together as concrete reality.

Ward: Oceanic Arrays of Platonic Possibilities

Affirming and problematizing the real ontological status of the Possible has been central throughout Keith Ward's corpus. With Leslie, he insists that we can and perhaps must hold to the necessarily reality of a "complete array of every possibility of any kind, something like the Platonic world of Forms" (PF, 131). One need not reify or essentialize this realm as "higher" or "more real" in comparison to actuality, however. Neither should they simply dismiss it as nonexistent. Rather, the Platonic world provides the intelligible archetypes, structures, and relationships presupposed not simply by our actual universe but also by "infinitely many other possible universes." Indeed, the "fundamental elements" of our actual universe, Ward states, are governed by a subset of mathematically pictured "Platonic possibilities." He likens these to the abstract "skeleton" or "map" of the universe, but he is quick to remind us that "skeletons are not living forms, and maps are not landscapes in which one can breathe and walk"—these are abstractions (GCN, 29).[19] Nevertheless, Ward remains fully "inclined" to say that "possibilities *do exist*; "even if no actual universe existed, its possibility would exist, together with the possibilities of every other possible universe, all comprising an infinite set of possibilities" (ibid., 36, emphasis mine). We can agree with Ward that it seems fully plausible that "if something is ever possible (exists in one possible world), then it is always possible (it is a possibility in every world)"; in this way "the complete array of possibles cannot be thought away in any world" (RC, 196).[20]

What riddles then do possibilities pose for Ward? He speaks to the queer ontological status of possibilities, saying, "It may seem rather odd . . . to think of a 'complete array of all possible states.' In what sense would such a thing exist? Things, it may be said, are either actual or non-existent"; he states, but "there cannot be actually existent possibles" (CIG, 93). The question thus stands for Ward: "How can mere possibilities exist" (GCN, 39)? He readily grants that the "existence" of possibilities may be an objectionable thesis; some will no doubt insist that they *cannot* and *do not exist*. Ward, however, holds firm: "the Platonic reminiscence continues to haunt us . . . the possibility of things is not a mere non-being. It has a potentiality to be. It has some form of existence. If so, it must have some form of actuality." This oceanic realm of Possibilities (what Boethius calls the "infinite ocean of being") harbors "all potentialities for being," but "not as actual, and yet not as simple nullities" (RC, 197). Indeed, possibilities on Ward's account should be *distinguished* from Nothingness and can scarcely just "exist" in some pseudo-real world between Being and Nothingness. "Possibilities cannot simply exist unsupported in a half-real world between non-being and actual-being," he states. "Half-existence is not good enough; you either exist or you do not. Yet it makes sense to speak of possible existents, of real potentialities, that are different from absolute nothingness" (GP, 48).

More so than Leslie, Ward thus problematizes the status and sustaining metaphysical framework of Possibilities in and for the universe. We not only have the problem of *how* possibilities can "exist" but also (with Leslie) *why* it is that "any possibility should be actualized at all" (GCN, 47). In the face of infinite possibilities and infinite possible universes, some principle or criterion of selection must be operative. It remains for Ward a "major problem" not only to consider the "sense in which such possible worlds really exist" but also "how some (or all?) of them get 'selected' for actuality" (PR, 38).

Like Leslie, primordial possibilities are, for Ward, far from value-neutral. Rather, the "array of possible states" retains "the values they necessarily have"; there can be a "goodness or intrinsic value" to possibilities "that is necessarily what it is" (CIG, 97). And if possibilities "exist" necessarily laden with values, this is not inconsequential for considerations as to their "selection." But *what* is it that *does* the selecting? Ward and Leslie remain resonant; but here, Ward hesitates where Leslie accelerates: For Ward, the abstract *Value* of possibilities is *not enough* to ontologically ground their "existence" or *actively* (creatively) *select* for them. It is precisely at this point, Ward holds, that we should turn to Mind.

Whitehead: The Temporalization of the Eternal

Whitehead's philosophy retains a richly suggestive (and technical) treatment of the reality of abstract "possibility," "potentiality," or "eternal objects" for a universe whose fundamental character is "a creative advance into novelty" (PR, 222).[21] The "metaphysical status" of an eternal object is "that of a possibility for actuality" and "every actual occasion is defined as to its character by how these possibilities are actualised for that occasion" (SMW, 159). Eternal objects are "objects" because they *do not have subjectivity*, and "eternal" because they are *immutable and transcend time*. Since the emergence of each actual occasion presupposes limited "selections from the realm of possibilities," Whitehead fully recognizes that "the ultimate character of how actual occasions have the general character they do have, must lie in an analysis of the general character of the realm of possibility" (ibid., 163). His analysis of this "character," moreover, is fully consistent with his conviction that "philosophy is explanatory of abstraction, and not of concreteness." He is confident that "it is by reason of their instinctive grasp of this ultimate truth that, in spite of much association with arbitrary fancifulness and atavistic mysticism, types of Platonic philosophy retain their abiding appeal; they seek the forms in the facts. Each fact is more than its forms, and each form 'participates' throughout the world of facts." Whitehead thus insists that "the true philosophic question is, How can concrete fact exhibit entities abstract from itself and yet participated in by its own nature" (PR, 20)?[22]

Although Whitehead at times also speaks of these aboriginal possibilities as "universals" or "platonic forms," he has his own relevant reasons for using "eternal objects" in distinction from these. While tradition has referred to these "transcendent entities" as "universals," Whitehead prefers "eternal objects" so that he might separate himself from problematic presuppositions associated with this term throughout the tradition. For Whitehead, eternal objects by their very nature are *abstract*. By "abstract," he means "that what an eternal object is in itself—that is to say, its essence—is comprehensible without reference to some one particular occasion of experience." "Abstraction" thus indicates that eternal objects transcend "particular concrete occasions of actual happening"; but Whitehead is quick to also insist that such transcendence does not mean being "disconnected" from them (SMW, 159). As such, Whitehead distinguishes between an *independent* and *relational* essence of eternal objects: "[Each eternal object] has an individual essence—whereby it is the same eternal object in diverse occasions, and it has a relational essence—whereby it has an infinitude of modes of entry into realization." In fact, Whitehead insists that eternal objects are "a first endeavor to get beyond the absurd simple-mindedness of the traditional universals." The key points to notice, he states, are the following: (1) that eternal objects carry potentiality into realization; (2) they thus carry mentality into matter of fact; (3) in their finite realization, no eternal object can exhibit the full potentialities of its nature.[23] Whitehead further distinguishes between *subjective* and *objective* species of eternal objects. Eternal objects of the objective species inform *only objects of experience*, not the experiences themselves; while eternal objects of the subjective species *do inform experiences*. As Whitehead differentiates them: objective eternal objects "are the mathematical Platonic forms," concerning the "world as a medium," while subjective eternal objects are elements in the "definiteness of the subjective form of feeling"—that is, the *emotive way* in which entities feel the data of their experience (PR, 291).

While Whitehead does say that the meaning of "eternal objects" corresponds to Platonic-like "forms" or "ideas," he also wants to distance himself from any restatement or "exegesis" of Plato. Eternal objects "are not necessarily restricted to those which [Plato] would recognize as 'forms,'" he states. He also holds that the term "idea" is inadequate because it "has a subjective suggestion in modern philosophy." So too does the term "essence" diverge from his intentions. "Accordingly," he concludes, "by way of employing a term devoid of misleading suggestions, I use the phrase 'eternal object.' . . . An entity whose conceptual recognition does not involve a necessary reference to any definite actual entities of the temporal world is called an 'eternal object'" (ibid., 44).[24] Nevertheless, Whitehead also reminds us that we need not follow his particular phraseology. "If the term 'eternal object' is disliked," he states, "the term 'potentials' would be suitable. The eternal objects are the *pure potentials* of the universe; and actual entities differ from each other in their realization of potentials" (ibid., 149, emphasis mine).

Let us remember that for Whitehead, "actual entities" or "occasions of experience" are "the final real things of which the world is made up"; they are "the real things which in their collective unities compose the evolving universe, ever plunging into creative advance" (ibid., 18; MT, 151). Creative activity belongs to the very "essence" of each occasion whose very life span Whitehead conceives as a "process of eliciting into actual being factors in the universe which antecedently to that process exist only in the mode of unrealized potentiates." Each entities "self-creation" is a feeling-laden (prehensive) transformation of potentiality into the actuality, and the "fact of such transformation includes the immediacy of self-enjoyment"—the *value* of achieved actuality (MT, 151).

Precisely because Whitehead conceives *creative process* to be the abiding "nature" and "character" of things, possibility and potentiality are indispensable. "The notion of potentiality is fundamental as soon as the notion of process is admitted," he states. Any notion of possibility or potentiality would simply vanish if the world was unchanging and static to its core, being only "morphological" on its surface. If process is conceived "as fundamental," however, then "the actualities of the present are deriving their characters from the process, and are bestowing their characters upon the future. Immediacy is the realization of the potentialities of the past, and is the storehouse of the potentialities of the future" (ibid., 99–100).

This reference to potentiality both in terms of the *past* and the *future* is helpful. Human experience is not only framed and limited by the potentialities of the past (what the past offers the present); Whitehead is also adamant that experience bears witnesses to the advent of the *radically new* (that which *transcends* what the past offers). In this way, we face *unrealized possibilities* whose very *unforeseeability* meets our present *from the future*. This "future" is the reservoir of the radically new—the *real*, but the "not yet" (GPW, 83).[25] Distinguishing these *two directions* of potentiality or possibility are vital for Whitehead. He insists that "the data of our experience are of two kinds. They can be analyzed into realized matter-of-fact and into potentialities for matter-of-fact. Further, these potentialities can be analyzed into *pure abstract potentialities apart from special relevance to realization . . .* and into *potentialities entertained by reason of some closeness of relevance to such realization*" (MT, 94, emphasis mine). These two *kinds* of potentiality correspond to what Whitehead calls "pure" or "general" potentiality as that *absolute* and *independent* Possibility presupposed by the creative advance of any and all cosmic epochs, and also "real potentiality"—what we might call "relevant possibility"—as that *immanent* and *related* mode of possibility that conditions, and is conditioned by, the actual world.[26]

While a universe of creative becoming in some deep sense presupposes the indispensability of these modes of possibility, Whitehead is not unaware of the constellation of metaphysical issues they create. These are related problems surrounding the *limitation, relevance, locus,* and *efficacy* of the possible for the actual in the creative advance of things. Whitehead has already pointed to the fundamental contours and law-like structures of our particular cosmic epoch as bearing witness to some kind of "arbitrary" limitation against an otherwise infinite backdrop of abstract Possibility. He is confident that the "spatio-temporal relationship, in terms of which the actual course of events is to be expressed, is nothing else than a *selective limitation* within the general systematic relationships among eternal objects" (SMW, 161, emphasis mine). The reality of the spatiotemporal continuum, in other words, presupposes a more fundamental *limitation* on Possibility as such. While this continuum itself is a "locus of relational possibility," it has been "*selected* from the more general realm of systematic relationship [among eternal objects]." These limits upon the "locus of relational possibility expresses *one* limitation of possibility inherent in the general system of the process of realisation" (ibid., emphasis mine).

In holding that there could have been many *other ways* Possibility *could have been* limited, Whitehead also fully realizes that not just *any limitation* upon the Possible would yield the emergence of an *ordered* cosmos such as our own. This is a vital point; rather, "rightness of limitation is essential for the growth of reality." Indeed, Whitehead holds that this determinate "rightness" is everywhere presupposed in the "whole process itself" (RM, 137). To speak of a selective *rightness* or limitation amid the maze of Possibility, moreover, is to assume the reality of *Value*—that some limitations are in fact *right* in order to procure anything *worthwhile* at all. "The fact that there is a process of actual occasions, and the fact that the occasions are the *emergence of values which require such limitation,* both require that the course of events should have developed amid an antecedent limitation composed of conditions, particularization, and *standards of value*" (ibid., emphasis mine). We thus run into a metaphysical problem that Whitehead fully confronts. Put simply: "There is a metaphysical need for a principle of determination"—a limiting ground governed by standards of Value. For Whitehead, one must appeal to this limitation not only in terms of the fundamental delimitations of our universe but also in terms of the emergence of each and every temporal actuality and what it *can* become for the world process (SMW, 178).

Within the problem of the *limitation* of Primordial Possibility is also the related problem of the *relevance* of possibilities to actualities in process. Whitehead is clear about this problem, asking, "In what sense can unrealized abstract form be relevant? What is the basis of this relevance" (PR, 32). This is not an inconsequential question; he is seeking the *basis* of the relevance of possibility to emerging actuality. "We require to understand how mere matter-of-fact refuses to be deprived of its relevance to potentialities beyond its own actuality of realization," he states. Why is it, however, that we are *required* to understand this? Precisely because "the very character of concrete realization—that is to say, of historic fact—is suffused with the potentialities which it excludes with varying types of relevance" (MT, 83–84).[27]

The relevance of eternal objects to concrescing occasions is such that they can actually take rise. Even if one should hold that the infinitude of general potentiality is in some way made present to each arising occasion, it seems hardly conceivable that occasions must first wade through this wild infinitude to grasp those narrow range of possibilities relevant to their own becoming. In facing the infinitude of possibility, how could a *finite* occasion ever come to be at all? In order for temporal process to be conceivable, therefore, a *limited provision* of relevant possibilities both *for* and *to* becoming actualities is required.[28] This is again connected directly to the "need" for some kind of principle of limitation.

Why could not *possibilities themselves* provide the rightness of limitation presupposed by the emergence of each occasion? This is problematic for Whitehead: *from where* would this take place and through *what causal means*? In addition to the problem of the axiological *limitation* of infinite pure possibilities and the *relevance* of real temporally related possibilities, Whitehead also points to the problem of the *locus* and *efficacy* of the possible. In what sense can *abstract* possibility actually *do* anything? Is not the womb of possibility causally barren? Possibilities themselves are not *active agents* any more than the number 2 is. Whitehead thus holds that "unlimited possibility and abstract creativity can procure nothing" (RM, 137). What is more, possibilities cannot just "exist" devoid of *ontological rootedness* in the soil of one's ontology. The *reality* and *relevance* of possibility must be traceable back to a metaphysical framework that properly integrates them. Whitehead's "ontological principle" holds that "it is a contradiction in terms to assume that some explanatory fact can float into the actual world out of nonentity." Rather, "nonentity is nothingness" (PR, 46). Alternatively, he insists that "apart from things that are *actual*, there is nothing—either in fact or in efficacy" (ibid., 40, emphasis mine). In this light, it makes little sense to say that "possibilities" or "potentials" are somewhere "out there," floating like hypothetical balloons in a sky-like metaphysical void, only to offer themselves when the time is right. Indeed, the adequacy of metaphysics demands that "there is nothing which floats into the world from nowhere" and that "there are no self-sustained facts, floating in nonentity" (ibid., 244, 11). What kind of "entity" then conceivably accounts for the riddles of the possible in terms of their determinate limitations, relevance, locus, and efficacy for the creative advance? For Whitehead, as we will soon see, a nontemporal Mental Actuality is an integrative solution to these metaphysical problems.

RIDDLES AND RIDDING

Leslie, Ward, and Whitehead thus each illuminate the riddles of possibility for their respective visions. Although Whitehead's analysis is considerably more detailed, Leslie and Ward also recognize the "suspicious" nature of the possible, both in terms of their ontological mode of "existence" (Leslie) and their Platonic whereabouts (Ward). In different ways, each of them remains haunted by Platonic intuitions. As we will begin to see in the next chapter, each is also driven toward affirming the reality of Mind and Value precisely as it relates to the riddles posed by possibility.

Before exploring this, however, it's worth considering whether or not we might approach possibility differently, in ways that do not tangle us in such riddles. These are contentious matters of metaphysics, to be sure, and philosophers will naturally disagree. While Leslie, Ward, and Whitehead each uniquely angle their treatment of possibility, they do so because of a philosophical need to *explain* the possible in relation to the world. For each of them, the reality of "God" conceived in terms of Mind and Value aids this quest. Other thinkers, however, unwilling to admit any divine reality, have taken different approaches and rest content with essentially *explaining away* the purely possible all together. Put differently, we might say that they have tried to *rid us of the riddles possibilities pose* and thus any theological context thought to be associated with them. Devoid of any ultimate recourse to Mind and Value, however, these modern attempts are deeply problematic. In moving now to briefly analyze some of them, my aim is to expose their inadequacies on the axianoetic grounds Leslie, Ward, and Whitehead provide.

NOTES

1. Recall the underlying axiological thrust of Camus' "fundamental question of philosophy." As long as we continue to go on living (thereby asserting "No!" to suicide), we presuppose the *worthiness* of being.

2. This is not to say, of course, that human beings are the only value-realizations in the universe or, for that matter, that they are the uniquely privileged bearers of mentality. On Whitehead's vision, rather, they lie upon (and contribute to) a layered continuum of psychophysical value-realizations ever happening in and as the cosmos itself. Value is inherent in actuality, and so is mind. Although "scientific reasoning is completely dominated by the presupposition that mental functionings are not properly

part of nature," Whitehead insists "that this sharp division between mentality and nature has no ground in our fundamental observation. We find ourselves living within nature ... I conclude that we should conceive mental operations as among the factors which make up the constituents of nature" (MT, 156). One should not immediately equate "mentality" with "consciousness," however. For the relevance of Whitehead's "panpsychism" or "panexperientialism" to the mind-body problem, refer to David Ray Griffin, *Unsnarling the World-Knot: Consciousness, Freedom and the Mind-Body Problem* (Eugene: Wipf & Stock, 1998).

3. The notions of possibility and anticipation are fundamental for understanding both the nature of human beings and the universe at large. Consider the following statements from Ingolf Dalferth and John F. Haught. Rather than being "deficient beings," Dalferth insists that "we live from a surplus of the possible that is not limited to what we actually are or could have been. What defines our humanity is not our reality and its possibilities ('Become what you are!') but rather the unforeseeable that comes our way as we live our lives, opening up possibilities that without the unforeseeable would never have been either conceivable or accessible ('Become what you can never be of your own accord!'). We live from possibilities over which we have no control. We are—in a radical sense—beings of possibility." Ingolf U. Dalferth, *Creatures of Possibility: The Theological Basis of Human Freedom* (Grand Rapids: Backer Academic, 2016), xx. Haught distinguishes an "anticipatory approach" to the universe from the inadequacies of respective "analogical" and "archaeonomic" approaches. "Anticipation offers a coherent alternative to both analogy and archaeonomy," he states. "It reads nature, life, mind, and religion as ways in which a whole universe is awakening to the coming of more-being on the horizon. It accepts both the new scientific narrative of gradual emergence and the sense that something ontologically richer and fuller is coming into the universe in the process. Instead of pretending to make complete sense of emergence archaeonomically, by looking back to the remote cosmic past, and instead of looking analogically for the 'more' to drop into the world of 'less' from up above, anticipation reads the universe as a story in which more-being and deeper meaning are always dawning on the horizon of the not-yet. Not-yet, however, is not the same as nonbeing. It exists as a reservoir of possibilities that have yet to be actualized. It is a realm of being that has future as it very essence." Haught, *The New Cosmic Story*, 38.

4. Dalferth, *Creatures of Possibility*, xv. Put differently: "We can possess capacities [potentialities] only if we exist, and we cannot construe our existence as an activity that results from practicing a capacity that makes our existence possible" (ibid). Many thinkers nevertheless use "possibility" and "potentiality" interchangeably.

5. Alternatively, "to account for the being of contingent existence at large, one has to imposes the burden of explanation on something that is itself entirely outside the realm of contingent existence and of existential fact. But where can one possibly look for explanatory resources if the realm of actuality, of 'what there is,' is not available? The answer is clear: we must look to the realm of possibility, of what *can possibly be*. For if reality is to have a basis, then *possibility* is the only available prospect" (ibid., 15).

6. See, for example, James Lindsay, "The Philosophy of Possibility," *The Monist*, 32, no. 3 (July 1922): 321–38; Ingolf U. Dalferth, "*Possibile Absolutum*: The Theological Discovery of the Ontological Priority of the Possible," in *Rethinking the Medieval Legacy for Contemporary Theology*, Anselm K. Min (ed.) (Notre Dame: University of Notre Dame Press, 2014), 91–130; Richard Kearney, *The God Who May Be: A Hermeneutics of Religion* (Bloomington: Indiana University Press, 2001), Ch. 5.

7. Quoted in Dalferth, "*Possibile Absolutum*," 91–92. Moltmann states, for example, "If we switch over from a metaphysics of reality [actuality] to a metaphysics of possibility, we can then view divine Being as the supreme possibility, as the source of possibilities, and as the transcendental making-possible of the possible." Jürgen Moltmann, "God's Kenosis in the Creation and Consummation of the World," in *The Work of Love: Creation as Kenosis*, John Polkinghorne (ed.) (Grand Rapids: Eerdmans, 2001), 150.

8. Karim Bschir, "Potentiality in Natural Philosophy," in *Physics and Speculative Philosophy: Potentiality in Modern Science*, Timothy E. Eastman, Michael Epperson, David Ray Griffin (eds.) (Berlin: De Gruyter, 2016).

9. Stuart A. Kauffman, *Humanity in a Creative Universe* (Oxford: Oxford University Press, 2016), 21, 23.

10. George Ellis, *How Can Physics Underlie the Mind?: Top-Down Causation in the Human Context* (Berlin: Springer-Verlag, 2016), 369. With Nancey Murphy, Ellis also argues for ethical possibility spaces in *On the Moral Nature of the Universe: Theology, Cosmology and Ethics* (Minneapolis: Fortress Press, 1996).

11. Howard J. Van Till, "From Calvinism to Claremont: Now That's Evolution! Or, From Calvin's Supernaturalism to Griffin's Theistic Naturalism," in Cobb, *Back to Darwin*, 356–57.

12. In part, both James Lindsay and Thomas Hosinski point directly to the kind of related questions one must engage:

"The philosophy of possibility," Lindsay states, "cannot evade the question of the origin of possibilities. Can we trace possibility simply to the human mind? Do possibilities not exist before the human mind comes into being? Will the possibilities not exist after the human mind has ceased to exist? Can we even ascribe the possibilities to the universe? If the universe were done away, would possibilities not remain in undiminished form? For, are the possible universes not infinite? And, is not possibility necessary and eternal? These are among the questions that may be asked. The philosophy of possibility can hardly be satisfied to accept these possibilities as accounting for themselves." Lindsay, "Philosophy of Possibility," 322–23. Similarly, for Hosinski: "Possibility is fascinating . . . the point I would make here is that possibility is not self-explanatory. Where do possibilities come from? Must we simply say, as we do for energy that possibilities just *are*? Must we simply assume them without being able to explain where they come from and how they function? Possibilities by definition are not *actual*, even though they are *real*. They are real in the sense that we can think of possibilities and interact mentally with them, but they are not actual in the sense that they are not *agents*, nor are they *actual* things. We cannot hold a possibility in our hands or take it on a walk. Possibilities must be actualized in and by some actual agent of the universe to be become actualized. How then, if they are not actual things, can they interact with actualities? These are not scientific questions but philosophical ones." Thomas Hosinski, *The Image of the Unseen God: Catholicity, Science and Our Evolving Understanding of God* (Maryknoll: Oribs, 2017), 77–78.

13. This assemblage must take account of any and all variety of human experience for Whitehead: "Nothing can be omitted, experience drunk and experience sober, experience sleeping and experience awake, experience drowsy and experience wide-awake, experience self-conscious and experiences self-forgetful, experience intellectual and experience physical, experience religious and experience skeptical, experience anxious and experience care-free, experience anticipatory and experience retrospective, experience happy and experience grieving, experience dominated by emotion and experience under self-restraint, experience in the light and experience in the dark, experience normal and experience abnormal" (AI, 226).

14. Whitehead was nothing short of haunted by the infinite possibilities that lie before humankind. These possibilities frame both human purpose and human hope. Lucian Price records one of his most compelling statements in this regard. "Our minds are finite, and yet even in these circumstances of finitude we are surrounded by possibilities that are infinite, and the purpose of human life is to grasp as much as we can out of that infinitude. I wish I could convey this sense I have of the infinity of possibilities that confront humanity—the limitless variation of choice, the possibility of novel and untried combinations, the happy turns of experiment, the endless horizons opening out. As long as we experiment, as longs as we keep this possibility of progressiveness, we and our societies are alive; when we lose them, both we and our societies are dead, no matter how externally active we and they may be, no matter how materially prosperous they and we may appear. And nothing is easier to lose than this element of novelty. It is the living principle in thought, which keeps all alive." Price, *Dialogues*, 160.

15. Of course, I reserve these comments to our own planet only. I fully agree with David Ray Griffin that "on other planets with the conditions for life to emerge and to evolve for many billions of years, we should expect there to be some with creatures that, no matter how different in physical constitution and appearance, would share some of our capacities, such as those for mathematics, music and morality, or, more generally, truth, beauty and goodness." David Ray Griffin, *Panentheism and Scientific Naturalism: Rethinking Evil, Morality, Religious Experience, Religious Pluralism and the Academic Study of Religion* (Claremont: Process Century Press, 2014), 88. Faber expresses a similar point with respect to the very possibility of life and mind in the universe. "The fact of life and mind on Earth is already an example that does not only imply that they are possible, but actualizations of universal potentials of the cosmic history. There is no rule restraining possibilities to be necessarily only realized once, only contingent reasons of serendipitous coalescence of causes. Whenever such causes or constellations would come together, we can expect such potentials to be realized—again." Roland Faber, *The Ocean of God: On the Transreligious Future of Religions* (London: Anthem, 2019), 160n52. For further discussions in this regard, refer to Steven J. Dick (ed.), *The Impact of Discovering Life Beyond Earth* (Cambridge: Cambridge University Press, 2016), part III.

16. Alternatively, "what distinguishes men from other animals, some humans from other humans, is the inclusion in their natures, wavering and dimly, of a disturbing element, which is the flight after the unattainable. This element is that touch of infinity which has goaded races onward, sometime to their destruction" (FR, 51).

17. Again, this is not to say for Whitehead, that prior to human emergence, mentality plays no role. Mentality in fact pervades the actualities of nature (each entity having a physical and mental pole), although he would remind us that "consciousness is no necessary element in mental experience." Rather, "the lowest form of mental experience is blind urge toward a *form* of experience, that is to say, an urge toward a *form for* realization." He continues, "In its essence mentality is the urge toward some vacuous definiteness, to include in matter-of-fact which is non-vacuous enjoyment. This urge is appetition. . . . Mental experience is the organ of novelty, the urge beyond" beckoned by novelties transcending the repetitions of the past. In this sense, "mental experience contains in itself a factor of anarchy" (FR, 26–27).

18. In light of the countless improbabilities that have been actualized in the universe, consider Paul Davies words: "All this prompts the question why, from the infinite range of possible values that nature could have selected for the fundamental constants, and from the infinite variety of initial conditions that could have characterized the primeval universe, the actual values and conditions conspire to produce the particular range of very special features that we observe. For clearly the universe is a special place: exceedingly uniform on a large scale, yet not so precisely uniform that galaxies could not form; extremely low entropy per proton and hence cool enough for chemistry to happen; almost zero cosmic repulsion and an expansion rate tuned to the energy content to unbelievable accuracy; value for the strength of its forces that permit nuclei to exist yet do not burn up all the cosmic hydrogen, and many more apparent accidents of fortune." Paul Davies, *The Accidental Universe* (New York: Cambridge University Press, 1982), 111.

19. Ward here appeals positively to Whitehead's "fallacy of misplaced concreteness," the mistaken tendency in pursuits in science, philosophy, and religion that misplaces the abstract for the concrete.

20. Alternatively, "if a thing is ever possible, surely it is always possible. That is, if it is ever true that *x* may be the case, then it must be always and immutably true that *x* may be the case, under suitably specified conditions" (RCG, 153).

21. These are terms that Whitehead often (but not always) uses interchangeably.

22. Alternatively, "we require to understand how the mere existence of unchanging form requires its own immersion in the creation of a changing historic world" (MT, 83).

23. Cited in Charles Hartshorne, *Whitehead's Philosophy: Selected Essays 1935–1970* (Lincoln: University of Nebraska Press, 1972), xi.

24. For many interprets of Whitehead, however, "eternal objects" have indeed been one of the most "misleading" and misunderstood dimensions of his philosophy. For a discussion of the ways in which Whitehead is *not* a "Platonist" in this regard, refer to William Hendrichs Leue, *Metaphysical Foundations for a Theory of Value in the Philosophy of Alfred North Whitehead* (Ashfield: Down-to-Earth Books, 2005), Ch. 3; and Faber, *God as Poet of the World* (GPW), § 18. Whitehead, we remember,

acknowledges that his philosophy stands in a "European tradition" that is inherently indebted to Plato, but he has not forgotten the "intervening two thousand years." This is important to keep in mind when considering the ways in which "eternal objects" are *different* from "Platonic forms." Randall E. Auxier and Gary L. Herstein comment rightly here: "[Eternal objects] are not Plato's forms, but, as Whitehead says, closer to what he imagines Plato would say if he lived in the twentieth century." Randal E. Auxier and Gary L. Herstein, *The Quantum of Explanation: Whitehead's Radical Empiricism* (London: Routledge, 2019), 240.

25. Consider Dalferth's comments in this regard: "Something new and unexpected takes place—new life when we begin our existence, and something new within our life when possibilities come our way that could not have been derived from our life hitherto or from everything we currently do or refrain from doing. . . . They cannot be anticipated; they take us by surprise; they are unforeseeable and unexpected, without specific purpose, unprovoked, unmerited, gratuitous. They are what turns every moment of life into an adventure, both in the positive and the negative sense." Dalferth, *Creatures of Possibility*, 7–8.

26. "Thus we have always to consider two meanings of potentiality: (a) the 'general' potentiality, which is the bundle of possibilities, mutually consistent or alternative, provided by the multiplicity of eternal objects, and (b) the 'real' potentiality, which is conditioned by the data provided by the actual world. General potentiality is absolute, and real potentiality is relative to some actual entity, taken as a standpoint whereby the actual world is defined" (PR, 65).

27. Whitehead continues, "In the present fact there are various characteristics of the past, partly reproduced and partly excluded; there are the characteristics of concurrent facts in the present, partly shared in and partly excluded; there are the possibilities for the future, partly prepared for and partly excluded. The discussion of present fact apart from reference to past, to concurrent present, and to future, and from reference to the preservation or destruction of forms of creation is to rob the universe of its essential importance" (ibid., 84).

28. Hosinski, *Stubborn Fact*, 158.

Chapter 7

Ridding the Possible

Modern attempts to rid us of facing the "reality" of nonactualized possibilities have come in a variety of forms and expressions, with different assumptions and concerns. In this chapter, we briefly consider three of these attempts and a few of the ways in which their deficiencies are linked to their rejection of any ultimate Mind and Value in the universe. These attempts differently come from W. V. Quine, Frederick Ferré, and David Lewis. We will see that while the attempts of Quine and Lewis are more broadly directed against the wider axianoetic metaphysics of Whitehead, Ward, and Leslie (and all other proposals inclusive of Platonic-like phenomena), those of Ferré are aimed directly at Whitehead in a reductive attempt to show that, contrary to what one must see as a major oversight on Whitehead's part, you can actually affirm "Whitehead without God." With the exception of Quine, each of these attempts of ridding the possible are imaginative and unique. We seek to show, however, that they are also insufficient in ways supported by Whitehead, Ward, and Leslie. This discussion, moreover, serves to further set the stage for considering in the next chapter how "God" conceived in terms of Mind and Value does indeed illuminate the riddles of possibility for Whitehead, Ward, and Lelise.

W. V. QUINE: THE PROBLEMATIC "EXISTENCE" OF NONBEING

Willard Van Quine is a representative example in modern philosophy of one who objects strongly to the existential status of Platonic phenomena.[1] Although he is arguably inconsistent in affirming the "indispensability" of abstract mathematical objects, he pushed strongly against the viability of "unactualized possibilities" or "possible worlds" as having any sort of coherent "existence" (MP, 110).² We saw above that difficulties surrounding the "existence" of such phenomena have already been clearly recognized by Leslie, Ward, and Whitehead. It is certainly worth asking: What sort of "existence" it is that possibilities have if indeed they are *not* Nothing and *not* something fully Actual? Often posed against a default "naturalism" harboring sensationist, atheist, and materialist commitments—to which Quine himself adhered—the difficulty of this question has led many modern thinkers to simply deny the existence of such phenomena all together.³ In reexpressing Plato's phraseology, Quine thus called this "the problem of non-being." In so doing, however, Derek Malone-France rightly comments that Quine (with others) simply "presupposes that there is *no form of being* that properly can be attributed to inconcretia [like possibilities]" (DE, 116, emphasis mine).

It seems clear that possibilities do not "exist" as physical "things" digestible by the physical senses. You cannot see, hear, taste, touch, or smell possibilities physically. As Hosinksi relayed in the last chapter, you cannot hold a possibility in the palm of your hand or take it for a walk.⁴ Rather, you contemplate, evaluate, and feel them *mentally*; you can, as a matter of speaking, "hold" them *in mind*. Quine's narrow commitments caused him to prematurely dismiss possible distinctions among *types* of existence as an "obfuscation of issues" (quoted DE, 118). Yet, is it really the case that anything the reality of which is *less than* fully actual can be tossed aside as mere nothingness? Malone-France notes rightly that Quine *does not* take seriously enough what Whitehead called the *subsistence* of possibilities.

Although "subsistence" is a traditional term, Whitehead reemploys this term in consonance with his "ontological principle," such that unactualized possibilities are not independently existing or somehow unqualified in their Platonic preeminence; rather, they are *relationally subsistent in Actuality*. To what actuality, however, can one possibly relate the subsistent infinitude of unactualized possibility—be it of the past, the present, or the future? "The notion of 'subsistence'" Whitehead states, "is merely the notion of how eternal objects can be components of the primordial nature of God" (PR, 120). Subsistence in this sense is a *form or mode of related existence* arguably required by a serious consideration of the reality of "inconcreta" (DE, 119). Such a Primordial Mental Actuality, however, was not an option for Quine; thus, the "problem of non-being" remains in full force.

Although Ward himself does not use the phraseology of "subsistence," he is quite close to Whitehead in expressing his own version of the "ontological principle" in terms of the explanatory power divine Actuality harbors for Possibility. We will encounter this more fully in the next chapter. Leslie, by contrast, while not dismissing Platonic Possibilities, appears to push back strongly against the claim that possibilities have any *dependent subsistence*—even upon God (a view often thought to epitomize "Platonism"). This too we will face in time. Nevertheless, we seek to show that he may be closer to Whitehead and Ward than first thought. For now, my point is that we must resist Quine's (and others) *narrow* ontological assumptions as they effectively create the "problem of non-being" in the first place. Platonic realities may have modes of *subsistent existence* much wider than basic (and often static) ontological categories like "Being," "Nothingness," or "Matter."[5] As many have argued, Quine's physicalist ontology was not expansive enough to include the transphysical spaces arguably required by the real status of unactualized possibilities.

FREDERICK FERRÉ: DECENTERING AND DIFFUSING THE POSSIBLE

Frederick Ferré has clearly realized the need for making coherent sense of Platonic-like possibilities in one's ontology. He greatly admires Whitehead and remains a skillful exegete of his "constructive postmodern metaphysics," including his affirmation of a form of naturalistic theism unhindered by the inadequacies of classical theism, on the one hand, and modern materialist metaphysics, on the other.[6] Nevertheless, his own preference ("inclination") is to *not affirm* as essential the roles Whitehead (mistakenly) reserves for God with respect to Possibility and Value. Particularly, Ferré points to God as the *locus* or *place* of Possibility. In subscribing to the coherence of Whitehead's ontological principle—at least in part—he can appreciate that this principle would establish "a [divine] 'place' for pure possibilities without falling foul of the objection to the Platonic 'realm' of Forms as somehow unintelligibly subsisting independent of and even prior to any actuality in which they participate." Ferré too rules out "a mysterious realm of pure characteristics without anything characterized"; but the question remains for him as to "whether all the fundamental forms of definiteness need to be located in a *single* great actual entity, as god would provide, or whether they might be distributed through the infinitely many finite entities . . . of the kosmos itself." This latter alternative, Ferré admits, lacks "the neatness of a central repository graded and maintained by a single cosmic mind," but he questions whether a "central locus" is either logically or valuationally supported (BV, 364). "Whitehead's god," he states, "provides a 'where' for all abstract possibilities, but is it logically necessary—logically appropriate—to require a 'where' for characteristics which are admittedly devoid of a 'when'" (ibid., 368)? This is a wonderfully phrased question; and it may indeed *not* be *logically necessary*, but *ethically or axiologically* necessary that Possibility find residence in divine Mentality. On Ferré's reductive affirmation of the ontological principle, it is *necessary* that possibilities do reside in actualities, but *not* a centralized divine Actuality. Admittedly humble, Ferré is inclined instead toward a "decentralized" theory of possibility as diffused among the infinitude of actualities (ibid., 370). Pure possibility would then seem to vanish into real possibility. Contrary to Whitehead's own inclinations then, God as the locus of the purely possible is not actually required.

It is difficult to not see Ferré's comments as simply reflecting an anti-theological preference. Not only must he question Whitehead's integrity when he insisted clearly that he would "never have included [God] if [God] had not been strictly required for descriptive completeness," he has in fact *not* shown it any more plausible—beyond a few imaginative sentences—that, in the absence of "God," anything like Whitehead's aesthetic (what Ferré calls "kalogenic") universe is plausible at all.[7] What is more, as seen in the last chapter, the "place" or locus of possibilities is only *one* of several problems included in Whitehead's analysis of possibility for a processive universe. We will see more fully in the next chapter that God is not simply (or only) the "place" of unrealized Possibility in Whitehead (and Ward) but also the presupposed axiological condition under which possibilities ingress into and as the value of worldly actualities in the collective creation of beauty ("kalogenesis").[8] On Whitehead's account, it remains inconceivable that finite actualities provide the determinate limitations among possibility required for their own emergence and, indeed, the emergence of all unrealized future actualities. Nor is it plausible that actualities themselves can constitute the kalogenic standard at work in Ferré's reduced Whiteheadian universe. Actualities are in fact *already* achievements of value the persistent standard of which transcends their finitude.[9]

On Ferré's account, there is only value *for* and *to* finite actualities themselves; but in the absence of the receptive axianoetic Unity Whitehead imagines God to be, the entire universal process must be *devoid of Ultimate Significance*.[10] For Whitehead, however, it is clear that the fleeting finitude of value in the temporal world cannot be considered, nor fully appreciated, without recourse to the Value of the Whole. In fact, Whitehead stresses that to connect the value of the details with that of the Whole is to begin to grasp (however vaguely) that sense of sacredness presupposed by any truly "kalogenic" cosmos. Contrary to Ferré: would not any truly kalogenic universe have to support "the value of the world in its whole and in its parts" (RM, 105)? If so, it must affirm the ultimate axianoetic sense in which the whole can have Value beyond the flickering lives of occasions and humans. To do so, I claim, is to begin to bring "God" back into the discussion in a profound way, and thereby to reject a merely reductive account of value. Whitehead would express these sentiments in a profound and beautiful way worth quoting in full.

> [There is a] factor disclosed in our sense of the value, for its own sake, of the totality of historic fact in respect to its essential unity. There is a unity in the universe, enjoying value and (by its immanence) sharing value. For example, take the subtle beauty of a flower in some isolated glade of primeval forest. No animal has ever had the subtlety of experience to enjoy its full beauty. And yet this beauty is a grand fact in the universe. When we survey nature and think however flitting and superficial has been the animal enjoyment of its wonders, and when we realize how incapable the separate cells and pulsations of each flower are of enjoying the total effect—then our sense for the value of the details for the totality dawn upon our consciousness. This is the intuition of holiness, the intuition of the sacred, which is at the foundation of all religion . . . the sense of being one actuality in a world of actualities—is the gift of aesthetic significance. This experience claims a relevance beyond the finite immediacy of any one occasion of experience. If in that occasion, there is a failure consciously to discern that significance, so much the worse for that occasion. Our intuitions of righteousness disclose an absoluteness in the nature of things. (MT, 120–21)

The details of this brief discussion have been thoroughly *intra-Whiteheadian*. As such, they have not overtly concerned Ward and Leslie. On this final point surrounding the ultimate Value of the Whole, however, it suffices to say that all three thinkers come together in affirmation. In some deep sense, the *Value* of the Whole is precisely *why* the Whole exists.

DAVID LEWIS: POSSIBILITY, PLENTITUDE, AND ETHICAL REPUGNANCE

We briefly encountered the extreme plentitude of Davis Lewis's "modal realism" in chapter 2. Modal realism, he claims, "holds that our world is but one world among many. There are countless other worlds . . . many and varied" (quoted ME, 27). In fact, absolutely any possible way a universe *could be* from the perspective of our world is a way a universe *actually is* beyond and unrelated to our world. At the heart of Lewis's proposal is the denial of any real distinction between the "possible" and the "actual." These are merely perspectival terms. Although the "actual" world is *our particular world*, "possible" worlds are only those referenced from the *perspective* of our actual world. They appear possible from *our standpoint*, but in and of themselves, they are *as fully actual as our own*. Indeed, Lewis insists there are no unactualized possible worlds at all; every possible world is an actual world—and infinitely so.

This perspectival collapse between the possible and the actual is equally a collapse between the contingent and the necessary. "Contingency" is ultimately a façade arising from one's own limited perspective of their world; the final reality of the matter is unhindered Brute Necessity.[11] Lewis is thus adamant that there are "uncountable infinities of donkeys and protons and puddles and stars, and of planets very like Earth, and of cities very like Melbourne, and of people very like yourself" (quoted ME, 30). What is more, he remains undisturbed by "incredulous stares" gesturing that "modal realism fails the test" of common sense. The "price is right, high as it is," he claims; "modal realism ought to be accepted as true. The theoretical benefits are worth it" (ibid.).

One might find any number of reasons to reject Lewis's modal realism. We should ask immediately whether or not the benefits really are "worth" the costs of such an extreme proposal that we "ought" to accept. Is there not a deeper "test" beyond that of "common sense," which should govern one's assent to such a view? In denying possibility and contingency altogether, Lewis may indeed offer a bizarre way of making sense of our particular cosmological existence, but the price paid is *axiological*—and it is far too high. Not only is it implausible that all possibilities are *really actualities*, albeit *elsewhere*; it is also ethically and aesthetically ruinous. The question of Value does not seem to irritate Lewis any more than the incredulous stares of his critics. For these critics, however, the complete lack of Value renders his proposal nothing short of holocaustal on a grand scale. Truly, his is an acute expression of the fact that cold, hard necessity, stripped of any ultimate adjudication of Value and Mind, produces endless demonic worlds without meaning, purpose, and ethical motivation.[12] God forbid this dreadful fact not haunt Lewis. For Ward, Leslie, and Whitehead, however, this is precisely the "test" that modal realism fails.

Ward holds clearly to vital distinctions between the possible and the actual, the necessary and the contingent; and he points directly to the moral repugnance inherent in theories like those of Lewis.

> The most repugnant aspects of some versions of the multiverse theory is that, according to them there must exist universes that are totally morally repugnant, in which sentient beings are totally irrational and in which they all suffer unending and excruciating torments for no reason . . . nothing at all would be too strange, too irrational or too immoral to exist. Any sane human mind must draw back in horror from such a thought. In such a system, there would not just be one Hell, which would be bad enough. There would be an endless series of Hells, each bad in its own way. (PF, 137–38)

We have seen already that should Mind and Value have any divine Ultimacy in the nature of things—as we think plausible—then *not every possibility* will be actualized. The divine Mind will be restricted by the Value through which it lives. "God is limited precisely by being God," Ward states, "by being . . . necessarily good" (SDN, 112–13).[13] Ward, Leslie, and Whitehead all agree on this point. For Ward, "if the creator has any decency, the possibly enormous set of extremely bad universes, in which there is endless and totally pointless suffering, will not be actualized. Some selection between possible universes will be needed." The criterion of selecting possibilities is precisely that of value: "if possibilities exist in the mind of God . . . then only those possibilities will be actualized that exhibit some preponderance of value" such that "each actual universe will retain its own unique distinctive value" (ibid., 138). What is more, Ward follows Augustine in having no qualms about a "principle of plentitude" as an essential "characteristic of primordial mind." This principle, he tells us, would hold "that it is good that every possible sort of good should exist, as long as its existence does not come at the price of excessive and pointless harm. . . . Perhaps there is something in the divine nature," he admits, "that causes it to generate many possible sorts of goods, even though some kinds will inevitably incur suffering" (ibid.).[14] For Ward, this "something" in the divine nature is the supremacy of Value and its plentitudinous expression in this, and perhaps many, worthwhile worlds.

Although Leslie has engaged Lewis's thought more so than Ward, he is remarkably close to Ward's affirmations, albeit admitting infinite divine Minds as determined by Value. He recognizes fully that Lewis refuses to see "logical possibilities" as "useful fictions" or mere linguistic truths. This much Leslie also holds, but Lewis then oddly concludes that *all possibilities* really must *be actual* (ME, 20). In this, he escapes any need to explicate the meaning of *purely possible existence*, that is, Leslie clarifies, "possible existence which isn't, as in the case of our world, a case of real existence *as well*." For Lewis, there is no real sense in which *pure possibilities* exists except as *real actualities* somewhere. For Leslie (like Ward), this view is not only steeped in grim problems of Value rightly deemed horrific, but it also dissolves any ground for our basic inductive confidence in the persistence (and value) of the world's order. Here, Leslie is also worth quoting in full.

> In trying to get a handle on the distinction between really existing and being purely possible, it can help to say that pure possibilities *don't matter*. Innumerable logical possible beings undergo tortures far more frightful than all tortures ever inflicted in our world. It doesn't matter does it? Not because we can't do anything about it, but instead there's nothing awful to do anything about. Those tortured beings are nothing more than possible—not unless Lewis is right. But if Lewis is right then the tortures really are happening somewhere:

indeed, in infinitely many somewheres. Although we couldn't do anything about it, this ought to fill us with horror. It would matter. Now, likewise with suddenly turning into elephants. There's no logically firm guarantee we won't, but the possibility of our doing so doesn't matter, we can tell ourselves, because it will never happen anywhere. The innumerable ways in which Logic would allow it (big elephants? small ones? gray ones? pink?) can be disregarded because, we can tell ourselves, they will none of them be real in any world, let alone in our world. Lewis, however, cannot tell himself this. Instead of just recognizing that our future *conceivably might* be very different from what past experience would lead us to expect, his theory, could seem to say that it almost surely will be very different—if not elephantine then cabbage-like or swirling-dust or whatever. (Ibid., 21)

We have already seen that for Leslie, "ethical needs" or "requirements" for the existence of a good cosmos or, indeed, the nonexistence of "a world of unalleviated misery" are real independent of actually rejoicing or sorrowing people. They are unconditionally real in a robust Platonic sense (U, 170). It is the Supremacy of creative Value that lies at the explanatory base of infinite divine Mentalities whose existence consists in fully contemplating all possible worlds *worth* knowing. Implicit in this proposal is the fact that some possible words—those of horrendous torment or senseless chaos—are *not* valuable enough for divine contemplation and, therefore, *not* worth intricately thinking about. "Detailed knowledge of messy worlds, such as ones which suddenly began behaving crazily, would be knowledge *not* worth having," Leslie states. "A divine mind therefore wouldn't contemplate such worlds and [no one] need fear that he or she inhabits one of them" (IM, 30). Put differently, the "matters God contemplates in detail are those which are worth contemplating in detail. Worlds in which the laws of physics suddenly break down are not. Any knowledge worth calling divine would no doubt include a recognition that immensely many such worlds were possible, but it wouldn't involve knowing their structures in full" (ibid., 37).

This distinction between divine *recognition* of chaotic or evil worlds housed in the "kingdom of possibility" and *fully intricate divine knowledge* of such worlds is of utmost importance for Leslie. On his vision, in fact, this distinction is that between *the possible* and *the actual*—the difference between *worthless* possibilities forever banished to the land of the possible and valuable possibilities selected for and divinely *thought into* actual existence. An ethically required divine Mind, therefore, only actualizes good worlds ethically marked out for existence. Contrary to Lewis, necessity on Leslie's account is not *unhindered* actualization of all possibilities, but "ethical" necessity which hinders the existence of horrible universes and creatively procures the existence of valuable ones. Moreover, in ways much stronger than Ward, Leslie insists upon the ethically required plentitude not only of infinite divine Minds (as more divine Minds are *better* than less) but also of infinite valuable worlds as actualized through their oceanic thought.[15]

Whitehead too holds strongly to the difference between the actual and possible as fundamental to a processive cosmos on all levels. Microcosmically, every event emerges from its "actual world" amid a horizon "real possibility" conditioned by the past, and "pure possibility" as the unconditioned novelty of the future (TDM, 243–44). In each event, the actual and possible converge through the self-creation of events into and as the concrete world. Macroscopically, we have already seen that the determinate limitations of our "cosmic epoch" bear witness to real limitations among infinitudes of *other possible ways epochs might be*. While Whitehead does fully acknowledge "other epochs" of which ours is but one among a vast "primordial society," he will *not* insist upon the actualization of *every possibility*. This would not only destroy creative process as the essential condition of any cosmic epoch, but also render void the fact that this process is precisely that of aesthetic value attainment. The drive inherent in the universe is not a free-for-all devoid of direction; rather, ideals and values pervade the rhythms and reasons of the cosmos. "The teleology of the universe," we remember, "is directed toward the production of Beauty" (AI, 165). The world bears witness to an "aesthetic order" and this order "is derived from the immanence of God" (RM, 92).

Since God's existence "is founded in Value" and indeed "limited" by divine Goodness, not every possible world is worth striving for (Imm., 98; RM, 138). The divine "World of Value" is to be understood precisely in relation to the World of Possibility *for* the World of Fact. Its character is that of a "timeless co-ordination of the infinitude of possibility for realization" (Imm., 99–100). Such coordination involves aesthetic limitations, which move the world toward "truth, beauty and goodness" (PR, 346). Like Ward and Leslie, therefore, Whitehead insists that the aesthetic destruction inherent in purely chaotic possible worlds is contested on divine axianoetic grounds. As Whitehead puts it, "The immanence of God gives reason for the belief that pure chaos is intrinsically impossible" (ibid., 111).

RETAINING MIND, VALUE, AND POSSIBILITY

The critiques worth offering to Quine, Ferré, and Lewis are differently shaded, but resonant in their axianoetic basis. Quine's skeptical view of Platonic possibilities is based in his narrow physicalist vision of what kinds of "existence" there are. If widened by the notion of "subsistence," however, we must ask: what is it *in* which nonphysical, unactualized possibilities can subsist? What is the metaphysical medium? For Whitehead, Ward, and arguably Leslie, it is Mentality. This Mentality, moreover, would not only be inclusive of Quine's "indispensable," yet oddly free-floating mathematical objects, but also reincorporate his hasty dismissal of objective moral and aesthetic values.[16]

While far less dismissive of Platonic modes of being, Ferré "decenters" them from subsisting in divine Mentality, only to unconvincingly diffuse them among infinite actualities. His reduced ontological principle, moreover, suffers axiologically to the extent that it leaves no firm "place" from which to affirm the *total Value of the universal process* beyond fleeting occasions and all that emerges from their baffling combinations. Why not instead preserve the Value of the Whole and its Possibility at any one moment by including the ultimacy of Mind and Value? As in Whitehead (and Ward), this would require what Malone-France insists is a "cosmological application of the ontological principle" (DE, 155). Ferré, however, simply inclines otherwise.

Lewis, far more so than Ferré, suffers from a barbaric imagination devoid of any true Possibility and Value whatsoever. The only remedy to this horror is to insist upon the reality of unactualized Possibility *and* its metaphysical limitation by objective criterions of Value. Here, Mind and Value emerge in a form of ethical (Leslie) or aesthetic (Whitehead and Ward) necessity far more sane than the completely unhindered necessity of Lewis.

With these insights in hand, we can now turn to a deeper investigation of the axianoetic proposals of Whitehead, Ward, and Leslie. We remain concerned with the riddles of possibility, the place of Mind, and the question of their relationality.

NOTES

1. Refer to W. V. Quine, "On What There Is," in *Contemporary Readings in the Foundations of Metaphysics*, Stephen Laurence and Cynthia MacDonald (eds.) (Oxford: Blackwell Publishers, 1998).

2. For a discussion of Quine's inconsistencies as it relates to our considerations, see Derek Malone-France, *Deep Empiricism: Kant, Whitehead, and the Necessity of Philosophical Theism* (DE) (Lanham: Lexington, 2007), Ch. 5.

3. Although it is widely agreed that the scientific worldview requires "naturalism," relevant distinctions between *kinds* of "naturalism" are not often made. Over and against the inadequacies of the dominant form of "naturalism" conceived in terms of sensationism, atheism, and materialism (SAM), David Ray Griffin has argued forcefully for a Whiteheadian naturalism conceived in terms of prehension, panexperientialism, and panentheism (PPP). Not only is naturalism "SAM" not required by science, it cannot even do justice to what Griffin calls our "hard-core common sense notions," including causation, induction, the past, time, the external world, and

objective mathematical, moral, and aesthetic truths/ideals. Accordingly, a deeper naturalism is required that will better support science and these indispensable features of experience. Rather than "hardcore common sense notions," I prefer to call these "presuppositional imperatives." See Griffin, *Reenchantment without Supernaturalism: A Process Philosophy of Religion* (RWS) (Ithaca: Cornell University Press, 2001). See also alternative approaches in Alvin Plantinga, *Where the Conflict Really Lies: Science, Religion and Naturalism* (Oxford: Oxford University Press, 2011) and Peter Forrest, *God without the Supernatural* (GWS) (Ithaca: Cornell University Press, 1996).

4. Refer to note 14.

5. See, for example, Paul Davies and John Gribbin, *The Matter Myth: Dramatic Discoveries that Challenge Our Understanding of Physical Reality* (New York: Simon & Schuster, 1992).

6. Refer to Ferré's impressive trilogy in *Being and Value* (BV); *Knowing and Value: Toward a Constructive Postmodern Epistemology* (Albany: SUNY, 1998); *Living and Value: Toward a Constructive Postmodern Ethics* (Albany: SUNY, 2001). For praises and critiques of his work, see George Allan and Merle F. Allshouse (eds.), *Nature, Truth, and Value: Exploring the Thinking of Frederick to Ferré* (Lanham: Lexington, 2005).

7. I would thus agree with Griffin's comments in this regard. "The question is not whether the arguments for some position or another are coercive but which view, as Plato put it, provides the most likely account. And in terms of this question, I cannot believe that many readers will find that Ferré shows his own alternative to Whitehead's position—according to which finite actual occasions can perform all the functions Whitehead assigned to God—to be more likely." David Ray Griffin, "Theism and the Crisis in Moral Theory," in Allan and Allshouse, *Nature, Truth and Value*, 209. Griffin's comments equally hit Donald A. Crosby's attempt to address the problem of novelty in Whitehead without recourse to God. He does so by denying any reality to "pure possibility" and affirming only the "real possibility" inherent in the past as the storehouse of novelty for the future. See Donald A. Crosby, *Novelty* (Lanham: Lexington, 2005). Crosby, however, fails to appreciate the weddedness of "pure" and "real" possibility in Whitehead. As Lewis Ford states, "Real possibilities" link "pure possibilities to particular spatio-temporal loci." Lewis Ford, "The Nontemporality of Whitehead's God," *International Philosophical Quarterly* 8/3 (1973): 362.

8. Faber clarifies this saying: "God's primordial nature is not simply the 'locus' of all possible worlds, but rather their concrescence, that is, their free *valuation*." Faber, *God as Poet*, 185. Alternatively, "the primordial nature of God is not just a 'place' of potential, possibilities, alternative realities, or possible scenarios, but the 'mother' who harbors all possibilities, potentials, alternatives, and possible worlds as such, as unrealized . . . the primordial nature is not only a reservoir of potentials and infinite worlds but a divine event, actually uniting and proposing potentials to any event in its own becoming as values to be realized" (TGR, 190).

9. Contra Ferré, John Cobb states, "It is my impression of the earth's history that it reflects a kalogenic tilt that is too consistent to be attributed to local causes, and I

do believe that the universe as a whole has basic similarities . . . the view that there is a kalogenic tilt that is somewhat more than [what Ferré says is] 'barely detectable' is consistent with the present state of scientific interpretation. . . . Ferré thinks that the general role of value in the world requires no theistic explanation. Purpose and self-determination are simply part of what is. Hence the only thing that a nontheistic nature would not explain would be a cosmos-wide bias toward increasing value. Since I do not see how a nontheistic account explains purposiveness and self-determination in general, I find that God's role in the world is far more extensive and far more crucial." John B. Cobb Jr., "God Revisited," in Allan and Allshouse, *Nature, Truth and Value*, 231–32, 238.

10. Consider William L. Power's statements in this regard: "In Whitehead's metaphysics, God is viewed as that actual entity that takes up into his own unique subjective concrescence the unique subjective concrescences of all spatio-temporal actual entities. As such, God suffers with them in their weal and woe and cherishes them forever. In doing so the world is given everlasting significance and worth in the ultimate scheme of things. Whiteheadians without God cannot make the above claim. . . . [W]ith a kalogenic ecological naturalism such as Ferré's, one can claim that all creatures great and small have penultimate significance and worth in the whole cosmic scheme of things, and that is perhaps all that one can hope for if there is no ultimate producer and preserver of value." William L. Power, "Ferré without God: A Shift to a Neo-Whiteheadian Humanistic Naturalism," in Allan and Allshouse, *Nature, Truth and Value*, 252.

11. Faber confirms this of Lewis: "Although any world, from its own perspective, can be considered contingent, considered as part of a whole that is all possible worlds, as they are actualized in themselves, per definition really none of them is contingent, but just a *variant of necessity*" (TDM, 243).

12. Consider Faber's comments in this regard. "If all possible worlds are realized, while any given 'world' remains contingent in its structure, the deep question of value and meaning becomes *irrelevant*, because we must then imagine even the worst world in its utmost meaninglessness to be actualized" (TDM, 243). Faber protests further saying: "Not only does [modal realism] not intend to accept any Reality that in goodness, love, and peace infuses itself into the infinite worlds as their eros and compassionate context, but [it] withholds itself from differentiating possibilities as mere abstraction from actualization as events of becoming. By doing so, it deprives itself not only of any *meaningful* alternatives to this world in and beyond itself (as all worlds are realized, just not here), that is, any *direction* possibly taken by motivation of goodness, love, and peace to transform the world, but also instills in us the horror that any abomination we have ever heard of and can ever think of (and beyond) is realized somewhere. (I need to pause at this thought for a moment!) In escaping any restrictions, such as goodness, love, and peace, this view leaves us neither with any aesthetic motivation for existence nor with any ethical drive for change since it has for the better or worse already happened somewhere anyway" (TGR, 204).

13. Ward's full quote runs: "God is limited precisely by being God, by being good, wise, powerful, and loving. These are ways in which God is, and they exclude

their opposites. God is not evil, stupid, weak, and malevolent. . . . However, if God is necessarily good, then God *could not ever*, in fact, do evil. God's power is limited by God's goodness. That is not bad, but good. Therefore some limitation (some defining properties of God) must exist in God" (ibid., 112–13).

14. For Ward's recent discussion of the "principle of plentitude" as it relates to "the perennial philosophy," see RMW, Ch. 13.

15. See Leslie, "What God Might Be."

16. Griffin, *God Exists but Gawd Does Not*, 182.

Chapter 8

The Mutual Immanence of the Possible and the Actual

In chapter 6, we saw that the "riddles" of the possible are differently angled by Whitehead, Ward, and Leslie. Each of them express these riddles in relation to the resolving abilities of a divine axianoetic framework. We must not say this too hastily, however. We will find below that while Whitehead and Ward come close together in their resolution of these riddles through their *dependent relation* upon the *Actuality* of divine Mentality, Leslie, while arguably close himself, nevertheless pushes us to pose still deeper riddles as to God's relationship to the Possible. Put simply: Should God exist, does not the *fact* that God *is possible* mean that Possibility as such *does not* and *cannot* depend upon the divine Mind? This is an excellent question and a robust stimulus to clarify how it is that Actuality and Possibility might relate in God. Where, after all, does the priority lie? It does not seem one can avoid this question and still hope to fully resolve the riddles of Possibility by appealing to a divine Mind. Yet we seek to unveil the ways in which Whitehead, Ward, and Leslie each harbor unique spaces for affirming a mutually immanent, and thus also mutually transcendent, mode of relationality between Possibility and Actuality in God. Through this *kind* of relationality, we may discover that the riddles Possibility poses for the world, and even for God, find plausible resolution. We turn first to Whitehead and Ward.

WHITEHEAD: POSSIBILITY AND "THE GENERAL ARISTOTELIAN PRINCIPLE"

Whitehead's expression of the "ontological principle" is his way of capturing the "general Aristotelian principle" that "apart from things that are *actual*, there is nothing—nothing either in fact or in efficacy" (PR, 40, emphasis mine). Elevating the explanatory power of Actuality, this principle has had a long-standing foothold in the philosophical tradition. From Aristotle, Augustine, and Aquinas to Descartes, Kant, Leibniz, and Whitehead himself, this principle, although differently expressed, has been vital to discussions of ultimacy and explanation.[1] We have seen already that Whitehead articulates this principle in different ways: "Every explanatory fact refers to the decision and to the efficacy of an actual thing," for example; or "everything must be somewhere; and here 'somewhere' means 'some actual entity.'" This principle aims to secure a mode of explanatory coherence such that "there are no self-sustained facts, floating in nonentity." For Whitehead, not only does this principle aid one in avoiding any "contradiction in terms," it is also central to any coherent explanation in and of the actual world itself (ibid., 46, 11). Nowhere is this expressed more acutely than in terms of the Infinite Possibilities presupposed by the world in process.

Whitehead recognizes immediately that upholding the ontological principle means that the "general potentiality of the universe *must be somewhere*; since it retains its proximate *relevance* to actual entities for which it is unrealized" (ibid., 46, emphasis mine). We saw already that the *locus* and *relevance* of possibility constitute key riddles for Whitehead. It is not only that the actual process of the universe at any one point presupposes the infinite fullness of its Possibility but also that each actual entity is an emergence of potentials relevant to that entity as it decides how to contribute itself to the world process. No single finite actual entity can account for the "general potentiality of the universe," and no finite actual entity can provide relevant potentialities *for its own emergence*; rather, it chooses among these potentialities as *already given*. This seems rather straightforward. Both of these statements make recourse to a certain *transcendence* Possibility retains in relation to finite actuality. Neither on Whitehead's vision, however, can it be said that possibility "procures" anything due to its abstractness. Infinite Possibilities alone cannot coherently limit themselves as relevant to the world process. The *efficacy* and *limitation* of possibilities constitute the other riddles encountered in chapter 6.

In seeking to resolve these problems, Whitehead must, in consonance with the ontological principle, refer the locus of Infinite Possibility, as well as its limited/ordered relevance and efficacy to the world process, to something both Nontemporal *and* Actual. What could this "somewhere" and "something" be? Whitehead answers: "This 'somewhere' is the non-temporal actual entity" and "'proximate relevance' means 'relevance as in the *primordial mind of God*'" (ibid., emphasis mine). In part, this divine Mind must be *nontemporal* to account for the *timeless infinitude* of Possibility, and *Actual* to account for its limited/ordered relevance for the world. The eternal objects *in* God's primordial Mentality, Whitehead holds, thus "constitute the Platonic world of ideas"; although, as stressed already, these are "forms *of process*" and rather *unlike* reified renderings of traditional "Platonic Ideas" (ibid.; cf. MT, Lect. 5).[2]

As "the unlimited conceptual realization of the absolute wealth of potentiality," Whitehead conceives this primordial Mind to be nothing other than the *presupposed reason* for the relevance of eternal objects to the world process. This Mind, he states, "is the unconditioned actuality of conceptual feeling at the base of things; so that, by reason of this primordial actuality, there is an order in the relevance of eternal objects to the process of creation" (PR, 344). So essential is the divine *appetitive* ordering of Possibility that without it the world would halt in disjointed stagnation. Whitehead communicates this vividly.

> The final entity is the divine element in the world, by which the barren inefficient disjunction of abstract potentialities obtains primordially the efficient conjunction of ideal realization. This ideal realization of potentialities in a primordial actual entity constitutes the metaphysical stability whereby the actual process exemplifies general principles of metaphysics, and attains the ends proper to specific types of emergent order. By reason of the actuality of this primordial valuation of pure potentials, each eternal object has a definite, effective relevance to each concrescent process. Apart from such orderings, there would be a complete disjunction of eternal objects unrealized in the temporal world. Novelty would be meaningless, and inconceivable. (Ibid., 40)

Whitehead thus holds that the Non-Temporal Actuality of God is included in every creative phase of emergence in the actual world. We remember that every "event on its finer side introduces God into the world" such that "the world lives by its incarnation of God in itself" (RM, 140). Considered alone, the unlimited wealth of abstract possibility "would leave each creative phase still indeterminate." Conceived in terms their "bare isolated multiplicity," possibility lacks any "existent character." Whitehead thus holds that eternal objects "require the transition to the conception of them as efficaciously existent by reason of God's conceptual realization of them." It is this divine "conceptual realization" that performs "an efficacious role in multiple unifications of the universe, which are free creations of actualities arising out of decided situations" (ibid., 81–82; PR, 349). Devoid of subsistence and actualization, these possibilities would also hold *no real value* on Whitehead's account. Possibilities in themselves "represent no achievement of actual value" devoid of fusion with actuality (RM, 141). The definite determination, which gifts ordered balance and value to the world, therefore, requires a divine axianoetic entity which shares "its own unchanged consistency of character on every phase" (ibid., 81–82).

How is this "character" to be conceived? For Whitehead, the consistency of this unchanged divine *character* must be an expression of the very *nature* of God. This nature, as we have seen, is "founded on Value," both "moral and aesthetic"; it is characterized by "necessary goodness" and thus divides "the good from the evil" (Imm., 98, 101; PR, 345; SMW, 179). There is indeed a "character permanently inherent in the nature of things," he insists, and it expresses this very nature as a "character of *permanent rightness*" whose inherence in the world effectively modifies efficient and final causes, such that "the one conforms to harmonious conditions, and the other contrasts itself with the ideal." The ordered harmony in the actual world, therefore, is due to the world's conformity *with* the axiological steadfastness of this divine character (RM, 50). Indeed, Whitehead articulates the interplay of Mind, Value, and Possibility in a vision of God whose very purpose is the "attainment of Value in the temporal world" (ibid., 87).

> God, who is the ground antecedent to transition [or process], must include all possibilities of physical value conceptually, thereby holding the ideal forms apart in equal, conceptual realization of knowledge. Thus, as concepts, they are grasped together in the synthesis of omniscience. . . . He is complete in the sense that his vision determines every possibility of value. Such a complete vision coordinates and adjusts every detail. . . . This ideal world of conceptual harmonization is merely a description of God himself. Thus the nature of God is the complete conceptual realization of the realm of ideal forms. The kingdom of heaven is God. But these forms are not realized by him in mere bare isolation, but as element in the value of his conceptual experience. Also, the ideal forms are in God's vision as contributing to his complete experience, by reason of his conceptual realization of their possibilities as elements of value in any creature. (Ibid., 137–39)

Whitehead thus integrates and explains the riddles of pure and real possibility through their *subsistent residence* within the evaluative understanding of an axianoetic divinity. The functions of this divine Actuality at once reason the very possibility, order, and value of the world and the actual entities which variously comprise it.[3] Considered from its highest altitude, the "ontological principle" expresses the fundamental commitment that without the Actuality of God in relation to every event, there would be *nothing* either possible or actual, no order, and thus no world at all. "Apart from God, the remaining formative elements would fail in their functions. There would be no creatures, since, apart from harmonious order, the perceptive fusion would be a confusion neutralizing achieved feeling. . . . If there were no order there would be no world. . . . The ordering entity is a necessary element in the metaphysical situation presented by the actual world (RM, 90–91).

WARD: POSSIBILITY, NECESSITY, AND THE "PLATONIC-AUGUSTINIAN MODEL"

Ward has consistently advocated a "Platonic-Augustinian" model to resolve the riddles of possibility.[4] He has expressed variously the explanatory force in that "ancient saying," holding that "anything actual must either be caused by something actual and with at least as much actuality as it has, or be such that it could not possibly be caused by anything" (GCN, 48). Aquinas inherited this Aristotelian tradition and put it succinctly: "Actual existence takes precedence of potential existence" (RCG, 35; CIG, 93; SDN, 84). This statement, for Ward, is not a denial of possibility, but an affirmation of its *necessary weddedness to Actuality* (CC, Ch. 5). We remember that for Ward one of the principal riddles of possibility is the odd sense in which one can affirm their "existence" at all. In *what sense* would an infinite "array of all possible states" plausibly exist—and *how*? If, for example, our "laws of nature" are but a set of many possible laws, then a clear problem presents itself as to the ontological status and nature of those laws. "Do they really exist," Ward asks, "and if so, where? How can one be sure they will continue to apply to nature" (CIG, 93; GCN, 39, 53–54).

For Ward, as we have seen, it seems fully plausible to affirm that many possibilities do necessarily exist. This conclusion seems difficult to deny. It is not helpful, however, to leave them unintegrated (as Plato arguably did) in some void-like, half-real realm. If possibilities exist at all, they must, in virtue of the "ancient saying," have subsistent dependence upon some actual being. Ward is thus adamant that "one must be logically ruthless, and say that either there are really no possibilities or that they exist in something actual" (GCN, 36). It seems obvious that it is not *possible* to deny the reality of possibility without assuming its reality. Human existence and experience confirms this. On Ward's account then, we are continually forced toward Actuality as inclusive of Possibility. Indeed, he often frames the existence of a "necessary being" precisely as it relates to such riddles. "If one asks what a necessary being could be, the answer is that it is that being which is the ground of all possibilities. The specification of his nature defines the whole realm of possibility and constitutes him as the actual ground of that realm" (RCG, 35).[5]

Ward has expressed the necessity of God through the problem of possibility in different ways. "A definition of a 'necessarily existing being,'" he states, "is that it is a being which exists in every possible logical world (where 'a world' is taken to cover absolutely everything that actually exists." If anything at all is ever possible then "there exists an actual being which contains that possibility, and if that actual being is the same in all possible worlds, then by definition that actual being is a necessarily existing being" (GCN, 36). Put differently, this being is the only thing that must be *Actual* if anything at all is

Possible; and there cannot be any possible alternatives to it, because it is the condition of the possibility of alternatives (PF, 132). What is more, if one is to seek after *what* this "being" must be like in order to include the infinitude of nonphysical possibility in its own nature, Ward answers: "Theists call it the mind of God, and the doctrine of creation is that this universe comes into being out of nothing except the mind of God" (ibid., 37).

Ward therefore is entirely comfortable with putting forth a "basically Platonic" vision, which, he claims, has been revived in a variety of proposals in recent years, not least in those of Leslie and Roger Penrose (CIG, 84).[6] Yet, in contrast to these thinkers, he has repeatedly stressed the integrative value of Augustine's Middle Platonic move as a necessary complement to the Platonic vision of "Forms" or "Ideas." "It was Augustine who formulated an elegant integration between these elements by placing the world of the Forms in the mind of the primordial intellect, and making the physical cosmos a 'moving image of eternity,' a world selected by intellect out of the world of Forms for the sake of making many sorts of goodness actual" (MAG, 107–8). This Augustinian move, moreover, "eased the problem of what it could mean to speak of the actual existence of a mere possibility; for their actuality becomes that of the mind in which they inhere" (RCG, 153). Ward thus follows this Augustinian approach in showing how it aids one's inquiry into the nature of ultimacy and explanation.

> I have suggested, following Augustine, that mind or consciousness is somehow involved in such an ultimate explanation, because it is mind that stores possibilities non-physically and mind that can act for a reason—that is, in order to make actual some possible states. This is just to say that mind is a fundamental constituent of ultimate reality and is necessarily prior to all physical entities. For they are actualisations of possibilities apprehended by cosmic mind, the only actuality that is not capable of being brought into being or of not existing or of being other than it is, precisely because it is a condition of the existence of any possibilities whatsoever. Cosmic consciousness is the condition of any and all possibilities existing . . . and not merely a very complex thing that just happens to exist. (CIG, 98)

For Ward, as in Whitehead, far from just happening to exist, the ground of divine Mentality, as the presupposed condition of the Possible, is the supremacy of divine Value or Goodness. This is the divine nature—even what Ward too calls the divine "character."[7]

In an axianoetic universe, all possibilities are possibilities of *Value*. To speak both of their Necessity and their Value, therefore, is to begin to form a coherent basis from which to speak of purpose in the actualization of anything at all. "For a full and adequate explanation of a contingent universe,"

Ward states, "one needs to employ the concepts of necessity, purpose and value. Without necessity, values would be arbitrary and inexplicable; without value, necessity would be blind and pointless; without purpose, both would be immobile and unproductive" (RCG, 172). That Ultimate Mind is the binding element among these notions is not at all a "vacuous explanation" for Ward; rather, "positing an underlying mind-like reality that is expressed in the cosmos explains how intelligibility, value and beauty can be found in objective reality" (CIG, 69). It follows for Ward that "without mind, there will be no value and purpose in the universe" at all. Yet, if human existence and experience does witness to such realities, then there are grounds for affirming that "something mind-like may be the basis of the physical reality." Ward is confident, moreover, that without this divine axianoetic reality, "there would exist nothing at all" (ibid., 49).

LESLIE'S CHALLENGE AND THE QUESTION OF RELATIONALITY

How then does Leslie approach the riddles of Possibility in relation to divine Mentality? We do well to remember that his proposal pictures the *abstract*, conceived in terms of "ethical needs" or "requirements," as *not depending* upon the existence of actualities—either finite or divine. The *possibility* of things *transcends* the actuality of things; however "suspicious," possibilities are *Platonic necessities* marked out for existence because of their Value. They would be every bit as real if nothing actual existed at all. Moreover, some of them have an ethical weight so heavy that they are creatively effectual in actually bringing about the reality "required." God conceived as a divine Mentality is the supreme exemplification of this case. Leslie therefore strongly challenges that tradition that would prioritize *Actuality* in quest for ultimate explanations of abstraction. This includes the Actuality of God as stressed by Whitehead's "Aristotelian" or "ontological principle," as well as Ward's "Platonic-Augustinian" model—both of which can be seen (at first glance) to prioritize Actuality in resolving the ontological riddles posed by abstract possibilities. For both, the Actuality of the divine Mind is the existential ground of the Possible.

This is not easily the case for Leslie, however.[8] Not only does Value have an eternal unilateral claim on the actual existence of divine Mentality, such that ultimacy is properly conceived in terms of the Abstract, it would be the same to say that the eternally value-laden *Possibility* for divine Actuality does not depend upon the existence of that Mentality, but rather unilaterally procures this Mind as supremely worthwhile over and above the infinitude of other Platonic possibilities vying for existence. Leslie then, while holding that

God is *Actual*, insists that this is so *because* the abstract, indefatigable Value of *God's Possibility* eternally acquires God's Actuality. This very possibility, as well as its procurement, however, is *independent* of God and cannot *depend* upon God.

In chapter 3, we saw Leslie express this clearly with respect to Leibniz. Instead of inquiring as to "why mere possibilities could not have both ethical and creative importance," Leslie finds Leibniz too hastily transferring "the war among them to God's mind" (ME, 121). Have Whitehead and Ward done this as well? Rather than being required for greater coherence and explanatory power, Leslie thinks this move by Leibniz was perhaps a result of societal pressure from a culture that would enact "serious consequences" upon those who denied God "the ultimate foundation of all explanations." Just as Whitehead insisted that Leibniz's affirmation of the "best possible world" was an "audacious fudge" to "save the face of the Creator," so too does Leslie think that in making possibilities *dependent* upon divine Mentality, Leibniz was effectively saving his own face!

The culture has changed, and this cannot easily be said of Whitehead and Ward. Nevertheless, as Leslie would have it, the correct position is to insist that "God Himself, even when infinitely sure to succeed in any struggle between possibilities, had actually been compelled to take part in such a struggle, a creative process occurring *independently* of His will" (ibid., 106, emphasis mine). God's own possibility, therefore, along with a host of other Platonic realities, do not depend upon God. Leslie has stated these convictions in full force, and yet in ways that might also open up interesting dialogical spaces with Whitehead and Ward on God's relationship to the Possible.

> God's own possibility cannot have been under God's control, and the logical, mathematical, and ethical truths which God supposedly knows wouldn't be under God's control either. God couldn't have made misery into something very good in itself. God couldn't have made two and two make five. But in any case, something 'outside God's control' wouldn't necessarily mean something *outside God*. There is only a verbal difference between declaring that God owes his existence to an ethical requirement that he exist and declaring instead that he owes his existence *to his own ethical requiredness*. (IM, 183)

This is a deeply intriguing statement by Leslie. What can it mean, however, that these Platonic realities, though seemingly beyond the control of God, are nevertheless *not*—and never have been—*outside God*? What is more, one might conceivably argue that there is not simply a "verbal difference," but a *metaphysical difference*, between the claim that such realities are *independent* of the divine Mind and the claim that they in fact constitute something of the *infinite depths of this Mind's abstract nature*. The difference here, we might say, is that between Leslie's thoroughgoing Platonic sensibilities on the one hand and Whitehead and Ward's more Middle Platonic sensibilities on the other. These are tedious distinctions to be sure, but they do raise the question as to how best to conceive the relationship between the divine Mind and Platonic possibilities.

Leslie has insisted that he *does not* locate the infinity of possibilities *in* the mind of God, if by "in" one means that possibilities *depend* on this Mind. Possibilities, in other words, are not possibilities *only* because they are *thought or contemplated* by the divine Mind; rather, even if this Mind were removed from the metaphysical picture altogether, they would still constitute robust Platonic realities preeminent in their independence. The issue, of course, is that there is no possible scenario in which the necessary reality of divine Mentality can be coherently *removed* from Leslie's metaphysics. We find him admitting this below. How then could one ever know that abstract Possibilities—including this Mind's own—do not in fact depend upon the Actuality of this Mind? This is a striking question. Leslie's thought experiment may indeed be helpful in articulating his own position, but it also seems to constitute its own challenge.

> Even if God didn't exist—(which in my view is an impossibility, since in God's case ethical requiredness is creatively effective, not by chance but instead by necessity)—God's existence would still be ethically required: it really would be the case, even if nothing actually existed, that there was a need (but if nothing existed it would be an unfulfilled need) for God to exist. My belief is that if, *per impossibile* (as the medievals would say), God suddenly vanished, then there would be an ethical need for God to reappear, and therefore (since on my theory the ethical need for God to exist explains God's existence) God would reappear.[9]

We can put these playful statements differently in terms of God's Possibility and Actuality. Hypothetically, we *can* separate the divine Mind's Possibility from its Actuality, such that there remains the *Possibility* of God without the *Actuality* of God. There is, however, *no* metaphysical state of affairs for Leslie in which this really is (or ever could be) achieved. Rather, the Supreme Value of God's Possibility ever acquires its Actuality with eternal creative success. Leslie's statements again prioritize abstract Value and Possibility over Actuality, yet it is not clear that this is demanded of us when there is, despite their distinction, *never a separation between divine Possibility and divine Actuality*. The question as to their mode of relationality can and should be raised here, especially when facing the honest Platonic problem, which despite Leslie, many still feel when considering how the abstract "kingdom" of Possibility and Value—including God's own—can be explained on the one hand and be creatively effectual on the other. We seem to require at once both abstract Possibility and concrete Actuality. Leslie, Ward, and Whitehead include both, but the way is now opened for a more detailed consideration as to that *mode* of relationality that may obtain between Possibility and Actuality in God.

THE MUTUAL IMMANENCE OF THE POSSIBLE AND THE ACTUAL IN GOD

For Leslie, Ward, and Whitehead, the presupposition of anything actual is its possibility. For each of them, possibility and actuality are intricately linked. But is this also the case for the Actuality of the Divine Mind and its *own Possibility*? Leslie reminds us that we cannot evade the fact that, *if* God is Actual, *then* God is also Possible, and that *this* Platonic Possibility must transcend any dependence upon God. God depends upon it, but it—being utter Platonic—does not depend upon God. How should one conceive this problem and its relation to ultimacy, explanation, and the riddles of the possible? Is there a way to understand the relationality between the Possible and Actual in God that might help resolve this final riddle?

We saw above that Leslie clearly prioritizes *the Possibility of God* for the Actuality of God (and indeed for all actualities), while Ward and Whitehead seemingly prioritize *the Actuality of God* for the Possibility of God (and, indeed, for all possibilities). Although these priorities may at first glance seem utterly exclusive, the *mutual immanence* of the Possible and the Actual in God reveals them to be *abstractions* from their wider relationality to one another. What this allows us to affirm is not the ultimacy of Possibility over and against Actuality, nor the ultimacy of Actuality over and against Possibility, but rather the *ultimacy of their relationality* through mutual immanence. We will find these insights surface below though a unique back-and-forth between Leslie and Ward precisely on these points. My goal is to show how mutual immanence emerges as an interpretive framework between their respective insights. We will then find that Whitehead's own insights complement the discussion.

From Leslie to Ward and Back Again

More so than above, Leslie has expressed clearly his Platonic position as to why God's Possibility *cannot* depend upon the Mind of God. For him there is an "obvious" difficulty at hand, which cannot be easily solved.

> There's at least one very obvious case of a Platonic reality that is necessary as a prerequisite of the existence of any divine being, and which cannot itself in any

way depend on the actuality of such a being: namely, the reality of the logical possibility of there being such a being. To make the divine being's logical possibility itself depend on the divine being's actual existence would be a particularly unconvincing case of somebody pulling himself into the air by tugging upwards on his own pigtail (as in Baron Munchausen's story of how he rescued himself from a swamp).[10]

How should one respond to these comments? In the first place, when considering *finite* beings, it does indeed seem fully "obvious" that the "logical possibility" of such a being cannot depend upon the "actuality of such a being." To the contrary, it is quite the reverse; finite beings *come into existence*. Yet, is not the *infinite necessary* reality of God a completely different matter? If one seeks an integrative total explanation of things, might there be a way of achieving what Leslie seeks, albeit without the difficulty of imagining how abstractions can be creatively effective *on their own*? On Leslie's account, the incomparable Value (ethical demand) of the divine Mind's Possibility *eternally procures* this Mind's Actuality such that the *Possibility* of this Mind and the *Actuality* of this Mind, although distinct, are *utterly inseparable* from one another. The question then arises as to why we should privilege the divine Mind's Possibility over its Actuality and whether or not there might be a mode of relationality between them that is *mutual* instead of *unilateral*.

Why should one be concerned with this? It is because they may be *unconvinced* that Platonic Possibilities, while indispensable, can utterly stand alone. Leslie envisions the Value of God's Possibility as eternally acquiring God's Actuality in a unilateral fashion. But does not the Actuality of God offer *something back* to the Possibility of God? Even on Leslie's account, one might provocatively say that it does: The Actuality of God eternally *satisfies* the Possibility of God. Put in terms of mutual immanence, we can say that the Possibility of the Divine Mind is the *abstract presupposition* of the *Actual Existence* of this Mind, just as the *Actual Existence* of this Mind is the *concrete presupposition* of the Existence (or Subsistence) of this Possibility. Only in the mutual immanence and transcendence of both for each other, do we arguably arrive at a total explanation of the Possible and the Actual in God. Through *mutual immanence*, we find these distinct realties to be inseparable from each other; through *mutual transcendence*, we find this inseparability based in the claim that neither of them by themselves can provide the function the other offers. Perhaps this is a plausible way of imaginatively conceiving how it is that God (as a manner of speaking) does pull the divine self "into the air by tugging upwards on [the divine] pigtail."

These statements constitute a set of fascinating and difficult issues. Through my own encouragement, both Ward and Leslie have responded to each other precisely on their account. Consider the ways in which Ward's response to Leslie's comments above open unique spaces for affirming the mutual immanence of the Possible and the Actual in God.

> It is true that God is logically possible, and if possible God is actual (Anselm was right here, though we cannot be sure that God is logically possible!). The possibility does not precede the actuality, but is co-existent with it (it is not first in the swamp, then pulled out of it; God is never in the swamp). If possibles exist, they are in some sense actual. Perhaps uniquely, in God's case the possibility of God is actual both as possibility and as instantiated. In fact it may seem that there must be some instantiated possibility if there are to be any sheerly logical possibilities at all.[11]

This is a remarkable statement. In saying that the "possibility *does not* precede the actuality, but is *co-existent* with it," Ward assumes, but does not elaborate upon, a kind of coexistent relationality *between* God's Possibility and Actuality.[12] What can it mean, however, that the uniqueness of God's existence may be found in the fact that "the possibility of God is actual *both as possibility and as instantiated*"? This is rather like John Polkinghorne's comment in chapter 5 that God is "supreme goodness and its instantiation in a divine bootstrap of virtue" (FP, 58). Naturally, this is difficult and speculative, but a relationship of mutual immanence may indeed illuminate to a greater extent not only the insight that there is a relational *coexistence* between Possibility and Actuality in God, such that *neither* takes precedence over the other, but also how the abstractness of God's Possibility is *instantiated* as God's Actuality. Mutual immanence would offer a way in which each is necessary for the other: divine Possibility requires its instantiation in divine Actuality, just as divine Actuality requires its Possibility as instantiated. In God there is the coexistent, coinherence of both for the other in ways immanent and transcendent.

In responding to Ward, Leslie articulates again the discomfort he feels in a God who pulls the divine self into existence by divine "pig tales" (or bootstraps!). Nevertheless, his comments also reveal some manner of deep resonance with Ward on this issue.

> I stick by my claim that making God's logical possibility depend on God's actuality would be rather too similar to what Munchausen pictured. Yes, IF (which is what I, too, think) God (suitably understood, not necessarily as an almighty Person) has an existence that's eternally necessary, hence eternally actual (so that there was never a time at which God didn't exist), then God's logical possibility didn't precede God's existence in time, and God "was never in the swamp from which he'd need to extract himself by pulling upwards on his own pigtail." But it still seems to me clear enough that a PREREQUISITE of anything, even

God, having actuality is that its actuality is (unlike the supposed actuality of a round square or of a married bachelor) logically possible.[13]

The question as to whether it is a "temporal" or "logical" relation that God's Actuality has to God's Possibility is an important point worth clarifying. Leslie rightly rejects a "temporal" relation, precisely because God is "eternally necessary" and "eternally actual." To affirm a temporal relation here would be to insist that there was a time when the Actuality of God *was not*, while the Possibility of God *was*. This is what Leslie and Ward rightly deny. Necessity, as they conceive it, *does not* allow the Possibility of God to temporally precede the Actuality of God. Nevertheless, despite their agreement, Leslie still bows toward the abstract. We can, of course, fully agree that the "prerequisite" of God's Actuality *is* God's Possibility, but it is *not* so clear—given their eternal inseparability—that this must be a *unilateral relation* flowing from divine Possibility to the divine Actuality, but *not* from divine Actuality to divine Possibility. Ward is uncomfortable with any free-floating Platonic Possibility and is, therefore, more willing to equate both Possibility and Actuality with each other in the existence of God. His response to Leslie, moreover, draws out their similarities, their divergence, and the necessary humility required by all in venturing such wild discourse.

> We both accept that God is necessarily and eternally actual, and we both agree that therefore God must be logically possible, and we both agree, I think, that if God is logically possible, then God is actual. That's not bad! I just have a bad feeling about logical possibilities without any actualities. If there are some, then there is something actual—the logical possibility! But it is paradoxical to say that a possibility is actual; so what I do is to equate the possibility with the actuality, and say that in this unique case what is possible is necessarily actual. But we are all breathing very thin air at this point; much turns on the word prerequisite. Logically prerequisite, yes; temporally pre-requisite, no (but the word temporal wouldn't apply here either).[14]

Far from coming into existence temporally, therefore, the necessity of God has to match the necessity of the Possible itself. Possibility cannot come into being or be "created" (and this is different from *becoming actualized*); for if it did, it will have been *possible* that it did. For Ward, then, these Possibilities—including God's own—are not independent of God, but part of the abstract nature of God. He expresses this clearly, saying, "Possibilities cannot come into being or pass away. So, like God himself, they must be eternal and uncreated. If follows that they are not brought into being, even by God, but are parts of his immutable nature. God does not decide which possibilities to create; all possibilities are specified completely by the uncreated being of God"

(RCG, 153).[15] It remains vague, however, to insist that in God Possibility and Actuality are *equated* such that God's Possibility is necessarily Actual. How does this work? True clarity on such questions will forever evade us; and this is perhaps a good thing. Still, one wants to say more. Mutual immanence, I claim, may illuminate these intuitions through a mode of relational ultimacy at the heart of divinity. Arguably, it is a way of preserving both the essential claims and worries of Leslie and Ward.

Enter Whitehead: The Mutuality of Ultimate Modes of Existence

Where does Whitehead stand in terms of this discussion? We have seen that "mutual immanence"—which is also mutual transcendence—is his way of expressing the *ultimacy of relationality*, and we find him stating with upmost clarity the inherent mutuality between the Possible and the Actual in God. What is more, contrary to shortsighted critiques that he unjustly privileges Actuality with his "ontological principle," mutual immanence reveals that this principle can be equally expressed from the perspective of Possibility. One is therefore fully justified in prioritizing or angling their philosophical approach from one side or the other *as long as* it is remembered that this is *abstraction* from the mutual immanence of both for the other.

One of the central tasks of philosophy, Whitehead reminds us, is "to elucidate the *relevance to each other* of various types of existence." Put differently, the task of philosophy is to understand "the *interfusion* of modes of existence" (MT, 69–71, emphasis mine). Knowing fully well that one cannot "exhaust" such modes, which must be "unending" in number, Whitehead nevertheless points to "two extreme types," neither of which are "fundamentally more ultimate." These are the "Type of Actuality" and the "Type of Pure Potentiality," each of which is "requiring of the other," such that "actuality is the exemplification of potentiality, and potentiality is the characterization of actuality, either in fact or in concept." "What is the meaning of actuality conceived as the extreme contrast to potentiality?" Whitehead asks; he answers: "We recur to the statement: actuality and potentiality require each other" (ibid., 70–71).

For Whitehead, this is not only the case in the world but also in God who *chiefly exemplifies* these ultimately related modes of existence.[16] We have seen that eternal possibilities ("eternal objects") do not "float in non-entity," but constitute something of the abstract and necessary primordial nature of God. Through the ontological principle, God is conceived to be a "non-temporal actual entity" who includes in the divine Self the infinitude of Abstract Possibility, and renders it effective and relevant for the world process.

Does this necessary nature include *God's own Possibility*, however? It seems that it must. Although Whitehead does not put it in this way, God's own Possibility might be conceived as an "Eternal Object" of an utterly preeminent kind. As an Actuality, however, God is not an eternal object, but the *Eternal Subject*—indeed, the eternal subjective ground of eternal objects, that uniquely includes its own Possibility in the Actuality of its own nature. Again, Whitehead does not express this explicitly, but it nevertheless does seem to be a coherent extension of his commitment to the mutual immanence of ultimate modes of existence in Possibility and Actuality. God "does not create eternal objects"; Whitehead tells us, "For his nature *requires* them in the same degree that they *require* him" (PR, 257, emphasis mine).[17] Considered in light of God's own Possibility, this mutually immanent requirement flows both ways. It is precisely the mystery of relationality that lies at the core of God's existence. Put as Whitehead does above: divine Actuality is the *exemplification* of divine Possibility, and divine Possibility is the *characterization* of divine Actuality. Both coincide in existential depths of divinity.

A critique of Whitehead, however, remains to be addressed. Both Donald Crosby and Justus Buchler have insisted that Whitehead's ontological principle, that "apart from things that are actual, there is nothing—nothing either in fact or in efficacy," unjustly *prioritizes actuality* over and against possibility.[18] We have seen, however, that Whitehead has several different expressions of this principle, and not just one. While Malone-France is right to say that this formulation "does *rhetorically* privilege actuality," he is fully aware of Whitehead's other formulations that lean toward possibility. Whitehead also insists, for example, that "the things which are temporal *arise by their participation in the things which are eternal*." Indeed, the *other side* of the ontological principle, we might say, is precisely the indispensability of possibility *for* actuality. The mutuality expressed in Malone-France's intuitions, I think nicely align with Whitehead's own. In reference to Whitehead's above quote, he states correctly that

> [Whitehead's statement] would seem to suggest (given his equation of "possibilities" and "eternal objects") that he was perfectly cognizant of the equally fundamental status of possibilities and could have consistently endorsed a possibility-centric formulation of the ontological principle as representing the logical and metaphysical flip-side of the "actuality-centric" formulation. Indeed, on my reading, Whitehead's point in this passage is precisely that, just as nothing actual can enter into the world without relation to some prefiguring possibility, no such possibility can affect the world except though its inclusion or instantiation in some actuality. (DE, 166 n. 15)

This is a beautiful statement as to mutual immanence of the possible and actual. It expresses Whitehead's fundamental intuition that neither Possibility nor Actuality is "fundamentally more ultimate," but each "requiring of the other." A mutual understanding Whitehead's ontological principle will hold not simply that Actuality conditions Possibility but equally that Possibility conditions Actuality. This must be exemplified, for Whitehead, not simply in the finite actualities comprising the becoming world, but chiefly so in life of God where Possibility and Actuality interfuse, "each side lending to the other a factor necessary for [God's] reality" (PR, 126).[19]

Leslie, Ward, and Whitehead thus each offer unique spaces for affirming the mutual immanence of the Possible and Actual in God. At first glance, Leslie is seen to emphasize the *abstract and possible* as conditioning the concrete actuality of God, while Ward and Whitehead are seen to emphasize the *actual* as conditioning the possible, including the possibility of God. But these are not mutually exclusive for each thinker, especially when read through the relationality of mutual immanence. For each of them, it may be said that the necessary correlate to the Possible *is* the Actual, just as the necessary correlate to the Actual *is* the Possible. Mutual immanence thus balances Leslie's abstract unilateralism through its *relationality* to Actuality; it clarifies Ward's intuitions as to how Possibility can be *instantiated* in, and *equated* with, Actuality; and it names for Whitehead *how* these ultimate notions are chiefly *interfused* in the life of God.

We mentioned in chapter 6 that discussions in philosophy and theology have taken different priorities with respect to the possible and the actual. Greek roots and the scholastic tradition prioritized actuality over possibility (Aristotle and Aquinas); but key voices of modern thought came to prioritize possibility over actuality (Wolff, Heidegger, Jüngel, and Moltmann). When read through mutual immanence, however, these priorities are *relativized* against their *wider relationality to each other*. They become different starting points which nevertheless live through what the other provides.

IN VIEW OF THE WORLD

From philosophy and theology, to physics, cosmology, and biology, the universe riddles in possibility. The axianoetic nature of *Homo Quaerens* continues to be uniquely haunted by this fact and what it suggests about the nature of things and their ultimate explanation. We remain linked inexorably to the past, but we are fundamentally oriented to an open future where the *radically new* can and does spring. The actualization of our own possibility is nothing short of a baffling expression of such novelty. We thus continue to dream of what *can be*, of what *might be*, and we do so with anxiety and adventure as mind and value blend into our hopes and fears. Philosophy begins in wonder; and we wonder as to the *conditions* and *grounds* of such possibility and how it is that anything is possible, let alone actual at all.

My goal in Part III has been to engage the riddles of the possible as they uniquely arise in Whitehead, Ward, and Leslie, as well as in other prominent thinkers including Quine, Ferré, and Lewis who would seek to effectively *rid us* the riddles possibilities pose. I have sought to do so in ways that deepen our focus on Mind and Value, both in human experience and at the foundations of existence—including God's own. That we ourselves are axiological expressions of this universe, which necessarily harbored our possibility, and labored to bring it into actualization, is profoundly suggestive. No less than in human experience, I have suggested through engaging Leslie, Ward, and Whitehead that a universe that riddles in such Possibility is a universe wherein Mind and Value, Possibility and Actuality, are divinely entangled in the ultimacy of mutually immanent relationality.

That this divine Actuality of Mind lives *reciprocally* through its own Possibility and Value is not insignificant for the open strivings of the universe. The existence of the world, and ourselves as worldly beings, testifies that the universe stretches in reach for deeper actuality and deeper possibility, deeper value and deeper mind. In doing so, it reflects and refracts the infinite Possibilities of the axianoetic nature of divinity as it is shared in and for the world. Beneath these comments, however, still remain a series of fundamental inquiries that have yet to be adequately addressed. These are questions about the nature of the world itself, the mystery of its actualization, and how it relates to the reality of God. Put in more traditional terms, such inquiries ask after the status and character of "creation" in relation to the "creator." This is the focus our final two chapters, which together constitute the final part of our investigation into the nature of ultimacy, explanation, and relation.

NOTES

1. Whitehead, for example, references the ontological principle as the "true general principle" underlying the following statements from Descartes' fourth *Meditation*: "'For this reason, when we perceive any attribute, we therefore conclude that some existing thing or substance to which it may be attributed is necessarily present.' And again: 'For every clear and distinct conception (*perceptio*) is without doubt something, and hence cannot derive its origin from what is nought'" (quoted ibid).

2. Malone-France states rightly that Whitehead "does *not* claim any *extra* or *independent* existence for the 'possibles' (or 'impossibles') entertained by actualities. Their 'existence' is, therefore, according to Whitehead, *nothing other than this entertainment*. Even in the case of possibles or impossibles that are not, and never have been entertained by human understanding, the existence imputed to them in Whitehead's theory is nonreified. The *only* mode of existence that is attributed to eternal objects that do not find inclusion in any *other* actual entity is their inclusion in the *divine* actual entity" (DE, 121, emphasis his).

3. For a detailed discussion, see Hosinski, *Stubborn Fact*, Ch. 7.

4. This is found to be the case not only in *Rational Theology and the Creativity of God* (RCG), published in 1982, but also in *The Christian Idea of God* (CIG), recently published in 2017. See, for example, RCG, 153, and CIG, 98, 100.

5. In part, Ward also follows Kant here, but not without necessary critiques. See Ward, RCG, 36–39. In his *Only Possible Argument in Support for the Demonstration of the Existence of God*, Kant had insisted that "every possibility presupposes something actual, in and through which everything is given that can be thought." Similarly, in his *Lectures on the Philosophical Doctrine of Religion*, he points to the need to "ground" the possible: "every possibility presupposes something actually given, since if everything were merely possible, then the possible itself would have no ground." That which grounds the possible is that without which there is no possibility at all; this is "God." Quoted in Dalferth, "Possible Absolutum," 105. For a deeper discussion of Kant's approach in this regard, refer to Nicholas F. Stang, "Kant's Possibility Proof," *History of Philosophy Quarterly* 27, no. 3 (2010): 275–99; and Robert Merrihew Adams, "God, Possibility, and Kant," *Faith and Philosophy* 17, no. 4 (2000): 425–40.

6. Refer to Roger Penrose, *Shadows of the Mind* (Oxford University Press, 1994).

7. In *Rational Theology and the Creativity of God* (RCG) in particular, Ward used the analogy of a person's character and the acts that express or realize that character. Similarly, Ward elsewhere states that "it is the 'character' or nature of God which is necessary and immutable, while he is a causal agent, expressing this character in creatively free relation to the universe which he has brought into being" (CG, 162).

8. Although "many strong modern philosophers want to make all logical possibilities, and truths about them, depend on there being at least one actuality," Leslie insists that "this has always seemed to me very hard to accept." He continues, "Bertrand Russell wanted to make 'two plus two equals four' into a truth about all collections of two plus two existing things, but I'd say that 'two plus two equals four' would be true even if nothing existed: I'm a card-carrying Platonist. The claim that two plus two would suddenly cease to make four when the fourth-to-last existing thing vanished strikes me as almost as bizarre as Descartes' idea (Did he truly accept it, or was this instead just a case of wanting to get published to avoid being burned as a heretic?) that God could have made two and two equal five." Personal e-mail correspondence, September 20, 2019, 3:10 pm.

9. Personal e-mail correspondence, September 20, 2019, 3:10 pm.

10. Personal e-mail correspondence, May 9, 2019, 9:27 am.

11. Personal e-mail correspondence, May 23, 2019, 1:15 am.

12. Elsewhere, Ward has stated that "the possibility of [God's] non-existence must be excluded just by the possibility of God. God's possibility uniquely entails his actuality" (RCG, 20–21). That God includes God's own possibility is central to Kant's own comment that the "[divine] ground of possibility must itself be given not merely as possible but also as actual." Quoted in Dalferth, *Possible Absolutum*, 105. Consider also James Lindsay's statement: "for, metaphysical as may be the entity which is the real basis of possibility, the possible essence must obviously be logically

pre-contained in that existence which is the only basis of its reality." Lindsay, "The Philosophy of Possibility," 325.

13. Personal e-mail correspondence, September 20, 3:10 pm.

14. Personal e-mail correspondence, September 23, 9:14 am.

15. Nevertheless, Ward consistently seeks to qualify such statements on behalf of real creativity in the universe: "A common way of thinking about a complete array of all possible states is to think of them as simultaneously present in detail, fully specified. Any created or contingent future would have to consist in the selection of some of these possible states. In a sense, there would never be anything that was radically new and that had not already existed, as a possibility, in the mind of God. But once we have introduced the idea of mind as the container of possibilities, there is an alternative conception. A truly creative mind could perhaps generate radically new possibilities (which would not exist even as possibilities before they were conceived). For such a mind, some possibilities could be generated by imaginative mental activity. We might think, by analogy, of the activity of a creative human mind; for instance, that of Mozart writing a new symphony. There would exist an array of possible states (the notes). There would exist a set of rules for combining those notes (the rule of harmony). Working with those states and rules, Mozart can compose a new work that perhaps did not previously exist as a complete possibility even in the mind of God. Genuine creativity might thereby have a place in the universe" (CIG, 94–95).

16. "God is not to be treated as an exception to all metaphysical principles, invoked to save their collapse. He is their chief exemplification" (PR, 343).

17. Malone-France elaborates saying, "God is not responsible for (does not 'create' the totality of eternal objects from which God selects an order set in the realization of conditions of actuality . . . the divine existence no less than any other, presupposes certain formal conditions of *its own possibility*. Reciprocally, in accordance with the ontological principle, these formal conditions (i.e. eternal objects) presuppose the existence of some actuality, to which their own existence is referable, precisely as the formal constituents thereof" (DE, 170–71, emphasis mine).

18. Donald Crosby, "Whitehead's God and the Dilemma of Pure Possibility," in *God, Value, and Empiricism: Issues in Philosophical Theology*, Larry E. Axel and Creighton Peden (eds.) (Georgia: Mercer University Press, 1989), 33–40. Referenced in DE, 166.

19. While possibility was traditionally derivative from actuality, so that actuality was prior and necessary, Auxier and Herstein speak rightly to the different approach taken by "process metaphysics" generally and Whitehead in particular. They do so such that mutual immanence is the unspoken undercurrent of their words: "Process metaphysics does not fully accept this [traditional] view, and certainly Whitehead does not. While it is true that everything that *comes to be* actual becomes actual through the agency of some prior actuality (God's contribution to creative synthesis), it does not follow that possibility is derivative of actuality. Indeed it is equally true that everything that becomes actual must first be possible. Process philosophers, while not holding to the absolute independence of possibilities from actualities, nevertheless explore and explain the nature of possibility as

a fundamental metaphysical notion at least coeval with actuality." Auxier and Herstein, *The Quantum of Exploration*, 246. In saying that there is no "absolute independence" between possibility and actuality, and that possibilities are metaphysically fundamental in ways "coeval with actuality," Auxier and Herstein have not yet spoken to their mode of relationality. That this relationship is one of *mutual immanence* is just below the surface of their comments.

Part IV

THE WORLD AND ITS ACTUALIZATION

Chapter 9

Mind and the Making of Actuality

We have been navigating a wilderness of fundamental questions. These questions are at home in the universe; they are posed from the earth, and yet they extend like vast trees into upmost philosophical and theological skies. Having awoken amid an existential clearing (*lichtung*) in this wilderness, we find ourselves surrounded by dense mysteries with heights insurmountable and breadths forbidding any clear vision of the heavens. It has, nevertheless, been my conviction that the unique dimensions of *Homo Quaerens*—our wandering, wondering mental life, and the deep fathoms of our axiological experience—do shed light upon a means of approaching the nature of ultimacy and explanation. Through the various axianoetic insights of Whitehead, Ward, and Leslie, we have looked to the divinity of both Mind and Value. We have seen, however, that it is not enough to speak to the *necessary status* of these divine domains in an isolated or unilateral fashion; rather we have inquired into their *relationality* to one another in *mutually upholding* such necessity. In doing so, we have found our way into a *relational vision of ultimacy* wherein Mind and Value, Possibility and Actuality are mutually immanent presuppositions of divine and worldly reality. In God, we have seen that this relationality helps imaginatively resolve some key issues that arise from privileging or emphasizing one side of these realities to the neglect of the other. We have thus addressed something of the metaphysical presuppositions involved in the existence of God, ourselves, and the world we inhabit.

A further task remains, however. We have yet to adequately address *the world itself* in light of these convictions and the insights Leslie, Ward, and Whitehead offer. While we have been attempting to ascend certain philosophical and theological heights in order to see further, the time has come to return to the ground and consider the world directly in light of what we have seen. To return to the ground, however, is *not* to leave these divine heights behind—but rather to find them in the very depths of the world.

THE MYSTERY OF THE WORLD

The actual world is no less mysterious than its possibility. Having grounded the Possibility and Value of the world in relation to the Actuality of divine Mentality, we have next to inquire as to *how* such possibility and value *attains actualization* in and as the world. Our goal in this and the final chapter, therefore, is to entertain a collection of questions as they relate to the mystery of the world and the respective axianoetic intuitions of Leslie, Ward, and Whitehead. These questions are alluring and difficult: What properly speaking is *the world*? How should we conceive its *status*, *character*, and *constituents*? How does it *become actual* and what role does divine Mentality play? How should we conceive its *relation* to this Mind and this Mind's *relation* to it? Leslie, Ward, and Whitehead have different, but resonant, perspectives on these questions. We must further ask whether or not the interrelationality of the divine Life, as we have conceived it, also applies to the way in which God relates to the world? Put differently: Is mutual immanence only an insight into the nature God? Or, is it also an insight into the God–World relationship as such? We will find that fascinating differences emerge for Leslie, Ward, and Whitehead, largely as a result of how they conceive the role of divine Mentality in the *making of actuality*. Arguably, we will see that one will be more or less moved by their different proposals to the extent that they think it coherent or incoherent to claim that *divine thinking alone*—as in the case of Ward and Leslie—is what *makes things actual*.

In this chapter we focus on Leslie and Ward's proposals, as well as raise some challenges to them. Leslie insists that actuality is *identical to divine thinking*. In his Spinozistic pantheist proposal, the actuality of the world is *nothing other* than divine thought *intricately thinking this world*. There really is no "otherness" between the world and divine thought. Ward's more kenotic panentheistic proposal, however, is grounded in a free relationship of love. The world of actuality, therefore, needs to be in some sense "other" than divine thinking (as love must assume a true "other") and *not* be identical to it. Actuality is therefore grounded *in* God, but "other" than God by virtue of *being actual*. God actualizes a world out of the divine Mind, but it is "other" than the divine Mind. While this issue of identity and otherness between divine Mentality and worldly actuality is an important difference between Leslie and Ward, they nevertheless both insist that divine thought *is* what makes things actual.

It is this exact claim, however, that may be the problem. Whitehead *does not* make this claim. In fact, one may begin to see the value of his inclusion of the World of Actuality as *primordially related* to God precisely on issues of identity, otherness, and difference, and related problems of suffering and dissatisfaction, that arguably challenge Leslie and Ward's proposals. We will see that contours of these related issues are raised in part by Hugh Rice, who we encountered briefly in chapter 5, and also by Leslie and Ward themselves. One can legitimately ask: how is it that thinking—however intricate and however divine—could ever make things actual *by itself*? Indeed, one might very well doubt that thinking, be it divine or human, could ever produce actuality (Rice, for example), or at least not do so in a unilateral or nonrelational way. Even if it could, how could actuality ever be truly *other* than such thinking? If divine thinking is *all* that produces actuality, then it seems plausible to hold that divine thinking is *all* that actuality is. This is enough for Leslie, and for him, it would not really encumber normal human life. This is not the case for Ward. He raises an interesting point as to the *real value* of otherness, relationship, and love, which, on his proposal, necessitates a true difference between the divine Mind and the world. If the world really is governed by Value, after all, would not the value of *true otherness*—and the possibilities of relationship it affords—really obtain between God and the world? Leslie may be rather weak here; and while Ward answers affirmatively, he *still* holds that divine thought is ultimately all that makes for actuality. As with Leslie, however, it is this claim that may put the world's true otherness in doubt.

These are complicated and speculative issues. Nevertheless, we seek to show in our final chapter that they are issues that Whitehead actually avoids by making the creative process of Actuality ("the World") necessarily and eternally *other than* (transcendent), but intimately related to (immanent), the divine Mind. Arguably, on his unique proposal, the true value of otherness and relationship is ever sustained between God and the World, and what they each relationally offer other. Neither "pantheism" nor "panentheism," but "transpantheism" is the distinguishing designation that Faber assigns Whitehead's position in this regard. Such a position, moreover, might also illuminate honest difficulties inherent in shared questions Leslie and Ward pose as to why a divine Mind that lives through Value does not produce something *much better* than (arguably) "inferior" beings with such dissatisfactory lives. For Whitehead, however, Creative Actuality is necessarily presupposed as an everlasting coexistent "other." With this conviction, he can evade potential difficulties harbored in such questions: for God does not unilaterally produce actuality *as such*, but is rather the *poet of actuality*, inaugurating the creative firing of finitude through the provision of divine aims, such that events can actually create themselves. In a deep sense then, God primordially *requires* the co-creative actuality of the World process for the real achievement of Value—thereby endowing a grandeur upon the World. So too the World process *requires* God primordially for its possibility and axiological aim. In this way, God and the world are indivisible co-laborers on behalf of the creation of value.

LESLIE'S PANTHEISM: RIPPLES ON THE SEA OF DIVINE REALITY

In chapter 7, we mentioned in passing a vital distinction that Leslie makes between the divine Mind's *recognition* of certain possible universes and that same Mind's *intricate contemplation* of these universes in their utter totality. Eternally sustained through its own Value ("ethical requiredness"), we saw that the divine Mind is *aware* of the possibilities of all variety of mediocre and positively evil worlds, but that this Mind does not *think through them in their structural entirety*. Why not? It is not only the case that such universes are not *worth* thinking, but that *thinking them* would mean *their actual being*. Indeed, for Leslie, the intricacy of divine thinking *is* the actual reality of *that which is thought*. Put differently, the *immensely detailed* nature of this thinking is what distinguishes actual existence *from* possible existence. Leslie refers to this vision as "pantheism" and follows Spinoza in holding that "we, like all other intricately structured things of our universe, exist merely because that [divine] mind in question thinks of this universe in all its details" (ID, 3).[1] These wildly intricate patterns will have always been "available for the divine minds contemplation" as possibilities, but only when such structures "are contemplated in all their intricacy" are they then "more than merely possible." This thinking has made them genuinely existent. Leslie therefore holds that a "vastly intricate divine universe-picture is what the universe *is*," and that "apart from divine thinking there exists nothing whatever" (ibid., emphasis his). In God, moreover, he envisions that both *thinking* and *being a Mind* are "rolled into one," such that this mind would not generate thoughts, but "eternally possess them all; or rather, it would itself be those thoughts joined together in an unchanging whole" (ibid., 6).

Some Difficulties: Objects, Finite Minds, Time, Freedom

This Spinozistic vision is vast and compelling, but it is not without some interesting difficulties. Leslie confronts these and holds daringly firm to the viability of his pantheistic vision. We can briefly mention a few of these challenges and Leslie's responses. In the first place, if we and the universe we inhabit are "only very tiny elements of divine thought," what does this do to the status of, say, rocks, trees, and other objects? This is a fair question that Leslie anticipates: "Picturing rocks and trees in absolutely all their structured intricacy, would this immensely intricate mind be picturing things that thought they existed as part of it?" He answers: "Certainly not, for rocks and trees do not themselves think anything," but they "would exist as parts of it nevertheless" (ibid., 5). Leslie admits to defending of *kind* of "panpsychism" in this regard, where the "stuff of the universe has mental properties"; but he is right to say that it is *not* a "panpsychism" in which "trees and flowers, perhaps even rocks, have consciousness of a kind." The constituent parts of such things, Leslie holds, would not have the kind of unity needed "to form a whole that has consciousness intrinsically worthy of having." Nevertheless, it is still the case that such things are *only* elements in a divine Mind and, by that fact, involve mentality in and as their existence. While Leslie denies that "stars and planets and water molecules, sand piles etcetera" would exist in the *absence* of divine consciousness, he does not hold that they are "themselves conscious." He thus agrees with the distinction Forrest makes between the notion that things "have the property of there being consciousness of them" and "that all things have the property of being conscious" (ibid., 51; IM, 93; GWS, 203).[2] There is, to be sure, an important difference here.

What about the lives of human beings with their own finite and frail thoughts? Leslie insists that when the divine Mind formed fully intricate thoughts about human beings, they too would exist within this Mind whether they knew it or not, as would their limited, and often ignorant, thoughts. Indeed, divine knowledge could include "areas filled with ignorance" as the very ignorant thoughts of individuals themselves, but this would not then imply that the divine Mind itself is somehow ignorant. Hypothetically, Leslie grants that if telepathy was a reality (he is suspect that it is), the divine Mind would be aware of the ignorance of finite minds without thereby admitting this ignorance into its own (IM, 42, 105). Neither for Leslie is time or human freedom illusory on such a pantheistic scheme of things. Although Spinoza held that God *cannot change* due to the supremacy of divine perfection, Leslie holds that this does not require that we hold that the "world's unceasing variations are illusory."

Einstein's theory of relativity is of much help to Leslie here, because it situates reality in a *four-dimensional existence* rather than an evolutionary three-dimensional existence (ID, 6). On such a model, there could plausibly be a true *relativity* to what we consider the "past," "present," and "future." *Our time*, therefore, would just be a domain of a four-dimensional continuum, which, in its totality, is completely unchanging. Leslie concludes that a divine Mind could conceivably "contemplate an entire life, and its thoughts about that life could be the only reality which the life possessed, while that mind was itself eternally unchanging" (IM, 111).[3] Pantheists, for Leslie, also need not deny the "freedom that humans do have"; they are not puppets of divinity, but "parts of God" that are nevertheless able to influence and affect the world in ways both good and evil (ID, 41).[4] "Being a part of a system of divine thinking would not render us powerless to influence events," he states, any more than "a system of billiard balls set in motion by an expert player" would disallow "one ball from influencing another" (ibid., 39). Leslie thus communicates his expansive pantheist vision such that nothing in our universe is excluded from the divine Mind. It is rather the *thoughts* of divine Mentality that comprise concrete reality.

> On my Spinozistic or pantheistic theory, the structures of galaxies, planets, and continents, of mice and of elephants, and you and me as well as of the houses, fields, and streams with which we interact, are nothing but the structures of various thought in the divine mind. The divine mind does not contemplate any universe that exists outside it. Its thinking about our universe is what our universe *is*. When God contemplates various physical possibilities in full detail they do not remain "merely possible" like the golden mountains of our dreams. They are genuinely real, existent, actualized, non-fictitious. (IM, 8, emphasis his)

It is important to stress that Leslie's imaginative pantheistic vision is not detached from the world, but emerges, in part, from reflective considerations of the character of the world as revealed by modern physics. We will find that this is also the case for Ward and Whitehead, albeit differently.

The Universe as an Existentially Unified Whole

What is it about the constituent character of world that could suggest such a vast pantheistic vision for Leslie? We must admit that in consideration of the world, it seems a remarkable display of unity in diversity and diversity in unity. The world is both One unifying Many and Many unified into One. It can be viewed not only from the perspective of its utter multiplicity—its so-called constituent "parts" (mysterious as they are)—but also in terms of how such multiplicity unifies together into a whole *transcending* the simple sum of its parts. The immensity of such unity, in fact, may dissolve the notion that there are "individual" or "separate" parts at all.

Is the world rather like this? For Leslie, the world, and ourselves as a unified existents, must mean something other than "a collection of things each with an existence genuinely separate from that of the others." Truly, the advent of quantum mechanics has dissolved the notion of independent substances in a mechanical cosmos. The world, he states, can be rather viewed as "an existentially unified whole" such that "any components that it has are *abstractions* rather like the length of a pond or a ripple on its surface, or the grin on a face" (IM, 49–50, emphasis mine). This unity is not mere *structural unity* or *causal integration*, but rather something like "a union of sameness and diversity," as F. H. Bradley and others have described (ID, 42–43).

Many quantum physicists have held that the universe is an *entangled unity* in precisely this way. Paul Davies insists, for example, that the interaction and subsequent divergence of micro particles "can no longer be considered as independently real things." Lee Smolin confirms that "given any one electron, its properties are entangled with those of every particle it has interacted with, from the moment of its creation" (quoted ibid., 52). Wholes, therefore, cannot just be *reduced* to their "parts." Michael Redhead confirms that "the possibility of analyzing or reducing wholes in terms of their parts" is not plausible, rather we must reject the notion "that the component systems possess their own local properties independently of the holistic context." The substantialist Cartesian vision—it would roundly seem—has died. David Bohm thus states that "on the basis of modern physics even inanimate matter cannot be fully understood in terms of Descartes's notion that it is nothing but a substance occupying space and constituted of separate objects'; "the world cannot be analysed into independent and separately existing parts"; rather, interactions among particles are better conceived "as depending on a common pool of information belonging to system as a whole" (quoted ibid., 50).

These statements require imagination. From a bodily human perspective, the so-called *illusion* of separation itself seems illusory. Yet, Whitehead too would caution us here: "We think of ourselves as so intimately entwined in bodily life that a man is a complex unity—body and mind. But the body is part of the external world, continuous with it. In fact, it is just as much part of nature as anything else there—a river, or a mountain, or a cloud. Also, if we are fussily exact, we cannot define where a body begins and where the external nature ends" (MT, 21).[5] It remains difficult to express the reality of such unity or continuity in language. In reference to Whitehead's own philosophy, Leslie readily admits that his "extraordinary terminology could foreshadow a language we shall have to invent if we are to get a good grip on the existential unity in quantum mechanics and elsewhere" (ID, 55). We will encounter some of this language in our final chapter.

Human Consciousness, Existential Unity, and Value

What about the high mental functioning of human consciousness? Truly, it seems hard to deny any "existential unity" more robust and more immediately accessible than that of our own conscious states. Everything of which we are conscious at this very moment seems to indicate a remarkable union of diverse elements into holistic unity. This is not inconsequential for Leslie; for if our mental states exhibit a kind of existential unity that the universe as a whole might exhibit, this may aid the viability of a pantheist proposal. Our own consciousness, we remember, is in some deep sense an expression of the universe. It would be odd if the universe were any *less* existentially unified than the human (and perhaps alien) consciousness it brought into being. Philosophers will no doubt disagree on these matters, but that the elements of our own conscious states "can be united to one another in their existence" is what many philosophers have affirmed for Leslie. Moreover, whatever disagreements they may have, he is confident that this much is widely accepted: "At least some ingredients of our universe, namely, conscious lives or particular conscious states, or particular groups of elements inside such states, can be known (that is, just through being experienced) to be wholes whose constituents are abstractions, not separately existing entities." Indeed, the notion that human consciousness is "always just a matter of *separately existing whatnots arranged in various spatial patterns and causal sequences* has been rejected by one after another of a long line of thinkers" (IM, 61, emphasis his). If such existential unity is a reality in human experience, the question is what this might suggest about the nature of reality, and more particularly, whether it lends plausibility to the notion that the entire universe itself exhibits an existential unity identifiable with divine Consciousness. Assuming people can "agree that groups of photos or elections show signs of existential unification: the kind of unification . . . that many philosophers view as characterizing minds and nothing else," would not this "do a little toward persuading us that our universe exists inside a divine mind?" Leslie asks. Supposing we did "find such unification in our own conscious states," might this "nudge us a bit nearer to the same conclusion" (ID, 54)? Perhaps, it would.

It is vital to this discussion to not overlook the relationship between existential unity and Value for Leslie, both in human consciousness and the universe which gave it rise. Leslie states, for example, that "it can seem . . . that unless such unity were found in conscious states they would have no intrinsic value." A future computer, for example, might far outweigh human beings in complexity, intellectual power, and ability, but if it "lacked unity-of-experience of the specially evident kind that is found in human consciousness, those thoughts would have no value in themselves." Their existence, Leslie insists, "could not be self-justifying" (ibid., 42–43). Leslie therefore draws a connection between the value, existential unity, and consciousness of human beings in a universe that is itself self-justifying because of its Value, Existential Unity, and identity with ethically required divine Consciousness. If the entire universe has Value, then it must be existentially unified; and if it is existentially unified, then it is the existential unity of divine Mentality.

For Leslie, a divine Mentality would never be *exhausted* by the patterned universe its thought concretizes; this Mind would always in some sense be *more than* and *transcend* any universe. Although eternally possessing such thoughts—such that it *is* the existential unity of those thoughts—Mind, it seems, must always be *more than its thoughts*. Nevertheless, thoughts are always a part of some Mind, and are arguably never really "other." These thoughts—you and I—remain nothing more than *abstractions* or Spinozistic "modes" of a unified divine reality whose own thinking extends over an infinite splendor of worthwhile things. Leslie reminds us, however, that we must go *beyond* Spinoza's odd restriction to *only one* divine Mind. If Value reigns as the ethical explanation of divine Mentality, then there is an infinite ocean of divine Minds thinking infinite universes into being. Ours is but one of these universes adrift in a sea of divine thought. We are, as Leslie puts it, ripples on the sea of a unified divine reality" (ibid., 42).

WARD'S RELATIONAL PANENTHEISM: THOUGHT OTHERIZED, THOUGHT LOVED

Like Leslie, Ward has stressed the divine Mind's ability to actualize the world from its own thought on behalf of Value. Although their positions are close, Ward's emphasis on the *creative otherness* of actuality, and the importance of *loving relationship* between divine and human minds, moves him away from a strict *pantheism* wherein we are "nothing but" divine thought abstracted from the fullness of divine Mentality. Rather, his position is more akin to a *relational panentheism*, where real otherness obtains, albeit still not "outside" the inclusive infinitude of divine Mentality.[6] Since this Mind will "know all possible things"—possibilities being contents of divine consciousness—it will also have "the creative power to make thoughts actual." This connection between *knowledge of possibilities* and the *ability to actualize them* seems a coherent one. For Ward, there must be a "power" able to actualize possibilities "because if something is possible, that means that it *could exist*. Some power must be able to make it exist, or it would not really be *possible*, and a reality which itself actually exists by necessity would possess in its own nature the power of existence." It is this power, for Ward, "which could bring possibilities into actuality" (CIG, 127–28, emphasis mine).

How does it do so? It is the nature of Mind to consist in evaluative thought about the possible, and that is precisely what the experience of such a Mind would consist in. Although Ward does not seem to stress the detailed *intricacy* of such thought in the making of actuality—as does Leslie—it is nevertheless "thoughts in the primordial mind will be what give rise to this universe, and perhaps to many other universes." In this way, "the world exists as the embodiment and expression of thought" (ibid., 26; MJ, 71). These thoughts would not come from anywhere except the divine Mind that thinks them; it would be a "world of pure thoughts"—however difficult to imagine. Knowing every possibility, the divine Mind would think of all that *could be*, albeit not in succession; "it would not have to think of one thing after another," Ward states; rather, it would necessarily contain or creatively generate these thoughts in ways unimaginable to human beings (CIG, 217).

It is important for Ward that the relationship between God and the world is not that of *separation and exclusion*, but rather that of *distinction with inclusion*. This "relationship is not a purely external one," he states, "as though two distinct persons were related to each other while remaining quite separate." Rather, Ward affirms "a form of *panentheism*, since the Supreme Mind, God, in a sense includes all other realities, including finite minds, in itself." He thus does "not think of God as a being separate from the cosmos who can only externally interfere with it," but rather "as the all-enveloping spiritual reality which is the deepest nature of the cosmos itself" (MJ, 74, emphasis his). One might be tempted to call Ward's position "pantheism"—as Leslie does—but his emphasis on the true "otherness" of finite beings and the world keeps him away from asserting that the world and its inhabitance are only ever just divine thoughts. Rather, he wants to say that it is the *actualization* of such thoughts that makes them "other" in a real sense.[7]

Otherness, Creativity, and Value

How is it that divine thought could ever produce something "other than" divine thought? On Leslie's account, it seems it does not; intense and detailed divine thinking is what *makes* possibilities actual, such that the only actuality those possibilities ever have *is* their *identity* with divine thinking. By contrast, Ward's more panentheistic intuitions emphasize the fact that, although the world is *thought into actuality*, this actuality, by virtue of *being actual*, is *other* than divine thought. Despite being sustained in existence by the divine Mind, the world of "creation" nevertheless has an integrity of its own that seems far less apparent in Leslie's pantheism. Ward makes this clear. In saying that "the universe is a making actual of a set of possible states which exist in the divine mind," he clarifies that "it is not just the eternal expression of ideas in the mind of God itself, but also an *external expression of ideas* in an objective created order, which give them a reality *apart from the divine mind*" (CIG, 131, emphasis his). Put differently, it may be that "finite goods have a district reality, which cannot exist within the divine being itself, and which therefore add some goods to reality which cannot exist in God alone" (RC, 182).

For Ward, however, to be "external" to or "apart from" this Mind is not to be "outside" it in any kind of truly "separate" or "dualistic" fashion. He would rather use words like "estrangement" or "alienation" as the necessary result of being an actualized "other." To be an "other" is to retain in some real sense the ability to resist the ever-benevolent directives of divine thinking. This does appear at least harder to imagine on Leslie's vision. Yet, for Ward, the actualization of a real "other" is what a truly *creative* Mind would do. "To be truly creative, God must create an 'other' even an opposing reality, with possibilities of novel value, but also with possible resistance to change. The maximally valuable being must create an alien world that is potentially good but often actually resistance to creatively changing goods" (MJ, 72). This otherness for Ward is essential, as it conditions the *unique value* of real *collaboration* or *co-creativity* between not just a Mind and its Thoughts, but between a Mind, its Thoughts, and something *truly other* that these thoughts actualize.

It is interesting to consider the *value of otherness* in a world governed by divine Value. If it is *more valuable* that divine Mentality and the actual world be truly "other"—such that collaboration, relationship, and love might become real possibilities—then might that be the way things actually are? Might it be the way things *have to be* if there is to be a truly valuable world at all? It is hard to say. Leslie, of course, does not want to deny free collaborative abilities to creatures on his pantheistic vision, but it is worthwhile to consider whether or not real "otherness" and "difference" may be *required* in a universe governed by Value. This *true otherness*, after all, might seem to be what Leslie is denying. For Ward, however, "the greatest form of creativity is the creation of 'other' conscious autonomous powers with which experiences can be shared, with which God can co-operate, but which may also oppose and resist God." Indeed, the *value* of this kind of relationship or "fellowship" is unique such that it would perhaps be lacking if the world was only abstracted thoughts of divine Mentality. There is no way of proving this, of course, but it does seem plausible. "It is clearly a good thing if there are other subjects of experiences besides God who can experience desirable value and perhaps even share in creating them," Ward states (RC, 222–23). There is value in "fellowship forged through persistence of love in the face of hardships endured and overcome—that is a unique form of value that only a temporal and developing creation can provide" (ibid., 73). Such a creation, for Ward, is never *just* divine Thought, but divine Thought *otherized* so that finite value can be achieved.

Love, Necessity, and Kenosis

Ward fully realizes that a divine Mind conceived in terms of Supreme Value seems *destined* to have a creation. Is it not the nature of Value or the Good to *necessarily diffuse* itself as the philosophical tradition has long insisted? What if this Supreme Value is conceived as *Love*? It is this distinctively Christian insight that Ward affirms: "the supreme value is ecstatic love, an overflowing of being to share value." This means that God cannot be conceived as "some sort of impersonal substance from which the universe arises by a natural and inevitable and unwilled emanation," somewhat like the Neoplatonic vision of the Many emanating from the One. God will rather be a "personal being of love and freedom, who affirms the divine existence as of supreme value and in that sense will it to be" (RC, 180). Still, Ward recognizes that the particular Christian insistence that "God is Love" (Jn. 4:16) requires a God who does not remain isolated in the contemplation of all things good and beautiful. He is right to say that "this seems to commit one to the belief that God *must* create a universe of finite persons, as a condition of realizing the divine nature as love." Put differently, if self-giving love is the highest form of Value, "then the creation of some universe may be *necessary* to God" (ibid., 223–24, my emphasis).

Ward is careful here, however. He does not want to say that God is *obligated* to create any one world or, for that matter, the greatest possible number of worlds. We remember that he distances himself from Leslie on this point. Necessity, he wants to affirm, is not *constraint* upon the nature of God *from without*, but rather free *expression* of this nature *from within*. Whatever constraints God has are *internal* to the divine nature—goodness for example—as we have already seen. But God may still be *compelled* by the divine nature in a real way: "the expressive aspect of the divine nature compels God to relate to autonomous finite beings," but this is not an "external compulsion." God therefore, it seems, *has* to create *some* universe because God's nature is what it is (namely, Love); but Ward also does not want to rid God of a mode of *creative freedom*—even contingency. "Divine creation," he states, "will be free, in the sense that no particular universe follows from the nature of God. Creation will not arise from any lack or limitation on God's part. It will be a natural expression of the being of God" (CIG, 135; RC, 224).

Yet, Ward has just as well advocated a *kenotic creation* where the divine mind *freely limits* its own capacities—"sacrifices divine beatitude"—in order to relate to creatures. These are certainly limitations, but they are *interior* limitations as is required by the "creation of conscious and rational beings." Ward expresses something of what the divine Mind must kenotically *give up* for the value of created others.

> [It] will involve a giving up of pure divine bliss and accepting many experiences of pain and suffering. It will involve giving up of complete control and accepting the freedom of created beings to make their own decisions. . . . It will involve giving up complete knowledge and accepting that much about the future must be unknown until it is determined by the action of creatures. These are real limitations, and this may be thought of as a sort of kenosis, a giving up of some

great good in order that free creatures may exist in independence, community and creativity. (CIG, 194–95)[8]

Ward thus envisions this divine kenosis as *free*. The difficulty, however, is that free kenosis seems to assume that the divine Mind could *not have done so*. But it is precisely the nature of this Mind—as Love—*to do so*. Ward acknowledges the tensions here, and at times seems rather ambivalent as to whether God could have remained *utterly alone* in "pure divine bliss." Following Whitehead's divine "dipolarity," he has wanted to affirm both a *necessary* divine nature that forms the archetypal preconditions of any and all possible worlds (Whitehead's "primordial nature") and a *contingent* divine nature that allows for free divine expression and reception in a free evolutionary world (Whitehead's "consequent nature"). Here, we remember the praise Ward gave Whitehead in showing how creation and necessity might be reconciled: "Only if God is temporal, can he be a free creator of a universe of free creatures; only if he is eternal, can he possess that necessity which is the foundation of the intelligibility of the world; only if he is dipolar, can he be both" (RCG, 230).

Dipolarity, Process, and Hope

In Whitehead, Ward recognizes the inclusion and transformation of Hegelian and Leibnizian elements into a "radically new metaphysical system" where God has an essential place (RC, 307). We have seen, however, that he also has his reservations with respect to Whitehead. He has wanted to distance himself from certain convictions thought to be at the heart of "process philosophy"—the necessity of the world, for example, or an uncertain eschatological future. Nevertheless, he strongly affirms a dipolar or "dual-aspect" understanding of God (CG, Ch. 8). The eternal and necessary nature of God is necessarily expressed though a contingent and temporal nature, thereby allowing mutability, passibilty, and complexity into the divine life. This, for Ward, is a much needed complement to the classical Thomistic-Aristotelian overemphasis on divine eternity and necessity to the exclusion of contingency and temporality.[9] One can, Ward reminds us, affirm dipolarity, however, without strictly following Whitehead. There remain "many variants of process theology" that share the general features of divine "dipolarity, all-inclusive infinity, temporality, creativity, and persuasive action," Ward states. These are all good things that must find a place in one's vision of divinity, but he hesitates because many process thinkers tend "to see creation, not as a freely willed act of God," or a result of divine ordination. What is more, some process thinkers have held that God "can never create a perfect heaven and earth by free decision," or for that matter, assure "individual resurrection or life after death" (RC, 308).[10] These points should not be overstated, however; many process thinkers have addressed them with both confidence and hope.[11] Still, for Ward, the affirmation of divine dipolarity "may survive dissociation from general process metaphysics, and may contribute to further discussion of the proper attributes of a being 'than which no greater can be conceived.'" Despite the heavy influence that Whitehead and process thought has had on his own thought, Ward's work has, in part, demonstrated this. His adjustments, however, have largely concerned a more robust sense in which God is both *creator* and *assurer of benevolent ends*.

> On the account I am suggesting, human freedom and creativity remain basic constituents of the universe, but God has a much more active and positive role to play than in most versions of process thought. God is the master Creator, laying down the pattern, influencing creaturely choices towards a goal whose general nature is given by God but whose specific character is, in many respects, determined by creatures. God creates our capacities and influences them towards the good. But we express them in specific ways. We can and should do so by free reliance upon God, who will ensure that their potential for good is realized. . . . God ensures that all the evil caused by misuse of creaturely freedom will finally be ordered to good. (RC, 308)

Seemingly more so than Leslie, Ward thus prizes creative temporality and otherness, both in creation and in God. If such temporality is a mode of *divine perfection and Value*, then it may seem that an Einsteinian four-dimensional cosmos, being unchanging from a total perspective, is inadequate. Admittedly, this is not a point I'm fully competent to make; it is rather a kind of intuition that if anything is ever *changing at all*, then nothing in its totality is ever *unchanging*—including God. Ward seems to share this intuition.[12] It has been said, of course, that Einstein wanted a God that "does not play dice." This statement seems to undergird his concern with classical timelessness and determinism of a certain kind. Ward, however, stresses a free creativity, temporality, and indeterminacy both in the world and in God.[13] Whitehead himself, in fact, wrote an alternative to Einstein's theory of relativity, in which he objected not to *relativity as such* but to its philosophical underpinnings.[14] It appears then for Ward—and certainly for Whitehead—that God and world roll dice for each other.[15]

Organic Mind in a Sacramental Cosmos

Ward remains convinced that the nature of the world and its constituent "parts," with their creative temporality, and inherent potentiality, means that the world must be *more than* brute matter and brute mechanism. In a deep sense, to even speak of the *potentiality* of mind is to already put one *outside* a reductive purely material world, where matter is composed of vacuous bits that are externally related and lumped together for no apparent reason. This, Ward assures us, is an obsolete view. Advances in physics are forcing us to now deal with "primitive elements" like "quarks or superstrings or something as yet undiscovered" that form the fundamental basis of things. We can agree with Ward that it remains inconceivable that such primitive elements "unexpectedly clump into atoms, which surprisingly form molecules, which accidentally generate proteins, which unforeseeably build organisms, which by pure chance produce brains and societies of organic beings, so that the whole present universe is a totally unexpected accident" (MM, 83). There must then be a place for "purposive causality" or *organic teleology* in the world, not simply in human beings, but in the world's *character* as such, so that the emergence of higher levels of experience, complexity, and mind can actually be justified. The world is not a machine, but much more an organism with a developmental trajectory that was inherent since the Big Bang. This trajectory has been one of "increasing integrated complexity, producing new sorts of properties, and eventually the ability to comprehend and consciously shape the future of the universe" (ibid.).[16]

Reflecting back upon this, Ward sees mind and consciousness "as a natural development of simpler properties inherent in all material things." This is not per se an outright, "panpsychism," but it does see the external and publicly observable appearance of matter as requiring complementation by an *interiority* that drives a "causal route through space time" (ibid., 82). This "inner structure," however, is not fully conscious or "mind" in any straightforward sense, but it does include a kind of *potency for mind*. Like Leslie, Ward clarifies that this does not mean that rocks have "a rich and vibrant inner life." To the contrary, "they do not even have the complex organization that would make such life possible" (ibid., 145). It is not until central nervous systems develop that anything recognizably conscious or feeling-laden seems to appear, Ward holds; still, the antecedents of such possibility must mean there is some kind of *inner side* to matter, which, along a certain evolutionary trajectory, dons life, mind, and consciousness. Ward's own "dual-aspect idealism" envisions the fundamental spatiotemporal constituents of the universe as both *physically* and *internally* constituted (ibid., 102). He is again indebted to Whitehead here; for these events are not closed off to each other—like Leibniz's windowless monads—but "essentially open to the totality of the space-time nexus."[17] Each is conceived as "receiving stimuli from all the others that surround it," integrating "those stimuli into a unity of being," and actively responding "in accordance with its own specific powers." These lay the groundwork for a creative evolutionary universe that teleologically anticipates the advent of mind.

Ward too would agree with both Leslie and Forrest that it is not necessarily that *all constituents* of the world must have *consciousness as a property*; but it *is* the case that they have the fundamental property of there being *consciousness of them*. Whereas Leslie, in part, moves from the world to the divine Mentality through the "existential unity" the world exhibits, Ward points to suggestive intuitions in quantum physics, namely, that there is *no observer-independent reality*. He points, in particular, to Hawking's "astonishing claim" that "we create history by our observation, rather than history creating us," so that "the universe does not have a unique observer-independent history" (quoted EG, 78).

Indeed, quantum mechanics has suggested that *observation* is what collapses wave functions into particulate reality—what, in a sense, *makes possibilities actual*. This is controversial, of course. If true, however, an obvious question arises: Must there then be an "Observer" that makes the entire universe actual? This is a kind of imaginary thought experiment, but the question is compelling. If so, *who* or *what* is this "Observer"? For Ward, "it is obvious" that it is no human being; humans come "late in the history of the universe" and it is admittedly "pushing things a bit far to say that the Big Bang was not actual until some human being 'observed it.'" This is not even possible. Rather, what seems to be called for—however imaginatively—is "an observer that existed even at the beginning of the universe." "A good candidate" is a cosmic Mind "that makes some possibilities actual—namely, God" (ibid., 79). Ward, of course, would want to emphasize that the divine Mind does more than just "observe" the universe, but actively participates in and through all reality at every moment, such that the universe is a *sacramental expression* of divine Mentality and Value. It is in its widest sense a "physical expression of a spiritual presence," Ward states. "In the beauty of mountains and forests, desert and sea, there exists a physical expression of one part of the infinite being of God." The natural world is "the medium through which infinity can be manifested in some of its myriad forms" (CIG, 110–11).

There remain some real (if at times ambiguous) differences between Leslie and Ward. These principally surround pantheism and panentheism, identity and otherness, necessity and contingency, unilaterality and relationality, compulsion and self-limitation. Leslie and Ward nevertheless share the view that it is *divine Thought* that makes for actuality. In line with key intuitions from quantum physics, they each point to different (but resonant) facets of the natural world in drawing these conclusions. The constituent character of this world is clearly hospitable to the advent of mind, such that conscious human experience must, in some way, be *read back* over the evolutionary development of things. Mind, or at least the *potency for mind*, is a fundamental part of the constituents of the universe. However, this universe—the mystery of all it contains and all that it is—remains utterly dependent upon the divine Mind for its actuality.

These proposals are not without imaginative challenge. However compelling, it is naturally difficult to grasp the reality of what they conceive. Can Mind alone really make for actuality? Can such actuality ever really escape being *identical* to this Mind, on the one hand, or truly *other* than this Mind, on the other? It seems that both Ward and Leslie's visions face some difficulties. Yet, that would not mean that the place and role of divine Mentality is itself undermined. It may just be that this Mind *does not* produce finite actuality *as such*, but rather is *ever related* to finite actuality. In this sense, the World might have a more fundamental status in the nature of things: a *stronger independence*, a *deeper necessity*, and a *primordial relationality* to—and *importance* for—divine Mentality than either Leslie or Ward seem to allow. Of course, there is no room for dogmatism on such enigmatic matters. Before turning in the next chapter to the potential value of Whitehead's processual vision of the God-World relationship in this regard, it is worthwhile to first raise some speculative challenges to Leslie and Ward's proposals, the intuitions of which come not only from Hugh Rice, in part, but also from Leslie and Ward themselves.

RAISING SOME CHALLENGES: MIND'S INABILITY AND THE "INFERIORITY" OF THINGS

In today's philosophical climate, challenges to Leslie and Ward's proposals may be myriad in form. With the prevalence of atheism and materialism, it is not a widespread philosophical opinion that Mind and Value have a mode of ultimacy and necessity in the nature of things; or that they must enter into any plausible explanation of these things; or that they constitute something of the essential notions involved in the concept of "God." Philosophers will scarcely agree on these matters. Nevertheless, these are theses I hold with them. I have attempted to show in previous chapters, and in positive resonance with their (and Whitehead's) insights, not only something of the explanatory viability of Mind and Value, Possibility and Actuality, but also their mutually immanent relationality in trying to illuminate some important philosophical and theological challenges.

Given then what we have seen above, what challenges may be posed for Leslie and Ward? Two challenges, I think, are worthy of speculative concentration. They are shades of each other and may lead us deeper into considering the significance of the world's *otherness* and *necessity* for God. These challenges are expressed by Hugh Rice in terms of Mind's seeming *inability* to create anything except thoughts, and by Leslie and Ward in terms of the seeming *inferiority* of feeble creatures such as ourselves. While these are not points that Leslie and Ward have left unaddressed, they do harbor certain imaginative difficulties that may be raised regarding the place of identity and otherness, and Mind and Value in their proposals.

Rice's Challenge: Questioning Mind's Creative Ability

We encountered Hugh Rice briefly in chapter 5. He is worth revisiting here to set the stage for considering contours of a possible challenge to Leslie and Ward. In discussing something of the relationship between Mind and Value, Rice preferred affirming abstract Value *without* Mind's mediation. While he admits that it "may well be that we do not have any experience of goodness affecting things other than minds; we also have no experience of minds creating laws of nature; or indeed of minds creating anything, except possibly thoughts *ex nihilo*." It may be the case, he states, that "the notion of mind's perceiving that something is good is a relatively familiar one," but "the notion of a mind's creating a universe is a very unfamiliar one, and (so it seems to me) at least as unfamiliar as the notion that the goodness of the universe is directly responsible for its existence" (GG, 51). While Rice prefers the latter of these two options, he does raise an honest question regarding *mediation* that we might pose differently. The difference is that while Rice questions whether *Mind's mediation* is needed for Value to create, I want to question whether Mind and its Thoughts can actually "create" without any *worldly mediation*. Despite their differences on identity, otherness, and collaboration, both Leslie and Ward hold that divine Thought can and does do this; it is *divine thinking* alone that makes for being.

Rice seems correct in suggesting that one may have trouble with this when considering the only possible analogy we have: our own experience. It would seem that our experience testifies to a strong sense in which we *do not* and *cannot* create something with our minds alone "except thoughts *ex nihilo*." Rather, our creative thoughts are *mediated* through (and by) our bodily members so that what we seek to create comes to have a reality apart from our body. However intense and intricate our thought, *what* we think does not just come into being by our thought alone. This is not to say, of course, that the divine Mind must somehow *exactly mirror* human mental experience—certainly it far exceeds it; but it may cause us to *pause* and raise a similar kind of imaginative challenge for divine Mentality. Can divine Thinking—however intricate—ever really achieve what it seeks with its own Thought alone? It is at least plausible that we hold (with Rice perhaps) that the divine Mind *cannot* conceivably do this. If true, this would seem to present a rather robust challenge to the proposals of both Leslie and Ward. What is more, even if one does hold that Mind alone can do this, the tangled questions of value, identity, and otherness still may suggest otherwise.

This line of thought is worth unpacking. Leslie might fully agree with Rice that the divine Mind can only ever produce "thoughts *ex nihilo*"—for that is *all we ever really are* on his pantheism. If, however, as Ward intuited above, a universe governed by Value may *require true otherness* as the presupposition of still deeper values of relationship, collaboration, and especially love, then the world and human beings can *never just* be identified with divine thought. Leslie's pantheism may be truly lacking here. To phrase it in a way familiar to him, it may require a more robust sense of otherness precisely because it is *good that it should*. On the other hand, while Ward clearly recognizes the value of otherness between God and the world, and seeks to preserve this otherness through his relational panentheism, he still sees the divine Mind and its Thoughts as the "master Creator" of finite actuality. One might insist, however, that as long as this is the case, there really can be *nothing other* than these Thoughts, and that he really is more of a "Christian pantheist" as Leslie held above. In this case, while certainly advocating the *importance* of this otherness, Ward may not really allow for it as long as the world is just an "embodiment and expression of thought." The Value of true otherness may require a deeper independence and collaboration between God and world than he is actually willing to admit. What is more, while Leslie and Ward's appeal to quantum insights—the seeming "existential unity" and "observer-dependent" nature of the world—does imaginatively suggest a fundamental place for Mind or Consciousness in the nature of things, it is debatable whether one can then conclude that it is *only* this Mind that exists (Leslie), or *only* this Mind that is ultimately responsible for finite actuality (Ward).

I suspect that Leslie and Ward will no doubt qualify these considerations. If viable, however, they do seem to point toward a solution that, at once, calls for the combined preservation of the *Value of true otherness* between God and the world, and their *mutuality* in being *fundamentally creative for each other*. Both, I claim, move us toward a vision of the world as *primordial medium*, as *necessarily related to*, but *always other than*, divine Mentality. This, to be sure, requires a different way of understanding the God-World relationship. We will soon see that Whitehead develops this vision in a unique way. Before turning to Whitehead, however, we should first turn to another potential challenge that Leslie and Ward raise and see if we might be led in the same direction.

Leslie and Ward's Challenge: Inferiority, Dissatisfaction, Suffering

That the world is so often characterized by suffering, dissatisfaction, and inferiority offers a deep challenge to any claim that it is solely a benevolent divine Mind that creates. Against advocates of an omnipotent divine "person," Leslie asks, "Why, after calling a divine mind omnipotent and supremely good, do people think it created hugely many beings all infinitely inferior to itself?" Put differently, why indeed would this Mind ever produce "outside himself" many "crowds of vastly inferior beings?" Leslie recognizes this problem clearly. By contrast, if Value is "in control," it is hard for him to see why there would not be "anything except divine thinking"—and infinitely so (ME, 108–9; ID, 84). For him, the joining of pantheism and Platonism may help this problem because pantheism locates us *within* a divine mind and Platonism provides a reason for that mind's existence (ID, 84).[18] There remains then nothing but infinite divine Mentalities thinking only worthwhile thoughts.

However, if the divine Mind lives through Value, and only Thinks benevolent and worthwhile thoughts—thoughts that alone actualize worlds—we can still ask why life is characterized by such dissatisfaction. Both Leslie and Ward recognize this and pose similar questions in this regard. "If our universe in all its intricacy is intricate divine thinking, why are our lives so unsatisfactory?" Leslie asks. "Why is God not thinking about something much better" (ibid., 7). So too Ward admits: "Why God should create beings like us, when he probably could have created hosts of happier and cleverer beings, is a bit of a mystery" (CRF, 35). Indeed, for both Leslie and Ward, the idea that only divine thought produces actuality may harbor deep difficulties here.

In response to such questions, both Leslie and Ward have resonant answers. For Leslie, God is, and must be, contemplating something far better than our particular universe. "God is thinking about that *also*," he states. The divine mind conceives the intimate structures of immensely many universes all of which exist within the divine mind, just as our does. This Mind contemplates everything *worthy* of contemplation; and while our universe must be "among the things worth contemplating"—otherwise it would not exist—Leslie, nevertheless, claims that it "may be far from the best of those things" (IM, 7). Ward too holds that God perhaps did create "happier and cleverer" beings than us, "but that they are not in this universe." He points to the fact that we are intimately wedded to *this* universe. "We are beings who can only exist in this universe, of which we are integral parts," he states. "Either we exist in a world like this, or we do not exist at all." One might very well "complain that God should have created a more perfect world than this one"; Ward thinks it important however "to point out that God could have done that, but you certainly would not have been in it. You would not have been at all" (CRF, 35).[19] For Ward, like Leslie, our world, despite its many imperfections, exists because it is valuable.

Both Leslie and Ward do hold that some suffering, imperfection, and inferiority will be unavoidable in any world. This is a fact that even God must face. Why is this? It is because not all values are compatible with one another; they cannot all be actualized by the divine Mind without conflict and incoherence. For example, it is often said that the real value of freedom, with its inherent risks and rewards, *overrides* whatever lesser value perfectly content puppets might sustain. Both cannot coherently be a reality at the same time. Neither Leslie nor Ward necessarily wants to rely on a "free will defense," however; rather, suffering and dissatisfaction are in some sense the necessary risk of having a divinely thought world—especially one governed by Value. Still, it is arguable whether or not they adequately link the notion of the *world's value* to the fact that it may *need* to be necessarily other than divine Mentality. Contra Leslie, it does not seem apparent at all that if Value is "in control" there would *only be divine Thinking*. To the contrary, if "otherness" and "relationship" are supremely valuable, then it might be *better* that the world is always necessarily "other" than divine Thinking. Ward's intuitions are more robust here, but the value he assigns to "otherness" and "relationship" may also require their necessary foothold in reality. Would God's relationship to any world really be contingent? We saw already that Ward seems to waver here.

These are difficult and speculative considerations. Nevertheless, they might positively adjust how Leslie and Ward orient themselves to the world's inferiorities and dissatisfactions, its evil and suffering, and its relationship to divine Mentality. Ward rightly seeks and values otherness; Leslie, far less so; but it is questionable that they can really achieve it when the being of the world is traceable to divine thought alone. Values may indeed clash, and divine thought may indeed sustain the world's being, but one might still wish that divine thought—on either proposal—would have intricately thought something other than the gas chambers of Auschwitz-Birkenau. I do hold with Leslie and Ward that the goodness of divine thought was doing this; but the reality of the horror seems to require rethinking claims or intuitions that intricate divine thinking *is* being, compelling as they may be. On Leslie's proposal it seems especially hard to conceive how Auschwitz-Birkenau would ever exist if it is eternally *unthinkable* by the divine Mind. That it did exist seems to suggest that it is not just benevolent divine thinking that procures actuality as such. There is a *true otherness* between divine thought and the actuality of what is. Ward himself wants to uphold this in saying that "God could experience the feelings of the torturer, not as God's own feelings, but precisely as the feelings of *another*. Such an experience would be set in a context of revulsion, grief, and condemnation, so it would *not* be the experience as the torturer has it" (RC, 251, emphasis mine; cf. IM, 20, 103). To preserve these intuitions, however, he should seemingly distance himself from claims that "whatever happens is an expression of aspects of the mind of God" (EG, 39).

However different Leslie and Ward are from each other on these points, true otherness, outside of divine thought, seems to help these considerations. The inferiorities of the world may not only be a result of the fact that values will clash in whatever world the divine Mind thinks, but more so a result of the fact that the world is *never* just a thought of God. In this case, the divine Mind does not—and perhaps cannot—just think worldly actuality into being, but is always related to worldly actuality on behalf of the Good. The actuality of the world might have a deep integrity and otherness of its own that is truly valuable to the divine Mind. Divine Mentality may ever collaborate with worldly actuality in exemplification of the value of *real otherness*. This *otherness* may be the metaphysical condition for the supreme value of *real relationship* between God and the world. But it is also a relationship that necessitates some manner of deviation from the benevolent aims of divine Thought. Faber thus states compellingly that evil, suffering, and dissatisfaction are the "price of existence" *because* it is "fundamentally *relational*"; the "world process does not remain merely a fanciful idea of God (God's 'dream'), but is always a real process 'outside' God, as process of self-creativity (of the *Other*)—and that means a process not merely of God's own inner creativity, but always of relational *inter*creativity whose 'inter' can never be reduced to an 'intra'" (GPW, 289, emphasis his). It is precisely this relational vision of *mutual otherness* that is uniquely formulated by Whitehead.

NOTES

1. Leslie states, however, that whether or not his position (and that of Spinoza) be labeled "pantheism" could "be entirely a matter of taste" (ibid., vi).

2. Leslie here also cites Nagel's *Moral Questions* (Cambridge: Cambridge University Press, 1979).

3. Leslie agrees moreover that the relativity of time in this way offers a mode of "immortality" with which Einstein comforted the relatives of a dead friend (and perhaps also himself). Now diseased persons would actually still be alive "back there along the fourth dimension." Leslie expresses a way of viewing this *kind* of immortality: "Extending along a time dimension of a reality that exists four-dimensionally, humans may not be immortal in the sense that their earthly careers stretch indefinitely far beyond their births; however the four-dimensional reality, human included, exists forever in time of another sort. The passage of this other kind of time, time in a somewhat different sense of the word 'time,' is not an affair of passing seconds, days, centuries. Instead it consists in the fact that alterations *could in principle be occurring* although they never in fact occur. They could in principle be occurring because there would be no contradiction in the entire four-dimensional situation changing. It could in principle be replaced by a series of other four-dimensional situations, each noticeably different from its predecessor. It could even be replaced by total emptiness.

Lack of all actual changes of this type would not mean that they were ruled out logically—that they couldn't conceivably be occurring. Well, the time in which they could conceivably be occurring is a time in which you and I can exist eternally, if our world is a four-dimensional whole that never in fact alters" (ID, 60–61). For two additional types of immortality consistent with Leslie's Platonic pantheism, see ID, Ch. 4.

4. Alternatively, "Pantheism, the belief that nothing exists except divine thinking, in no way denies all the obvious facts recognized by science and by common sense, one of them being that our efforts can affect the world well or badly" (ibid., 88).

5. Whitehead continues: "Consider one definite molecule. It is part of nature. It has moved about for millions of years. Perhaps it started from a distant nebula. It enters the body; it may also be as a factor in some edible vegetable; or it passes into the lunch as part of the air. At what exact point as it enters the mouth, or as it is absorbed thought the skin, is it part of the body? AT what exact moment, later on, does it cease to be part of the body. Exactness is out of the question" (ibid., 21).

6. Although some (including Leslie below) find that Ward's position does raise what he has called a "specter of pantheism," as the view that God and the universe should simply be identified with each other, Ward insists that "any form of pantheism" must ignore essential aspects of divinity that he affirms, namely "the transcendent and personal aspects of the divine being." Ward remains adamant that one must be "careful of the sense of 'identity' that is at issue" if indeed they speak of an "identity of God and the creation." In denying that "pantheism" is the position he espouses, Ward affirms instead that his view "seeks to include the universe within the transcendent being of God," such that human acts "can express the actions and purposes of God . . ., and that our feelings and experiences contribute something of importance to the life of God. In a sense God acts and experiences in new ways in and through us" (SDN, 144).

7. Leslie states, for example, that Ward's "pantheist views have become very close to mine" (ID, viii). Although Leslie acknowledges the discussion surrounding "panentheism"—of which Ward is a part—he has not found it necessary to enter the debate surrounding relevant distinctions between these views. "Panentheism," he states, is "a name sometimes given to any theory that the divine existence contains much in addition to a universe or set of universes." Referencing perhaps the most well-known discussion of "panentheism" in Philip Clayton and Arthur Peacock, *In Whom We Live and Move and Have Our Being: Panentheistic Reflections on God's Presence in a Scientific World* (Grand Rapids: Eerdmans, 2004), many contributors of which seek to distance themselves from "pantheism," Leslie nevertheless calls it "modern work on pantheism," which "concentrates on pantheistic Christianity" (ibid., 15). One might argue just as well perhaps that Leslie's "pantheism" is actually "panentheism" to the extent that divine thoughts are *distinct* from the divine Mind, albeit always *included* within it. I do, however, view "pantheism" as the better designation for his position, because there is no real sense in which we are truly "other" than the divine Mind: the only reality we have *is* divine thinking. Ward seeks this "otherness" and thereby avoids the "specter of pantheism," but we will question below whether he can really achieve it. For a discussion of

the place of "panentheism" among religions, see Loriliai Biernacki and Philip Clayton, *Panentheism across the Worlds Traditions* (New York: Oxford University Press, 2014). For a history and criticism of panentheism, refer to John W. Cooper, *Panentheism: The Other God of the Philosophers* (Grand Rapids: Baker Academic, 2006).

8. See also Keith Ward, "Cosmos and Kenosis," in Polkinghorne, *The Work of Love*, 152–66.

9. Indeed, critiquing Thomism and the Aristotelian philosophy on which it is based has been central to Ward's efforts throughout his career. This is not only the case for *Rational Theology and the Creativity of God* (RCG) but also in *Sharing in the Divine Nature* (SDN), recently published in 2020.

10. Charles Hartshorne, for example, did deny "immortality as a career after death." See Charles Hartshorne, *Omnipotence and Other Theological Mistakes* (Albany: SUNY, 1984).

11. See, for example, Marjorie Suchocki's groundbreaking work in *The End of Evil: Process Eschatology in Historical Context* (New York: SUNY, 1988). For responses, critiques, and alternative proposals, see Joseph A. Bracken, *World without End: Christian Eschatology in Process Perspective* (Grand Rapids: Eerdmans, 2005); David Ray Griffin, *Process Theology: On Postmodernism, Morality, Pluralism, Eschatology and Demonic Evil* (Anok: Process Century Press, 2017), Ch. 5; Paul S. Fiddes, *The Promised End: Eschatology in Theology and Literature* (Oxford: Blackwell, 2000).

12. Indeed, Ward appears conflicted (if humorously so) with Einstein's convictions regarding timelessness and immortality: "Albert Einstein thought that the whole of time, with all its constituent world-lines, actually exists, from the first moment to the last. We only seem to move through it one moment at a time. In reality both our past and our future are timelessly existent and never come into being or pass away. He apparently found great consolation in the fact that his dead friends were not really non-existent. They all existed timelessly, and only seem to be dead to the rest of us. I suspect that you would have to be a very advanced mathematical physicist to be consoled by the thought that dead people really exist, because time is an illusion. Most of us will continue to be more impressed by the thought that we will never meet them again in time, and if there was no time, there would be not time for good conversation. We would just have to stare at each other, frozen in changeless immobility. That might be all right for Einstein, but it would be very frustrating for most people, especially for the talkative ones" (MM, 84–85).

13. For a discussion of these themes, see Joseph Bracken, *Does God Roll Dice? Divine Providence for a World in the Making* (Collegeville: Liturgical Press, 2012); Davies, *The Mind of God* (MG), 191–93.

14. See Whitehead's *The Principle of Relativity* (Cambridge: Cambridge University Press, 1922). Whitehead clarifies: "I would not however be misunderstood to be lacking appreciation of the value of his recent work on general relativity which has the high merit of first disclosing the way in which mathematical physics should proceed in the light of the principle of relativity. But in my judgment he has cramped

the development of his brilliant mathematical method in the narrow bound of a very doubtful philosophy" (CN, x).

15. "God may not play dice with the universe," Ward states, "but it *looks* as if God does" (PF, 98)!

16. Ward admits the "machine model" of the universe is helpful in some interrogations of nature, but it is not a guide to the reality of the cosmos: "The cosmos is not a mindless, conscious, valueless, purposeless, yet somehow strangely intelligible, mechanism. Such a view is the result of extrapolating a machine model, very useful in many scientific contexts, to provide the most comprehensive and adequate picture of the real cosmos" (ibid., 58).

17. Whitehead points to the inconsistency in Leibniz in this regard: "Monads, according to this doctrine, are windowless for each other. Why have they windows towards God, and Why has God windows to them" (AI, 135–36)?

18. Refer also to Leslie, "Infinity and the Problem of Evil."

19. Alternatively, "we belong in this universe, and if we are going to exist at all, we just have to exist in this universe, with its particular laws. So if we sometimes wish we existed in a better universe, this argument reminds us that, while other beings might exist in better universes, we could not. We just have to put up with this one" (EG, 45).

Chapter 10

The Mutual Immanence of God and the World

Whitehead articulates a profoundly relational vision of collaboration between divine Mentality and finite actuality, each of which are primordial exemplifications of *Creative Value* for the other. Put differently, it is a vision that grounds the *value* of true otherness through the *mutuality* of God and the World in their *differential necessity* for each other. In this final chapter, we will further explicate these statements with their theological and cosmological implications, as well as in response to the issues posed to Leslie and Ward in the previous chapter. Our concerns remain focused on the concept and role of God, the status and character of the world, and their relationship to one another.

CONCEPTS OF GOD: EXTREMES AND THE COMPLEXITY OF MEDIATION

It is important to grasp how deeply dissatisfied Whitehead is with extremes. This applies equally to science, philosophy, and theology. On the one hand, Whitehead recognizes that the "Eastern Asiatic" concept of God (as he understands it) was largely conceived as "an impersonal order to which the world conforms." The order is "the self-ordering" of the world itself and not some obedience to "imposed rule." This concept therefore "expresses the extreme doctrine of immanence" (RM, 56–57). On the other hand, the "Semitic" concept of God is conceived as "a definite personal individual entity, whose existence is the one ultimate metaphysical fact, absolute and un-derivative, and who decreed and ordered the derivative existence which we call the actual world." As such, this concept "expresses the extreme doctrine of transcendence" (ibid., 57). What Whitehead calls the "Pantheistic concept" of God can be considered in light of each of these extremes. With respect to the Semitic concept, he describes the nature of the actual world in ways reminiscent to Leslie's own pantheism (less so to Ward's panentheism): The "actual world is a phase within the completed fact which is the ultimate individual entity. The actual world, conceived apart from God, is unreal. Its only reality is God's reality. The actual world has the reality of being a partial description of what God is. But in itself it is merely a certain mutuality of 'appearance,' which is a phase of the being of God" (ibid., 58). With respect to the East Asian concept, the pantheistic concept can be read as its inversion: "According to the former concept, when we speak about God we are saying something about the world," Whitehead states, "and according to the latter concept, when we speak about the world we are saying something about God" (ibid.).

Whitehead recognizes that the extreme transcendent and immanent tendencies of the Semitic and East Asian concepts of God, along with their pantheistic inversions, seem to be "directly opposed to each other," such that mediations between them lead to "complexity of thought" (ibid.). Whitehead is no stranger to complexity. That his own considerations of "God"—even to his latest writings—are far from simple is a testament to his own commitment to the *value of mediation* between such concepts.[1] We may recall his critique of "various doctrines of God," which "have not suffered chiefly from their complexity," but rather been "extremes of simplicity" (RM, 65). Such a claim cannot be put to Whitehead's considerations of God, however. He is adamant that the extremes involved in simple notions of God "should not represent mutually exclusive concepts, from among which we are to choose one and reject the other." Rather, the clashing of doctrines is an *opportunity* requiring the complexity of mediation so that deeper truths are attained. "Instead of looking to each other for deeper meanings," however, different doctrines have often "remained self-satisfied and unfertilized." Whitehead of course fully recognizes that it "cannot be true that contradictory notions can apply to the same fact"; but it is not always clear whether or not contradictions really arise—especially in theological matters. Thus, the "reconcilement" of perceived "contradictory concepts must be sought in a more searching analysis of the meaning of the terms in which they are phrased" (ibid., 131, 65).

For Whitehead, these statements apply directly to extreme visions of divine transcendence and immanence, and, more particularly, to visions of God as unilateral "Creator" and the world as wholly derivative "creation." These are both theological and cosmological considerations: they involve reconceiving not only a vision of God and God's relationship to the world but also the world itself, its status, character, and constituents. In looking to the Western developments of these disciplines, Whitehead affects important mediations between the extremes found in and between Plato, Newton, Aristotle,

Augustine, and Calvin—to name only a few. In doing so, his own position as to immanence and transcendence, Creator and creature, begins to emerge in distinction from these thinkers. We will look first to a few cosmological mediations he draws specifically between Plato and Newton, and then to theological mediations that are also inclusive of these other thinkers.

Cosmological Mediations between Plato and Newton

Whitehead identified the *Scholium* of Newton and the *Timaeus* of Plato as the two lasting cosmological statements that have chiefly influenced Western thought (PR, 93). Given his own intentions of doing the same, he finds it necessary (even "wise") to affect a "fusion" of these two cosmotheological endeavors, but not without necessary critiques, mediations, and modifications. In the first place, he aptly agrees that if the *Timaeus* is taken as a statement of scientific details, it is "foolish" in comparison to the *Scholium*. Nevertheless, the *Timaeus* makes up for this superficiality in terms of its suggestive philosophic depth and profound allegorical truth. Where the *Scholium* is a striking and truthful statement of abstract detail, it nevertheless offers "no hint of the limits of its own applicability," falling into what Whitehead called the "fallacy of misplaced concreteness" (ibid.). Bringing both systems together in light of advanced scientific knowledge and philosophical consistency is (among other things) central to Whitehead's cosmological task.

Plato's cosmology was built upon the notion of *inner relations*—on the power and efficacy of the unchanging and eminently real realm of Forms (or Ideas) and the world's imperfect imitation of them. Newton's system, by contrast, reduced everything to *external relations*—to the locomotive movements of vacuous bits of matter devoid of inner development (GPW, 70). While Whitehead recognizes the value of these approaches in *abstraction*, they nevertheless falter to the extent that they are totalizing and exclusive of the insights the other harbors. His own fusion of Plato and Newton in this regard seeks to remedy these abstractions in light of modern physics and quantum theory. He does this in terms of mutuality and transition, objectivity and subjectivity, both external relations and internal relations inherent in the swing of concresent prehension. Actual entities arise by constituting themselves *both* from the objectified objects of the past *and* their inner subjective determinations. What is most fundamental in the emergence of entities (*concresence*) is this feeling-laden (*prehensive*) mediation between objectivity and subjectivity, externality and internality, *kenesis* and *energeia*. The world for Whitehead then is neither a reflection of timeless Platonic Ideas *nor* the bumbling movement of dead particles, but rather a deeply related and mutually affective fusion of inner and outer relations through prehensive process (ibid.).

What follows from these mediations is Whitehead's *integrative causal scheme*, one that is different from, but inclusive of those of Plato and Newton. Whereas Plato's cosmos operated through the *teleological* means of final causation, Newton's physics exemplifies a *mechanistic* or deterministic causality based upon iron-clad natural laws. Whitehead again mediates and fuses these into his own *prehensive causality*, which is both efficacious and final in nature. *Efficient causality* is the power of the objectified past on the emerging occasion, while *final causality* is what that entity chooses to become. The entity, therefore, is not determined by the efficient causation of the past, but left to finally self-determine its own becoming. For Whitehead, we remember, each event exhibits psychophysical *dipolarity*: it is both physical and mental, both influenced by the past and productive of the achieved value of its own actuality. In this way, each event is also *axianoetic*. Evolution for Whitehead is *neither* vitalistic nor mechanistic in nature; rather, as Faber insists, it is *non-dual* and *non-reductionistic*. It is non-dual because Whitehead understands "*all* forms (including life) as emerging from the same antecedents"; and it is non-reductionistic because he pictures "the appearance of both life and mind as evolving as genuine 'emergences' from complex causal-final laws" (ibid., 70–71). The universe is thus built up from complex characters, societies, nexuses, and democracies of events that are layered and relationally ordered toward the emergence of things. With Leslie and Ward, however, Whitehead would agree that it is misleading to say these events are "conscious." Nevertheless, they are each first something *for themselves*—having an inner "mental" constitution—before they are something *for the world*—having also an outer "physical" constitution. They are thus *subjective and experiential* before they are *objective and physical* in the making of the world and the emergence of life and mind. In this way, they are *experiential antecedents* of the arrival of consciousness and freedom.[2]

Given that there was no real sense of "self-production" or "generation" in Newton's system, Whitehead rightly states that modern evolutionary doctrine and quantum theory would have "confused" and "surprised" him (PR, 93–94). After all, Whitehead strongly critiques a mechanistic-materialistic metaphysics as incapable of *real* evolution.[3] The Plato of the *Timaeus*, however, would have been "enlightened" and welcoming of modern evolutionary theory and rather expectant of modern quantum theory (PR, 93–95). Indeed, while Whitehead acknowledges many things in the *Timaeus* as "now foolish," he nevertheless admires Plato's relational and evolutionary intuitions as "ahead of his time" (ibid., 94). He praises Plato's "Receptacle" or "Khora," for example, as the "place" or "foster-mother of all becoming," which is near to ("almost exactly") the space-time of modern physics. In contrast to Newton who viewed space and time as absolute, independent, immovable, and occupied (or empty), Whitehead insists that space and time are not independent, but abstractions that relationally emerge together as part of the "extensive continuum." Indeed, for Whitehead, the "elbow room" of empty space is that vast relational nexus of events without novelty or dominant pattern, and time is the ever-present continuum of the objectified past hurling itself into the future. Both space and time then are abstractions from a fundamentally processual universe (AI, 150–51, 195; GPW, 66–70).

Theological Mediations between Plato, Newton, and Others

In light of these cosmological considerations, Whitehead also mediates between Plato, Newton, and others with respect to God and creation, transcendence and immanence. Newton had admitted to writing his treatise with an eye for including such principles that require "belief in a Deity." In his mind, accepting his system also meant accepting that a supernatural God "externally designed" a ready-made, nonevolutionary world *ex nihilo*. The fact that he "made no provision for the evolution of matter," Whitehead assures us, resulted in modern thought accepting the same tacit presupposition. Newton's "Semitic theory" required "a definite supernatural origin" and the transcendent will of the divine in assuring the regularity of natural law (PR, 93). In contrast to Newton, Plato *did* make provision for the evolution of matter and instead traced the cosmological order of the world to a primeval chaos, which was ordered as best as possible by the Demiurge. Whereas Newton had assumed that the present world came into being through divine fiat, Plato insisted upon a creation from an "aboriginal disorder, chaotic according to our ideals." Plato's vision, Whitehead insists, "has puzzled critics who are obsessed with the Semitic theory of a wholly transcendent God creating out of nothing an accidental universe" (ibid., 95). Even into modern times, Whitehead claims that the "sole alternatives" were thought to be "either the material universe, with its present type of order is eternal; or else it came into being, and will pass out of being, according to the fiat of Jehovah." "Thus on all sides," he holds, "Plato's allegory of the evolution of a new type of order based on new types of dominant societies became a day dream, puzzling to commentators" (ibid.).

Whitehead seeks to follow Plato's intuitions, but in a way that mediates between the "sole alternatives" of a world created out of nothingness and a world that has been eternally evolving in its current form. With the *Timaeus*, as we have seen, Whitehead views "the creation of the world" as "the incoming of a type of order establishing a cosmic epoch. It is not the beginning of matter of fact, but the incoming of a certain type of social order" (ibid., 96).[4] Newton had insisted on a transcendent God *imposing* the divine will on the world. In this, he followed the same transcendent intuitions of Augustine and Calvin before him. Whitehead comments that Augustine fused Plato with

Saint Paul and leaned "heavily towards the notion of a wholly transcendent God imposing his partial favors on the world."[5] Calvin also held rigidly to this same view, which suggested a "Manichean doctrine of a wholly evil material world partially rescued by God's arbitrary selection." On his vision, the "physical order of the world was an arbitrary imposition of God's will" (AI, 130). Whitehead, by contrast, insists upon an eternally related God who immanently shares the divine nature with the world in its evolution of different "cosmic epochs." He makes clear his own intentions to reconcile *imposed* and *immanent* extremes in his own vision of God.

> The primordial Being, who is the source of the inevitable recurrence of the world towards order, shares his nature with the world. In some sense, he is a component in the nature of all [finite things]. Thus, an understanding of the temporal things involves a comprehension of the immanence of the Eternal Being. This doctrine effects an important reconciliation between the doctrines of Imposed Law and Immanent Law. For, with this doctrine, the necessity of the trend toward order does not arise from the imposed will of a transcendent God. It arises from the fact that the existents in nature are sharing in the nature of the immanent God. (Ibid.)

Whitehead is thus unwilling to hold to extremes of transcendence and immanence. These have been exemplified in the "extreme monotheistic doctrine of God, as essentially transcendent and only accidentally immanent," on the one hand, and "the pantheistic doctrine of God, as essentially immanent and in no way transcendent," on the other (ibid., 121). When conceiving the creation of the world in light of his theory of becoming actual entities, Whitehead still sees these options as essentially the "two current doctrines as to this process." In the West, the transcendent vision has reigned; it is that of an "external Creator, eliciting this final togetherness out of nothing" (ibid., 236). Whitehead holds that this view is a result of tragic—even idolatrous—combinations of Greek and Christian overemphasis on nonrelation and brute power in their doctrine of God. Indeed, the combination of Aristotle's "unmoved mover" with the "eminently real" God of Christian theology made God into "aboriginal, eminently real, transcendent creator, at whose fiat the world came into being, and whose imposed will it obeys." Whitehead insists that this is the "fallacy which has infused tragedy into the histories of Christianity and [Islam]" (RM, 46–47).[6] The Western world would accept Christianity, Caesar would conquer, and "the received text of Western theology was edited by his lawyers," he states. The relational intuitions of love, humility, and gentleness—those exemplified the founding figure of Christianity—would flicker uncertainly through the ages, only to be in large part replaced by their opposite: "The deeper idolatry of the fashioning of God in the image of the

Egyptian, Persian, and Roman imperial rulers, was retained. The Church gave unto God the attributes which belonged exclusively to Caesar" (PR, 342).[7]

Moreover, in the developmental history of "theistic philosophy," Whitehead finds various stages of combination between three prime visons of God. Correspondingly respectively to the divine Caesars, the Hebrew prophets, and Aristotle, these three "schools of thought" fashioned God in the image of an "imperial ruler," a "personification of moral energy," and an "ultimate philosophical principle." Whitehead fully admits to Hume's fantastic critiques of these schools in his *Dialogues*, yet he points to the silent flickering ideals of the "Galilean origin of Christianity," which offered "another suggestion" not easily fitted to these three stains of thought.

> It does not emphasize the ruling Caesar, or the ruthless moralists, or the unmoved mover. It dwells upon the tender elements in the world, which slowly and in quietness operate by love; and it finds purpose in the present immediacy of a kingdom not of this world. Love neither rules, nor is it unmoved; also it is a little oblivious to morals. It does not look to the future; for it finds its own reward in the immediate present. (PR, 343)[8]

These are beautiful statements. It is no shortage of the truth that say that Whitehead is concerned with including these fundamental intuitions in his understanding of both cosmology and theology, both in the process of creation and the God-world relationship.

Transpantheism: The Relational Paradox of Immanence and Transcendence

If the world is not the result of pure transcendent fiat, but a relational process of creativity in and between actual entities and God, how should its character be conceived? How should God be conceived? "The other doctrine," Whitehead tells us, is that it belongs "to the nature of things, that there is nothing in the Universe other than instances of this [creative] passage and components of these instances." In adopting this view, Whitehead holds that the word "Creativity" nicely expresses "the notion that each event is a process issuing in novelty"—what Whitehead calls a "concrescence." Indeed the phrase "Immanent Creativity," or "Self-Creativity," he states, "avoids the implication of a transcendent Creator." Nevertheless, he admits that the mere word "Creativity" *does* suggest "Creator," such that "the whole doctrine acquires an air of paradox, or of pantheism" (AI, 236). Whitehead is adamant that "God is *in* the world, or nowhere, creating continually in us and around us . . . everywhere, in animate and so-called inanimate matter, in the ether, water, and earth human hearts."[9]

This "paradox" Whitehead speaks of can be conceived in terms of transcendence and immanence, of that between a strong theism and a diffused pantheism, both of which harbor insights Whitehead seeks to affirm, but not in ways that fall to the extremes of either—or ways that banish true otherness and relationship between God and the world. He thus states that his "notion of God" is "that of an actual entity *immanent in the actual world*, but *transcending any finite cosmic epoch*—a being at once actual, eternal, immanent, and transcendent." Yet, Whitehead clarifies that the "transcendence of God is *not peculiar to him*. Every actual entity, in virtue of its novelty transcends its universe, God included" (PR, 94, emphasis mine).

These statements as to the immanence and transcendence of God and the world *for each other* have made it rather difficult to find an agreeable label for Whitehead's vision of God. God is *not* the World and the World is *not* God, but they are nevertheless inseparable in their *distinction* from one another.[10] Although, Whitehead himself recognizes an "air" of pantheism in his vision (akin to the "specter of pantheism" in Ward), he nevertheless complicates this designation precisely by including paradoxical elements of *transcendence* and *distinction*. Following Charles Hartshorne and David Ray Griffin, more *rationally* inclined interpreters have often referred to Whitehead's position as "panentheism." Labeled as such, Hartshorne saw Whitehead's God as an "Eternal-Temporal Consciousness Knowing and Including the World." For him, Whitehead was a "chief recent representative" of panentheism "among philosophers."[11] Other more *empirically* inclined interpreters, such as Peter Hamilton and William A. Christian, however, have pushed back against Hartshorne and insisted that "panentheism" is in fact a misleading label for Whitehead's vision. Hamilton follows the intuitions of Christian in saying that "Whitehead is not strictly a 'panentheist'; his complete insistence on freedom means that although we are influenced and indeed surrounded by God, each of us remains a separate subject." Whereas Hartshorne's understanding of Whitehead's "panentheism" meant that God "literally contains" the world, Hamilton insists that this risks upsetting "Whitehead's superb balance and interrelation between God and the world, and between transcendence and immanence *of each in relation to the other*."[12]

Roland Faber has recently made these points anew. Expressing his own hesitancy to "subscribe without reservation to the use of the term panentheism for Whitehead's position," he has commented that "panentheism grants only asymmetric reciprocity" between God and the World. "God always remains the exceeding 'more than all' (God is in all, but exceeds the all of the world) to which creation conforms as the embedded 'less than all' (the world, per definition, cannot exceed God)." While Faber grants that interpreters of Whitehead continue to use "panentheism" to emphasize the relationship of *mutual immanence* between God and the world, he has nevertheless stressed that "panentheism"—to the extent that the world is envisioned as always and only *in* God—risks missing the fact that mutual immanence is always also *mutual transcendence* for Whitehead: "Both God and the world exceed one another and, only for that reason, can be seen by Whitehead to be mutual instruments of novelty for one another" (TBG, 158).

In not wanting to lose this essential insight into Whitehead's vision, Faber has thus sought a "more adequate" characterization of his position. Instead of "panentheism," he insists that Whitehead's position is better conceived as "transpantheism" (TBG, Ex. 11; TDM Ch. 13). Given a confusing diversity of definitions and forms of "panentheism," this may indeed be a better way of distinguishing Whitehead's position in order to emphasize not only the mutual immanence of God and the world but also their mutual transcendence.[13] We will encounter Whitehead's own statements in this regard below, and in light of the challenges posed to Leslie and Ward.

It may be worth noting here that one might very well agree with Leslie that labels such as "pantheism," "panentheism," or "transpantheism" are "entirely a matter of taste" (ID, vi). Perhaps, they are. Nevertheless, I do find these designations helpful in distinguishing real differences surrounding the otherness and independence of the world in their proposals. With reference to both Leslie and Ward, Faber thus rightly distinguishes Whitehead saying, "It is only in Whitehead that we realize that no event, organism, and society, and even a world and all words . . . in their own becoming of themselves *was ever only* a thought of God. To the contrary, in mutual immanence, God and the world also remain *mutually transcendent*" such that "any world happening owes it to its existence its *own* actualization as its own decision of unification of its relationality." On this vision, "all events . . . with God create the world and their future . . . together" (TGR, 205). We need to further clarify the vision of these statements and ask after the role of divine Mentality in the making of actuality.

CREATIVITY, MUTUAL IMMANENCE, AND POETIC CREATION

That "creation" is *not* the inauguration of "finite matter of fact" can be a point of confusion and difficulty. What then is the status and character of finite actuality in the nature of things? One may still want to ask: Where does it come from anyway? How does it *come*? And what does the divine Mind actually *do*? It is important to connect such questions to the fact that Whitehead refuses to entertain the static dichotomies inherent in the ontological question. "Existence," he reminds us, "is activity ever moving into the future" (MT, 169). Existence is *not* the *other side* of nothingness, but always the *outcome* of a more fundamental process. This "ever moving" is a creative process that is *older* than "existence," precisely because it is what existence presupposes. This can be expressed in different ways: *coming into existence* is older than existence; *becoming* is older than being; *process* is older than stasis; *creative activity* is older than "creation"; *the* "World" is older than *our* "world." Creative process, therefore, has a necessary footing in the nature of reality. Whatever *comes to be* must first *come*; it must *be-come* such that becoming is the necessary metaphysical condition of being. In this, Whitehead admits that his philosophy "seems to approximate more to some strains of Indian, or Chinese, thought, than to western Asiatic, or European, thought. One side makes process ultimate," he states, "the other side makes fact ultimate" (PR, 7). Yet, even here, one finds Whitehead actually refusing to choose one over the other. His vision is a mediation between process and fact and their significance for each other: "The creative advance of the world is the becoming, the perishing, and the objective immortalities of those things which jointly constitute *stubborn fact*" (ibid., xiv, emphasis his).

If creative process is primordial, then *something* must always be *in creative process*. Something must become and perish and be formative of stubborn fact in the universe. What could this *something* be? For Whitehead, it is finite actuality—actual occasions or entities—that embody "Creativity" as the ground of their processive emergence. The fact that entities embody "Creativity" is precisely why they temporally become. But they do not do so wholly on their own. Emerging finite entities are not the only embodiments of Creativity. While the infinite and necessary process of actuality (*the* "World") is grounded in finite embodiments of Creativity, it is also grounded in the aims of God, who, Whitehead holds, eternally and primordially embodies this *same* Creativity.

It is essential not to miss how fundamental the category of Creativity is for Whitehead. He is adamant that "in all philosophic theory there is an ultimate which is actual in virtue of its accidents. It is only then capable of characterization through its accidental embodiments, and apart from these accidents is devoid of actuality." For Whitehead, "Creativity" is this ultimate and it replaces Aristotle's notion of "primary substance" (ibid., 7, 21).[14] He calls it the "universal of universals," which characterizes all matter of fact; it is the "ultimate principle by which the many, which are universe disjunctively, become the one actual occasion, which is the universe conjunctively." "The many become one, and are increased by one," he states; "entities are disjunctively 'many' in process of passage into conjunctive unity" (ibid., 21).

Creativity, therefore, is the principle of novelty in the universe; it is what all entities embody as their very emergent process. This process is the coming together (concrescence) of the many objectified influences of the past—the entire universe—into a novel subjective unity attained by the particular emerging occasion. It is therefore not an isolated happening, or the result of one occasion causing another, but a result of the "whole antecedent world" conspiring "to produce a new occasion" (MT, 164). A fundamentally creative universe, Whitehead insists, lives through the Creativity it embodies.

How does God relate to Creativity and to the creative process of actuality? Clarifying God's relationship to Creativity has been a source of much debate and confusion in discussions of Whitehead's philosophy. Creativity, for Whitehead, is not something that can be "created"—even for God—since it is a presupposition of any and all creative activity, be it finite or divine. In fact, it is not "something" at all, but pure formless activity embodied in all actuality—and chiefly so in divine Actuality. Many interpreters have nevertheless misunderstood or sought to modify Whitehead's views here. Perspectives have differently ranged from insisting that God and Creativity are *essentially identical*; that Creativity is *subordinate to and derivative* from God; that God is *subordinate to and derivative* from Creativity; and that God and Creativity are *equally primordial and mutually immanent* (RWS, 264).

Whitehead is partly to blame for this diversity of opinions. Many passages can be read in a variety of these ways, and especially in ways that seem to clearly *subordinate* God to Creativity, such that Creativity is *more ultimate* and therefore responsible for "creating" God. Whitehead states, for example, that God is the "primordially created fact," the "primordial creature," a "creature of creativity," and even the "primordial non-temporal accident of creativity" (PR, 31, 7; quoted RWS, 265). Such statements have naturally led some interpreters to think that Whitehead holds a kind of Arian position where God is subordinated to the status of "creature" while the ultimate reality is really Creativity.[15] One must be careful here, however. In fact, neither direction of subordination nor pure identity between God and Creativity is the correct understanding of Whitehead's vision; for just as Creativity *conditions* all actualities, all actualities also *condition* and *characterize* Creativity. This is a relationship of *mutual immanence*—and it is supremely the case for God. While Whitehead holds that the ultimate freedom and creativity of the universe is not just "to be ascribed to God's volition," it is nevertheless not somehow *above* or *more ultimate* than God; rather, it is supremely exemplified in God's own existence as Supremely Creative. John Cobb makes a helpful distinction between "Creativity" as *ultimate reality* and "God" as *ultimate actuality*, neither of which are more ultimate, precisely because they are mutually immanent.

> Between reality as such and actual things there can be no raking of superior and inferior. Such ranking makes sense only among actualities. Among actualities [God] is ultimate ... [God] is ultimate actuality, and ultimate actuality is just as ultimate as ultimate reality. Although it is true that there can be no ultimate

actuality without ultimate reality, it is equally true that there can be no ultimate reality without ultimate actuality. Between the two there is complete mutuality of dependence.[16]

Indeed, just as we have emphasized the distinct, but mutually immanent, relations between Mind and Value, Possibility and Actuality in God, so too Whitehead includes Creativity as that which ever enlivens the essential functions of these domains for each other in grounding divine existence. "The true metaphysical position," Whitehead clarifies, "is that God is the *aboriginal instance of this creativity*, and is therefore the *aboriginal condition which qualifies its action*. It is the function of actuality to characterize creativity, and God is the *eternal primordial characte*r" (PR, 225, emphasis mine).

In what way does God "characterize" Creativity? If, as we saw in chapter 8, the divine "character" as "Permanent Rightness" flows from the divine nature as "founded in Value," then Creativity, I suggest, is characterized precisely as *Creative Value*. In this case, God is the primordial exemplification of *Self-Creative Value*. "God is a creature of *God's own* self-creativity," Faber states, a "*creator of Godself* and *creation of Godself* . . . God constitutes Godself from God's own self-creativity such that God primordially 'characterizes' the otherwise wholly undetermined activity." Nevertheless, it is also the nature of Creative Value to overflow into and for an "other." Faber underscores that "God is not only the subject of *God's own* creativity, but also the superject of God's creativity *for others*." As such, God is "creator in the primordial sense of 'making' all that which is produced 'in creativity' in order to 'make' or create itself" (GPW, 145, emphasis his). God is not, therefore, the unilateral creator of the "other," but the relational provider of those essential conditions allowing the "other" to make itself. It is God's offering of relevant possibilities such that creative events can actually arise with coherent direction. Whitehead thus imagines the Self-Creativity of God flowing into the self-creativity of the creature in every moment. Divine Mentality does not produce or determine actuality though its Thought alone; rather, divine Mentality axianoetically lures actuality through aims and ideals of value. These aims are the gift of self-creation to the world of actuality. Whitehead expresses this vision in the following way.

> The initial stage of [an events] aim is an endowment which the subject inherits from the inevitable ordering of things, conceptually realized in the nature of God. The immediacy of the concrescent subject is constituted by its living aim at its own constitution. Thus the initial stage of the aim is rooted in the nature of God, and its completion depends on the self-causation of the subject-superject . . . [God] is that actual entity from which each temporal concrescence receives that initial aim from which its own self creation starts. . . . [T]he transition

of the creativity from an actual world to the correlate novel concrescence is conditioned by the relevance of God's all-embracing conceptual valuations to the particular possibilities of transmission from the actual world, and by its relevance to the various possibilities . . . available for the initial feelings. (PR, 244)

In an inherently creative world with an otherness and integrity never reducible to divine Thought, the role of God is imagined to be *aesthetic and poetic* rather than *causal and productive*; it is *internal* and *teleological*, rather than *external* and *determinative*. "God's role is not the combat of productive force with productive force, or destructive force with destructive force," Whitehead states, "it lies in the patient operation of the overpowering rationality of his conceptual harmonization." For Whitehead, the world is "self-created" through its own alignment or deviation from divine aims. God cannot coerce the self-creativity of the world, but only guide it with divine vision and then preserve the value of what is achieved. In this way Whitehead states that "God does not create the world, he saves it: or, more accurately, he is the poet of the world, with tender patience leading it by his vision of truth, beauty, and goodness" (PR, 146).

ADDRESSING CHALLENGES: MIND, ACTUALITY, AND THE VALUE OF CO-CREATION

The creative "otherness" and relationality Whitehead imagines at the foundations of the God-world relationship mean that the world is never only a thought or product of the divine Mind alone. To the contrary, the otherness of the world is what this Thought *requires* in order to find *actualization at all*. The real otherness of the world therefore plays an essential role for God—just as the real otherness of God plays an essential role for the world. There is both a mutual immanence and mutual transcendence in this relationship: "It is as true to say that the World is immanent in God, as that God is immanent in the World. It is as true to say that God transcends the World as that the World transcends God" (PR, 348). Whitehead expresses this vision variously. God and the World, he states, express "the final metaphysical truth" that divine "appetitive vision" and worldly "physical enjoyment" have an "equal claim to priority in creation." *Divine vision* is what God gives to the World and *physical actualization* is what the World gives to God. Put differently, God as the "infinite ground of all mentality" addresses the world with a "unity of vision seeking physical multiplicity," while the world as the "multiplicity of . . . actualities" is "seeking perfected unity" through divine vision. In this way, the "static majesty of God's vision" accomplishes "its purpose of completion by absorption of the World's multiplicity of effort" (ibid., 348–49). Each of these statements is grounded in the mutuality of God and the world for each other. They express the fact that God is the eternal axianoetic condition that makes the world's self-creation *possible,* while the World is an everlasting finite process that makes the divine vision *actual.*[17]

With these comments, let us now return briefly to the challenges posed to Leslie and Ward in the previous chapter. Through Rice's skepticism regarding Mind's mediation of Value, we questioned whether or not it is really conceivable that Mind—however intricate its thoughts—can ever really "create" anything with these thoughts alone. If Mind cannot do this, we said that Leslie and Ward face serious challenges that might find remedy only though including the otherness of the world as necessarily related to God as a creative medium. Yet, even if one did hold with Leslie and Ward that it is ultimately divine Thought that makes for actuality, they would still face seemingly irreconcilable differences between them on the question of *identity* and *otherness* between God and the world. On the one hand, Leslie's pantheism affirms our *identity* with divine thought such that we are *nothing other* than this thought. For him, this poses no serious problem. On the other hand, Ward's relational panentheism affirms our *real otherness* from this thought as the condition for the value of true relationship and love. For him, it is important that we really are an *external expression* of divine thought. The difference between Leslie and Ward here surrounds the status of actuality *as actual*; but one cannot have it both ways. If the divine Mind thinks actuality into being, this actuality is either *no different* from this thinking or it is *truly different* from this thinking. This seems rather straightforward.

Assuming the above claims are coherent and plausible, Leslie and Ward's proposals require adjustments precisely on the status of the world. Two speculative considerations undergird this claim: (1) It may be that divine thought alone *cannot* make for actuality; and (2) It may be *more valuable* in an axianoetic universe that true "otherness" always obtain between God and the world so that supreme values of relationship, collaboration, and love can be a reality. Ward clearly follows his relational intuitions in this direction, but he arguably should follow them *deeper* into an affirmation of God's *necessary relatedness* to the world such that the value of otherness and collaboration has *always been exemplified* in the God-world relationship. We saw that he seems to waver regarding whether or not God necessarily creates. He wants to affirm both that it is God's nature as *kenotic love* to create an "other" and that God does so *freely* such that *any world is ultimately contingent*. Whitehead offers a relational and axiological depth to these intuitions such that God is *always necessarily related* to, and in *collaboration* with, an "other" (*the* World process)—but also that any "cosmic epoch" (*a* world) that God brings about is, nevertheless, always *contingent*. Put in another way, while Ward arguably recognizes mutual immanence as *internal* to the divine life in terms of the interrelationality of Value and Mind, Possibility and Actuality, he does not recognize mutual immanence between God and the World. Here, we might say that he affirms *contingent mutual immanence* while Whitehead affirms *necessary mutual immanence*. The difference lies in the status of the world.

While Leslie has consistently wanted to hold to what is "best" in terms of Platonic Value—and gone to rather extreme lengths to do so—his pantheistic affirmation that there really is no "otherness" between divine thought and worldly actualities might put this in serious doubt. This identity between divine thought and the world he finds unproblematic; yet, it might be very problematic *precisely* on grounds of Value. As mentioned above, it may be *better* that the world is truly *other* precisely because real relationship and collaboration between "others" is of *upmost value*—even for God. Despite, Whitehead's own "air of pantheism," we see that the world is never *only* a thought in the divine Mind, but a reality of its own that God *requires* for the *real* achievement of Value. In Leslie, it does not appear that the world can ever *transcend* the divine Mind in any real sense. Whitehead, however, affirms this transcendence as a necessary requirement for the true value of otherness.

Both Leslie and Ward also raised the question as to why the divine Mind did not actualize something much "better" than arguably "inferior" creatures in a world of dissatisfaction and suffering. If the divine Mind contemplates "everything that is superbly wonderful," such as "all beautiful mathematics" and "all fine music," Leslie states, then why would this Mind "go out of its way" to contemplate "our depressing selves"? Are we not "too second-rate" and do we not "dilute all the really good stuff" (ID, 84)? Leslie and Ward affirm that values inherently clash such that there is no possible scenario where all values are realized; and while Leslie affirms that God really is thinking something "better," Ward affirms that God could have (and may have) created something better, but our weddedness to this *particular* cosmos guarantees that we would never be in it. Nevertheless, for both of them *our* existence in *this* world is worthy of contemplation by the divine Mind; otherwise, it would not exist. Put differently, for both Leslie and Ward, the divine Mind must have seen that the value of our world ultimately outweighs any and all suffering and dissatisfaction that might also come with it.

Here too, the depth of Whitehead's relational affirmations between God and the world offer much insight. The suffering and dissatisfaction of our world is not simply (or only) a result of clashing and incompatible values that inevitably quarrel in any world the divine Mind thinks. Rather, suffering and disvalue are the *inherent* shadow side of the fact that the world is *never* just a thought of God. The world in its otherness, creativity, and freedom retains an integrity that *transcends* God. The divine Mind does not think *the* World into being, but is always co-creating *with* the World in quest for the value of *a* world. Whitehead thus states that "[God] is not *before* all creation but *with* all creation" (PR, 343). In this way, Marjorie Suchocki has argued that creation is never a result of unilateral production, but rather a matter of *divine call* and *creaturely response*: "God calls; creation responds. God then responds to the creation's response, and building upon it, calls yet again. Through call and response, the creation comes into being as world. It is incremental, gradual, with creation participating in its own becoming."[18] John Cobb also speaks of God as the "One Who Calls" creation from where it is, to where it *might be*.[19] While the world's real otherness and freedom from God is of supreme value, these also necessitate deviations from divine aims—tragic *responses* that make for inferiority, dissatisfaction, and evil in the world. Yet, Whitehead holds that each evil is met with another divine call for the good: "This transmutation of evil into good enters into the actual world by reason of the inclusion of the nature of God, which includes the ideal vision of each actual evil so met with a novel consequent as to issue in the restoration of goodness" (RM, 139). Put in another way, "The Adventure of the Universe starts with a [divine] dream and reaps tragic Beauty" (AI, 296). God therefore always seeks a "better" world, but it is never entirely up to God whether that world is achieved. Such is the inherent risk of a world that is truly other.

Whitehead's vision of the mutual immanence and transcendence of God and the World, therefore, can illuminate the related challenges posed to Leslie and Ward. One may come to recognize this if they are *unconvinced*, on the one hand, that divine thinking alone can produce actuality as such, and *convinced*, on the other, that true otherness conditioning true relationship is of upmost value in an axianoetic cosmos. Arguably, Whitehead's "transpantheistic" proposal draws both of these convictions into a vision of the world's necessity for God and God's necessity for the world. "What metaphysics requires," Whitehead states, "is a solution which exhibits the World as requiring its union with God, and God as requiring his union with the World . . . metaphysics requires that the relationships of God to the World should lie beyond the accidents of will, and that they be founded upon the necessities of the nature of God and the nature of the World" (ibid., 168).

MUTUAL IMMANENCE AND THE GRANDEUR OF THE WORLD

Our aim in Part IV has been to identify some of the distinctive ways that Leslie, Ward, and Whitehead conceive the status, character, and constituents of the world in the making of actuality, and in relation to divine Mentality. Each of them remains deeply indebted to the advances of modern science and quantum theory. They have differently offered a way of viewing both the world and the divine Mind that is consistent with this vision. This has required each of them to critique not only isolated and mechanistic models that still uphold Cartesian and Newtonian intuitions, but also problematic theological legacies yielding too much to divine externality, independence, and power. Contrary to these models, Leslie, Ward, and Whitehead each put forth more organic, spontaneous, and creative views such that mind—or something like mind—plays an essential role among the interior spaces of every event. While consciousness need not be required at this elemental level, one thing is unanimously affirmed between them: without divine Consciousness our world would not exist at all. They each conceive this Mind as immanent, inclusive, and related, but they do so rather differently. We pointed to both resonant and divergent ways in which they understand the role of divine Mentality in the making of actuality. These included tangled and speculative questions surrounding the abilities of divine Mentality, issues of identity, otherness, and suffering, and intuitions upholding the value of real relationship and collaboration in an axianoetic cosmos. In suggesting that Leslie and Ward may face real challenges on these matters, we pointed the way forward through Whitehead's vision of the mutual immanence and transcendence of God and the World, and indeed, of all realities of ultimate significance for this relationship. Mind and Value, Possibility and Actuality, Creativity and the World all lend each other factors and functions necessary for their own reality.

> [God] is the actual fact from which the other formative elements cannot be torn apart. . . . Apart from these forms, no rational description can be given either of God or of the actual world. Apart from God, there would be no actual world; and apart from the actual world with its creativity, there would be no rational explanation of the ideal vision which constitutes God. . . . [T]here is no meaning to "creativity" apart from its "creatures," and no meaning to "God" apart from the "creativity" and the "temporal creatures," and no meaning to the "temporal creatures" apart from "creativity" and "God." (RM, 140–41; PR, 225)

Far from being "inferior," this vast relational vision crowns the world with ultimate significance and ultimate purpose; for God *needs* the world for the actualization of divine value. The world's actualization of this value thus reveals God to be "the mirror which discloses to every creature its own greatness" (RM, 139). The world's "true destiny" is to be a "co-creator in the universe" and, thereby, find itself robed with "dignity" and "grandeur" (RM, 139).[20]

NOTES

1. Indeed, one of his latest statements on the concept of God precisely undergirds the complexity of mediating the Semitic and East Asian visions. He describes this

own vision as neither "the God of the learned tradition of Christian Theology" nor "the diffused God of the Hindu-Buddhistic traditions. The concept lies somewhere between the two" (Imm., 97–98).

2. Due in large part to Griffin's work, Whitehead's position has come to be known as "panexperientialism." This term helps avoid any misunderstanding or confusion often attached to the word "panpsychism." In fact, Victor Lowe, a former student of Whitehead, reported that Whitehead was unhappy when some students (Lowe included) referred to his position as "panpyschism." Experience remains *more fundamental* than consciousness, such that consciousness is *not* a necessary element in mental experience. As Griffin has said, experience "goes all the way down," but consciousness does not. Refer to Victor Lowe, "The Concept of Experience in Whitehead's Metaphysics," in Kline (ed), *Alfred North Whitehead: Essays on His Philosophy* and Griffin, *Unsnarling the World Knot.* Other process thinkers like Michel Weber have used "pancreativism" with their own nuances; see Michel Weber, *Pancreativism: The Basics* (Berlin: De Gruyter, 2006). David Skrbina I think is right to insist that "panexperientialism is at present the most fully articulated form of panpsychism" and that "process philosophers may be credited with keeping alive the debate over panpsychism in general, and they have marshaled a large amount of evidence, both to support their position and to criticize the dominant materialist and dualist ontologies." David Skrbina, *Panpsychism in the West* (Cambridge: MIT, 2007), 21–22. In the recent explosion of panpsychist literature, however, the influence of Whitehead's vision has not always been fully appreciated. Philip Goff, for example, in his recent argument for panpsychism, relies primarily on the insights of Arthur Eddington and Bertrand Russell to make his case; however, he neglects to engage the fact that Whitehead stood between them as their contemporary with a truly robust vision of mentality pervading the universe. In part, Eddington considered Whitehead an "ally," and the same might also be said of Russell (at least for a time) in his collaboration with Whitehead. See Philip Goff, *Galileo's Error: Foundations for a New Science of Consciousness* (New York: Pantheon Books, 2019), 120.

3. He expresses this clearly in terms of the deficiencies of materialism for evolution and, by contrast, what real evolution requires: "The aboriginal stuff, or material, from which a materialistic philosophy starts is incapable of evolution. This material is in itself the ultimate substance. Evolution, on the materialistic theory, is reduced to the role of being another word for the description of the changes of the external relations between portions of matter. There is nothing to evolve, because one set of external relations is as good as any other set of external relations. There can be merely change, purposeless and unprogressive. But the whole point of the modern doctrine is the evolution of complex organisms from antecedent states of less complex organisms. The doctrine thus cries aloud for a conception of organism as fundamental for nature. It also requires an underlying activity—a substantial activity—expressing itself in individual embodiments, and evolving in achievements of organism. The organism is a unity of emergent value, a real fusion of the character of eternal objects, emerging for its own sake" (SMW, 107).

4. In light of this, Griffin holds, "We can thereby give a 'both-and' answer to the long-standing debate, often portrayed as a debate between Jerusalem and Athens, as to whether the universe had a beginning. On the one hand, by understanding 'the universe' to mean our particular universe, we can endorse the view, associated with Jerusalem, that the universe had a beginning. On the other hand, by understanding 'the universe' to refer to a multiplicity of finite actualities whether ordered into a cosmos or existing in a state of chaos, we can endorse the idea, associated with Athens (and India), that the universe has always existed." Griffin, *Panentheism and Scientific Naturalism*, 82.

5. "Plato's God is a God of this world," Whitehead states, "Augustine combined Plato's God with St. Paul's and made a fearful job of it. Since then our concept of this world has enlarged to that of the Universe. I have envisioned a union of Plato's God with a God of the Universe." In Price, *Dialogues*, 214.

6. "This worship of glory arising from power is not only dangerous," Whitehead states, "it arises from a barbaric conception of God. I suppose not even the world itself could contain the bones of men intoxicated by its attraction. This view of the universe, in the guise of an Eastern empire ruled by a glorious tyrant . . . has broken more hearts than it has healed" (ibid.).

7. Whitehead, we remember, saw the very "essence" of Christianity as an appeal to the life of Christ as a revelation of the persuasive nature of God and of this divine agency in the world. However, "on the whole" Whitehead states that the "Gospel of love was turned into a Gospel of fear" (RM, 63). Indeed, Whitehead relays this clearly to Price, saying that "the trouble starts with the interpreters of Christianity. The disciples were admirably solid people. And there was at first hope that the powerful Greek notions which were abroad in the world at that time—ideas of liberty, democracy, the horror of brutality, and so on—would be blended with the best of Jewish thought—not all of which, of course, was equally good; but the gracious and merciful insights were there by flashes. But then the disaster starts. You get it in all of the following interpreters of Christianity from Augustine, even in Francis of Assisi; the gentleness and mercy of one side of Christianity, but based logically on the most appalling system of concepts. The old ferocious God is back, the Oriental despot, the Pharaoh, the Hitler; with everything to enforce obedience, from infinite damnation to eternal punishment. In Augustine you get admirable ideas, he is full of light; then you enquire into the ultimate bases of the doctrines and you find this abyss of horror. Their hearts were right but their heads were wrong. And there was no appeal from their heads. In Saint Francis, for example, it is hardly credible that the two worlds, that of grace and mercy, and that of eternal damnation, could exist in one and the same breast. This theological disaster is what I mean when I speak of the mischief which follows from banishing novelty, from trying to formularize your truth, from setting up to declare: 'This is all there is to be known on the subject, and discussion is closed.'" Price, *Dialogues*, 172–73. For an excellent Eastern orthodox critique of the tradition in ways strongly reminiscent to Whitehead's statements, see David Bentley Hart, *That All Shall Be Saved: Heaven, Hell and Universal Salvation* (New Haven: Yale University Press, 2019).

8. Indeed, for Whitehead, "the life of Christ is not an exhibition of over-ruling power. Its glory is for those who can discern it, and not for the world. Its power lies

in its absence of force. It has the decisiveness of a supreme ideal, and that is why the history of the world divides at this point of time" (RM, 47).

9. Price, *Dialogues*, 366, emphasis his.

10. In asking Whitehead whether or not it is possible to "indicate God's locus," A. H. Johnson reports: "Whitehead replied that in respect to the world, God is everywhere. Yet he is a distinct entity. The world (i.e., the events in it) has a (specific) locus with reference to him, but he has no locus with respect to the world. This is the basis for the distinction between finite and infinite. God and the world have the same [general] locus. It is a matter of emphasis which you pick out as occupying the locus. Whitehead does not want to set God over against the other actual entities." Johnson, "Some Conversations with Whitehead," 9.

11. Charles Hartshorne and William L. Reese, *Philosophers Speak of God* (Amherst: Humanity Books, 2000), v, 17. Thinkers like Griffin and Dombrowski follow Hartshorne in this regard. Griffin is the most well-known exponent of Whitehead's position as "panentheism": "The term 'panentheism' can be used either generically or more specifically" for Griffin. "The *generic* meaning is implicit in the term itself, which means 'all in God.' Panentheism is thus distinguished from pantheism, on the one hand, and traditional theism on the other. On the one hand, by saying that the world is *in* God, thereby saying that God is *more than* the world, panentheism is distinguished from pantheism, which, by saying that 'all *is* God,' simply identifies God and the world. On the other hand, by saying that the world is in God, panentheism is distinguished from all forms of traditional theism, according to which our world was created *ex nihilo* in such a way that the very existence of a realm of finite beings is contingent upon a divine decision. Panentheism, by contrast, holds that the existence of the world is integral to divine existence." Griffin, *Panentheism and Scientific Naturalism*, 13. For Dombrowski, Whitehead's "panentheism" might be viewed as a "higher synthesis that rises above both classical theism and pantheism." Daniel A. Dombrowski, *A History of the Concept of God: A Process Approach* (Albany: SUNY, 2016), 247.

12. Peter Hamilton, *The Living God and the Modern World* (Boston: United Church Press, 1967), 165. Emphasis mine. See also William A. Christian, *An Interpretation of Whitehead's Metaphysics* (New Haven: Yale University Press, 1967).

13. For a discussion of the definitional diversity surrounding "panentheism," see my unpublished paper, "Ambiguities in Panentheism: Definitions, Distinctions and Demarcations," available on academia.edu.

14. Whitehead further clarifies that "creativity is without a character of its own in exactly the same sense in which Aristotelian 'matter' is without a character of its own. It is that ultimate notion of the highest generality at the base of actuality" (ibid., 31).

15. See, for example, Laurence Wilmot, *Whitehead and God: Prolegomena to Theological Reconstruction* (Waterloo: Wilfrid Laurier University Press, 1979).

16. John B. Cobb Jr., "Being Itself and the Existence of God," in *The Existence of God*, John R. Jacobson and Robert Lloyd Mitchell (eds.) (Lewiston: Edwin Mellen, 1988), 19. Quoted RWS, 267–68.

17. Consider Hosinski's comments in this regard: "God is the infinite and eternal ground of possibility, order, value and novelty that is necessary for there to be any actual course of events, any universe, at all. This aspect of God makes the universe possible, but, we should note, [it] is an eternal vision of merely *possible* beauty and value. The actual agents of the universe, finite, temporal, and passing, incorporate this aspect of God in receiving their aims, their creativity and freedom, and their possibilities. In turn, these agents of the universe give God something God cannot otherwise acquire: *actualized* beauty and value. It is only through the agency of the temporal actual agents of the universe that the possibilities in God's eternal vision are gradually actualized." Hosinski, *Image of the Unseen God*, 158.

18. Marjorie Suchocki, *Divinity and Diversity: A Christian Affirmation of Religious Pluralism* (Nashville: Abingdon Press, 2003), 28–29.

19. John B. Cobb Jr., *God and the World* (Philadelphia: Westminster Press, 1998), 82.

20. Price, *Dialogues*, 366.

Conclusion
The Ultimacy of Relationality

Investigations into the nature of ultimacy and explanation remain one of the most long-standing and laudable endeavors of the Western tradition of philosophical theology. This book has been an attempt to contribute, however slightly, to this discussion. The tradition remains diverse and winding, but resonant claims of ultimacy echo from Plato, Aristotle, and Plotinus to Anselm and Aquinas, and from Descartes, Leibniz, Spinoza, and Hegel to Whitehead, Ward, and Leslie as the triadic stimulus for the investigation. In referring to this tradition as "axianoetic," I have sought to recognize more readily the ways in which these echoes fundamentally concern the ultimate status of Mind *and* Value.

With their own emphasis, priorities, and insights, Whitehead, Ward, and Leslie together form a deeply perceptive means of approaching these themes. I have tried to draw upon each of them (as well as several others) in ways relevant to their own axianoetic intuitions, particularly as they relate to key mysteries of existence, including the mystery of any and all existence (Part I); the mystery of necessary divine existence (Part II); the mystery of possibility and its various riddles (Part III); and the mystery of the world and its actualization (Part IV). For Whitehead, Ward, and Leslie, Mind and Value differently shine through each of these related mysteries.

In following Whitehead's intuitions, however, my focus has been deliberately *relational*. I have not simply wanted to point to Mind *or* Value, Possibility *or* Actuality, God *or* the World as "ultimate" in an isolated, either-or fashion. Rather, I have affirmed the relational and interdependent function of all of these notions for each other, such that the mystery of divine and worldly things, and the various challenges associated with them, might find novel illumination. The mystery of ultimacy, I have suggested, *is* the mystery of relationality. It is the mystery of mutual immanence and transcendence wherein multiple realities, conditions, and requirements coinhere with one another such that they each lend each other essential factors without which they could not be.

It is my conviction that the notions of Mind and Value, Possibility and Actuality, are essential to any consideration of ultimacy and explanation, as well as of God and the World. But they do not exhaust ultimate notions. Whitehead reminds us that there are in fact an "unending number of them" (MT, 70). I trust that Ward and Leslie would agree. Nevertheless, I think such notions are indispensable enough to allow a more fundamental point to be made about the ultimacy of their relationality. Before concluding with my final statements in this regard, let us remind ourselves of where we have been by returning to the framing quotations first encountered in the introduction.

- *Leslie:* "Necessarily, eternally, there can be ethical requirements for the existence of various things, needs for them to exist" (ME, 130).
- *Ward:* "The deepest reality is mind, eternal and necessary mind" (EG, 75).
- *Whitehead:* "The key to metaphysics is [the] doctrine of mutual immanence, each side lending to the other a factor necessary for its reality" (PR, 126).
- *Ewing:* "It would be as true to say that the [value] principle could not be true without God existing as to say that God could not exist without the [value] principle being true" (VR, 203).
- *Whitehead:* God does not create eternal [possibilities]; for [the divine] nature requires them in the same degree that they require [the divine nature]" (PR, 257).
- *Whitehead:* "It is as true to say that God transcends the World, as that the World transcends God. It is as true to say that God creates the World, as that the World creates God" (PR, 348).
- *Whitehead:* "Thus the task of philosophy is the understanding of the interfusion of modes of existence" (MT, 71).

As conceived in the preceding pages, this relational *interfusion* is such that Mind lends to Value what Value cannot lend itself, just as Value lends to Mind what Mind cannot lend itself. In so doing, Mind and Value live through each other in mutual immanence and transcendence. So too, Possibility lends to Actuality what Actuality cannot lend itself, just as Actuality lends to Possibility what Possibility cannot lend to itself. In so doing, Possibility and Actuality live through each other in mutual immanence and transcendence. So too, God lends to the World what the World cannot lend itself, just as the World lends to God what God cannot lend God's self. In so doing, God and the World live through each other in mutual immanence and transcendence. It is in consideration of the relational nature of ultimacy in this way that one comes to affirm that *relationality is what is ultimate.*

Bibliography

Adams, Robert Merrihew. "God, Possibility, and Kant." *Faith and Philosophy*, vol. 17/4 (2000): 425–440.
Allan, George and Merle F. Allshouse. Editors. *Nature, Truth, and Value: Exploring the Thinking of Frederick to Ferré*. Lanham: Lexington, 2005.
Attfield, Robin. *Wonder, Value and God*. New York: Routledge, 2018.
Axel, Larry E. and Creighton Peden. Editors. *God, Value, and Empiricism: Issues in Philosophical Theology*. Macon: Mercer University Press, 1989.
Barrow, John and Frank Tipler. *The Anthropic Cosmological Principle*. Oxford: Clarendon Press, 1986.
Bergson, Henri. *Creative Evolution*. Translated by A. Mitchell. New York: Modern Library, 1944.
Bracken, Joseph. *Does God Roll Dice? Divine Providence for a World in the Making*. Collegeville: Liturgical Press, 2012.
Bush, Randall B. *God, Morality, and Beauty: The Trinitarian Shape of Christian Ethics, Aesthetics, and the Problem of Evil*. Lanham: Lexington, 2019.
Camus, Albert. *The Myth of Sisyphus and Other Essays*. New York: Vintage International, 2018.
Christian, William A. *An Interpretation of Whitehead's Metaphysics*. New Haven: Yale University Press, 1967.
Cobb, John B. Jr. *A Christian Natural Theology: Based on the Thought of Alfred North Whitehead*. Second edition. Louisville: Westminster John Knox Press, 2007.
———. Editor. *Back to Darwin: A Richer Account of Evolution*. Grand Rapids: Eerdmans, 2008.
———. *God and the World*. Philadelphia: Westminster Press, 1998.
Conway Morris, Simon. *Life's Solution: Inevitable Humans in a Lonely Universe*. Cambridge: Cambridge University Press, 2003.
Craig, William Lane. *God and Abstract Objects: The Coherence of Theism: Aseity*. New York: Springer, 2017.

———. *God over All: Divine Aseity and the Challenge of Platonism*. Oxford: Oxford University Press, 2016.
Crosby, Donald A. *Novelty*. Lanham: Lexington, 2005.
Dalferth, Ingolf U. *Creatures of Possibility: The Theological Basis of Human Freedom*. Grand Rapids: Baker Academic, 2016.
Davis, Andrew M. and Philip Clayton. Editors. *How I Found God in Everyone and Everywhere: An Anthology of Spiritual Memoirs*. Rhinebeck: Monkfish, 2018.
———. "Ambiguities in Panentheism: Definitions, Distinctions, and Demarcations." Unpublished Paper. Available on Academica.edu.
Davies, Paul. *The Accidental Universe*. New York: Cambridge University Press, 1982.
———. *The Mind of God: The Scientific Basis for a Rational World*. New York: Simon & Schuster Paperbacks, 2005.
Davies, Paul and John Gribbin. *The Matter Myth: Dramatic Discoveries that Challenge Our Understanding of Physical Reality*. New York: Simon & Schuster, 1992.
Dick, Steven J. Editor. *The Impact of Discovering Life beyond Earth*. Cambridge: Cambridge University Press, 2016.
Dombrowski, Daniel A. *A History of the Concept of God: A Process Approach*. Albany: SUNY, 2016.
———. *Rethinking the Ontological Argument: A Neoclassical Theistic Response*. New York: Cambridge University Press, 2006.
———. *Whitehead's Religious Thought: From Mechanism to Organism, from Force to Persuasion*. Albany: SUNY, 2017.
Dubay, Thomas S. M. *The Evidential Power of Beauty: Science and Theology Meet*. San Francisco: Ignatius Press, 1999.
Eastman, Timothy E., Michael Epperson, and David Ray Griffin. Editors. *Physics and Speculative Philosophy: Potentiality in Modern Science*. Berlin: De Gruyter, 2016.
Ellis, Fiona. *God, Value, & Nature*. Oxford: Oxford University Press, 2014.
Ellis, George. *How Can Physics Underlie the Mind?: Top-Down Causation in the Human Context*. Berlin: Springer-Verlag, 2016.
Ewing, A. C. *Value and Reality*. London: George Allen & Unwin Ltd., 1973.
Faber, Roland. *The Becoming of God: Process Theology, Philosophy and Multireligious Engagement*. Eugene: Cascade, 2017.
———. *Depths as Yet Unspoken: Whiteheadian Excursions in Mysticism, Multiplicity and Divinity*. Edited by Andrew M. Davis. Eugene: Pickwick, 2020.
———. *The Divine Manifold*. Lanham: Lexington, 2014.
———. *The Garden of Reality: Transreligious Relativity in a World of Becoming*. Lanham: Lexington, 2018.
———. "My Faith in Baha'u'llah: A Declaration." *Baha'I Studies Review*, vol. 20 (2014): 149–174.
———. *The Ocean of God: On the Transreligious Future of Religions*. London: Anthem, 2019.
Ferré, Frederick. *Being and Value: Toward a Constructive Postmodern Metaphysics*. Albany: SUNY, 1996.

———. *Knowing and Value: Toward a Constructive Postmodern Epistemology.* Albany: SUNY, 1998.

———. *Living and Value: Toward a Constructive Postmodern Ethics.* Albany: SUNY, 2001.

Ford, Lewis. "The Nontemporality of Whitehead's God." *International Philosophical Quarterly,* vol. 8/3 (1973): 347–376.

Ford, Lewis and George L. Kline. Editors. *Explorations in the Whitehead's Philosophy.* New York: Fordham University Press, 1983.

Forrest, Peter. *God without the Supernatural.* Ithaca: Cornell University Press, 1996.

Goff, Philip. *Galileo's Error: Foundations for a New Science of Consciousness.* New York: Pantheon, 2019.

Griffin, David Ray. *God Exists But Gawd Does Not: From Evil to New Atheism to Fine-Tuning.* Anok: Process Century Press.

———. *Panentheism and Scientific Naturalism: Rethinking Evil, Morality, Religious Experience, Religious Pluralism and the Academic Study of Religion.* Claremont: Process Century Press, 2014.

———. *Reenchantment without Supernaturalism: A Process Philosophy of Religion.* Ithaca: Cornell University Press, 2001.

———. *Religion and Scientific Naturalism: Overcoming the Conflicts.* Albany: SUNY, 2000.

———. *Unsnarling the World-Knot: Consciousness, Freedom and the Mind-Body Problem.* Eugene: Wipf & Stock, 1998.

Hamilton, Peter. *The Living God and the Modern World.* Boston: United Church Press, 1967.

Hart, David Bentley. *That All Shall Be Saved: Heaven, Hell and Universal Salvation.* New Haven: Yale University Press, 2019.

Hartshorne, Charles. *Anselm's Discovery: A Re-Examination of the Ontological Proof of God's Existence.* Chicago: Open Court, 1991.

———. *Insights and Oversights of the Great Thinkers: An Evaluation of Western Philosophy.* Albany: SUNY, 1983.

———. *The Logic of Perfection.* Chicago: Open Court, 1991.

Hartshorne, Charles and William L. Reese. Editors. *Philosophers Speak of God.* Amherst: Humanity Books, 2000.

Haught, John F. *God after Darwin: A Theology of Evolution.* Boulder: Westview Press, 2000.

———. *The New Cosmos Story: Inside Our Awakening Universe.* New Haven: Yale University Press, 2017.

Hawking, Stephen. *A Brief History of Time.* London: Bantam Press, 1989.

Heidegger, Martin. *An Introduction to Metaphysics.* New Haven and London: Yale University Press, 1987.

Hosinski, Thomas. *The Image of the Unseen God: Catholicity, Science and Our Evolving Understanding of God.* Maryknoll: Oribs, 2017.

———. *Stubborn Fact and Creative Advance: An Introduction to the Metaphysics of Alfred North Whitehead.* Lanham: Rowman and Littlefield, 1993.

Johnson, A. H. *Whitehead's Theory of Reality.* New York: Dover, 1962.

Jones, Judith A. *Intensity: An Essay in Whiteheadian Ontology*. Nashville: Vanderbilt University Press, 1998.
Kauffman, Stuart A. *Humanity in a Creative Universe*. Oxford: Oxford University Press, 2016.
Kearney, Richard. *The God Who May Be: A Hermeneutics of Religion*. Bloomington: Indiana University Press, 2001.
Kline, George L. Editor. *Alfred North Whitehead: Essays on His Philosophy*. Englewood Cliffs: Prentice-Hall, 1963.
Kuhn, Robert Lawrence. "Levels of Nothing: There Are Multiple Answers to the Question of Why the Universe Exists." *Skeptic Magazine*, vol. 18/2 (2013): 34–37.
Laurence, Stephen and Cynthia MacDonald. Editors. *Contemporary Readings in the Foundations of Metaphysics*. Oxford: Blackwell Publishers, 1998.
Leslie, John. *The End of the World: The Science and Ethics of Human Extinction*. New York: Routledge, 1996.
———. *Immortality Defended*. Malden: Blackwell, 2007.
———. *Infinite Minds: A Philosophical Cosmology*. Oxford: Clarendon Press, 2001.
———. "Infinity and the Problem of Evil." *European Journal of Philosophy*, vol. 11/2 (2019): 111–117.
———. Editor. *Modern Cosmology & Philosophy*. Amherst: Prometheus Books, 1998.
———. "The Theory That the World Exists Because It Should." *American Philosophical Quarterly*, vol. 7 (1970): 286–298.
———. *Universes*. New York: Routledge, 1996.
———. *Value and Existence*. Totowa: Rowman & Littlefield, 1979.
———. "What God Might Be." *International Journal for Philosophy of Religion*, vol. 85 (2019): 63–75.
———. "Why Not Let Life Become Extinct?" *Philosophy*, vol. 58/225 (1983): 329–338.
Leslie, John and Robert Laurence Kuhn. Editors. *The Mystery of Existence: Why is There Anything at All?* Malden: Wiley-Blackwell, 2013.
Lindsay, James. "The Philosophy of Possibility." *The Monist*, vol. 32/3 (July, 1922): 321–338.
Loomer, Bernard. *The Size of God: The Theology of Bernard Loomer in Context*. Edited by William Dean and Larry E. Axel. Georgia: Mercer University Press, 1987.
Lowe, Victor. "A.N.W.: A Biographical Perspective." *Process Studies*, vol. 12/3 (1982): 137–147.
Malone-France, Derek. *Deep Empiricism: Kant, Whitehead, and the Necessity of Philosophical Theism*. Lanham: Lexington, 2007.
Murphy, Nancey and George F. R. Ellis. *On the Moral Nature of the Universe: Theology, Cosmology and Ethics*. Minneapolis: Fortress Press, 2009.
Min, Anselm K. Editor. *Rethinking the Medieval Legacy for Contemporary Theology*. Notre Dame: University of Notre Dame Press, 2014.
Nagel, Thomas. *Mind & Cosmos: Why the Materialist Neo-Darwinian Conception of Nature is Almost Certainly False*. Oxford: Oxford University Press, 2012.

———. *Moral Questions*. Cambridge: Cambridge University Press, 1979.
Neville, Robert Cummings. *Metaphysics of Goodness: Harmony and Form, Beauty and Art, Obligation and Personhood, Flourishing and Civilization*. New York: SUNY, 2019.
Nitecki, M. H. Editor. *Evolutionary Progress*. Chicago: University of Chicago Press, 1988.
Oddie, Graham. *Value, Reality, and Desire*. Oxford: Oxford University Press, 2005.
Penrose, Roger. *Shadows of the Mind*. New York: Oxford University Press, 1994.
Plantinga, Alvin. Editor. *The Ontological Argument: From St. Anselm to Contemporary Philosophers*. New York: Doubleday Anchor, 1965.
———. *Where the Conflict Really Lies: Science, Religion and Naturalism*. Oxford: Oxford University Press, 2011.
Polkinghorne, John. *Faith of a Physicist*. Minneapolis: Fortress Press, 1996.
———. *Reason and Reality*. London: SPCK, 1991.
———. Editor. *The Work of Love: Creation as Kenosis*. Grand Rapids: Eerdmans, 2001.
Price, Lucian. *Dialogues of Alfred North Whitehead*. Jaffrey: David R. Godine, 2001.
Pugliese, Marc and Gloria Schaab. Editors. *Seeking Common Ground: Evaluation and Critique of Joseph Bracken's Comprehensive Worldview*. Milwaukee: Marquette University Press, 2012.
Rawlette, Sharon Hewitt. *The Feeling of Value: Moral Realism Grounded in Phenomenal Consciousness*. King George: Dudley & White, 2016.
Rescher, Nicolas. *Axiogenesis: An Essay in Metaphysical Optimism*. Lanham: Lexington, 2010.
———. *Metaphysical Perspectives*. Notre Dame: University of Notre Dame Press, 2017.
Rice, Hugh. *God and Goodness*. Oxford: Oxford University Press, 2000.
Russell, Bertrand. *Why I am Not a Christian*. New York: Touchstone, 1957.
Sherburne, Donald W. Editor. *A Key to Whitehead's Process and Reality*. Chicago: University of Chicago Press, Free Press, 1981.
Skrbina, David. *Panpsychism in the West*. Cambridge: MIT, 2007.
Stang, Nicholas F. "Kant's Possibility Proof." *History of Philosophy Quarterly*, vol. 27/3 (2010): 275–299.
Suchocki, Marjorie. *Divinity and Diversity: A Christian Affirmation of Religious Pluralism*. Nashville: Abingdon Press, 2003.
Unger, Robert Mangabeira and Lee Smolin. *The Singular Universe and the Reality of Time*. Cambridge University Press, 2015.
Wagner, Andreas. *Arrival of the Fittest: How Nature Innovates*. New York: Current, 2015.
Ward, Keith. *The Big Questions in Science and Religion*. West Conshohocken: Templeton, 2008.
———. *The Christian Idea of God: A Philosophical Foundation for Faith*. Cambridge: Cambridge University Press, 2017.
———. *Concepts of God: Images of the Divine in Five Religious Traditions*. Oxford: Oneworld, 1998.

———. *Confessions of a Recovering Fundamentalist*. Eugene: Cascade, 2019.
———. *In Defense of the Soul*. London: Oneworld, 1998.
———. *The Evidence for God: The Case for the Existence of a Spiritual Dimension*. London: Darton, Longman and Todd, 2014.
———. *God: A Guide for the Perplexed*. London: One World, 2002.
———. *God and the Philosophers*. Minneapolis: Fortress Press, 2009.
———. *God, Chance, Necessity*. Oxford: Oneworld, 1996.
———. *More than Matter? Is There More to Life than Molecules?* Grand Rapids: Eerdmans, 2010.
———. *Pascal's Fire: Scientific Faith and Religious Understanding*. Oxford: Oneworld, 2006.
———. *Rational Theology and the Creativity of God*. Oxford: Basil Blackwell, 1982.
———. *Religion and Creation*. Oxford: Clarendon, 1996.
———. *Religion in the Modern World: Celebrating Pluralism and Diversity*. Cambridge: Cambridge University Press, 2019.
———. *Sharing in the Divine Nature: A Personalist Metaphysics*. Eugene: Cascade, 2020.
Weber, Michel. *Whitehead's Pancreativism: The Basics*. Berlin: De Gruyter, 2006.
Weinberg, Steven. *Dreams of a Final Theory*. London: Vintage, 1993.
———. *To Explain the World: The Discovery of Modern Science*. New York: Harper Perennial, 2015.
Whitehead, Alfred North. *Adventures of Ideas*. New York: Free Press, 1967.
———. *Aims of Education*. New York: Free Press, 1967.
———. *The Concept of Nature*. Cambridge: Cambridge University Press, 1964.
———. *The Function of Reason*. Princeton: Princeton University Press, 1929.
———. *Modes of Thought*. New York: Free Press, 1968.
———. *The Principle of Relativity*. Cambridge: Cambridge University Press, 1922.
———. *Process and Reality*. Corrected edition. Edited by David Ray Griffin and Donald Sherburne. New York: The Free Press, 1978.
———. *Religion in the Making*. Cambridge: Cambridge University Press, 1926.
———. *Science and Philosophy*. Paterson: Littlefield, Adams & Co., 1964.
———. *Science and the Modern World*. New York: The Free Press, 1967.
———. *Symbolism: Its Meaning and Effect*. New York: Fordham University Press, 1985.
Wilczek, Frank. *A Beautiful Question: Finding Nature's Deep Design*. New York: Penguin Books, 2016.
Wilmot, Laurence. *Whitehead and God: Prolegomena to Theological Reconstruction*. Waterloo: Wilfrid Laurier University Press, 1979.
Wynn, Mark. *God and Goodness*. New York: Routledge, 1999.

Index

absolute idealism, 84n4, 90
absolute spirit (Hegel), 77–78
abstraction, 4–5, 17, 19, 47, 66, 74, 87–88, 90, 96, 114, 117–18, 140n12, 149, 156, 193
abstract objects, 19, 46–47, 49n12
abstract priority, 55, 99
abstract requirements, 19
abstract value, 3–5, 47, 54, 66, 90, 99, 117, 151, 182
actual entity, 20, 64, 66n7, 89–90, 127n26, 131, 140n10, 144–45, 156, 159, 198, 202
actual occasion(s), 28, 83n5, 117, 120, 139n7, 200
actus purus (Aquinas), 74, 108
Adams, Robert Merrihew, 160n5
aesthetic, 2, 19, 22–23, 29, 32n13, 41, 63–64, 89–90, 94, 98, 102n2, 132–33, 137–40, 146, 203
aesthetic cosmological principle (Haught), 22
agency, 85, 94–95, 102n3, 161n19, 209n7, 211n17
agent, 73, 75, 93, 125n12, 160n7
air of pantheism (Whitehead), 198, 205
Anaxagoras, 56
ancient saying (Aquinas), 147

Anselm, 2, 58–59, 66n3, 70, 73, 101, 154, 213
anthropic cosmological principle, 22, 32n19
anticipation, 107, 123n3
Aquinas, 2, 34n31, 58–60, 70, 74, 76, 78, 108, 144, 147, 158, 213
Aristotle, 2, 28, 42, 57–58, 65, 70–74, 85–87, 101, 103n7, 108, 144, 158, 192, 197, 213
atheism, 33n28, 138n3, 181
attainment of value (God's purpose), 89, 146
Attfield, Robin, 29n1
Augustine, 7, 34n31, 60, 66n2, 78, 135, 144, 148, 193, 195, 209n5
Auschwitz-Birkenau, 185
Auxier, Randal E., 127n24, 161n19
awareness, 30n4, 71, 73, 95, 100, 107, 111
axianoetic, 2–11, 36–37, 54–55, 82, 93, 99, 101, 107, 110, 122, 129, 132, 138, 143, 145–49, 158–59, 165–66, 194, 204, 207, 213
axianoetic tradition, 3–5, 36, 55, 82, 99, 101
axiarchic tradition, 56, 59, 65
axiarchism, 5, 20, 53–65, 82, 91–95, 100

axiological, 4, 11–12, 19–23, 29n1, 41–47, 57, 63, 69, 74, 80, 88–90, 99–100, 112, 115, 121, 122n1, 132, 134, 146, 159, 165, 168, 204
axiological explanation, 46, 69, 100

barbaric, 138, 209n6
Barbour, Ian, 25
beautiful, the (Anselm), 73, 101
beginning(s), 28–29, 30n8, 34n31, 38, 78–79, 180, 195, 209n4
Bergson, Henri, 14, 36–37
Berkley, George, 69
best, the, 42–43, 56, 61, 71, 76, 77, 81, 97, 99, 184
best possible world, 76, 81, 150
better and worse, 32n16, 41, 111
beyond being, 58, 70, 72
Biernacki, Loriliai, 188n7
big bang, 28, 39, 44, 179–80
biological forms, 108
biology, 5, 28, 108, 158
Bohm, David, 171
bootstrap of virtue (Polkinghorne), 92, 154
Bracken, Joseph A, 13, 188n11
brutal fact (Heller), 38
brute fact, 38–39, 43–45
Buchler, Justus, 157
Bush, Randal B., 29

Caesar, 196–97
Calvin, John, 193, 195–96
Camus, Albert, 31n10, 122n1
Carroll, Sean, 28, 39
causality, 39, 111, 179, 194
causa sui, 98
causation, 60, 138n3, 194, 202
cause, 38–42, 46, 56–60, 67n10, 70–72, 77, 83n5, 91–92, 96, 101, 182
cause and effect, 91–92, 101
cause of God (Ewing), 96
chance, 4, 36, 40–42, 151, 179
chaos, 21, 56, 136–37, 195, 209n4
Christ, 102n3, 103n9, 209nn7–8

Christian, William A., 198
Christian theology, 88, 196, 208n1
classical rationalists, 76
classical theism, 79, 131, 210n11
Clayton, Philip, 187n7
Closer to Truth (PBS), 9, 48n1
Cobb, John B Jr., 33n21, 66n7, 139n9, 201, 206, 210n16, 211n19
coercive, 85, 139n7
Cogito ergo sum (Descartes), 75
coincidentia, 93
coinherence, 99, 154
collective explanation (Rescher), 40
concepts of God, 191–92
conceptual, 41, 64–65, 70–71, 79, 87–90, 100, 103n7, 107, 111–12, 118, 145–46, 203
conceptualism, 86
concrescence, 18, 139n8, 140n10, 197, 200, 203
concrete mind, 3–5
concrete priority (of mind), 55, 99
consciousness, 5, 11, 13, 24, 27, 36, 67n10, 69–71, 74–80, 92, 95, 103n7, 112, 123n2, 126n17, 133, 148, 169–73, 180, 183, 194, 198, 207, 208n2
consequent nature, 79, 87–90, 177
contemplation (divine), 57, 72, 78, 100, 136, 168, 176, 184, 205
contingency, 4, 23–26, 46, 134, 176–77, 180
contingent mutual immanence (Ward), 205
Cooper, John W., 188n7
Copleston, F. C., 38
cosmic consciousness, 74, 79, 80, 148
cosmic epoch, 26, 28, 120, 137, 195, 198, 204
cosmological conditions, 25–26
cosmological mediation, 193
cosmological question, 4, 15–16, 21, 24–26, 46, 108
cosmology, 5, 7, 28, 45, 77, 108, 158, 193, 197
Craig, William Lane, 46, 49n12

creation, 28, 33n27, 34n31, 55–56, 58, 70, 79–83, 96, 126n22, 127n27, 132, 145, 148, 159, 174–78, 187n6, 192, 195–206
creation (as ultimate priority), 55, 66
creative activity, 34n31, 65, 119, 200–201
creatively effective, value as, 43, 59, 93, 151, 153
creative value, 82, 136, 191, 202
creativity (as ultimate), 22, 28, 30n8, 45, 64, 197, 199–202, 207, 210n14
creator, 29, 34n31, 44, 49n10, 63, 73, 79, 135, 150, 159, 177–78, 183, 192–93, 196–97, 202
Crosby, Donald, 139n7, 157, 161n18

Dalferth, Ingolf, 107, 123nn3–4, 124nn6–7, 127n25, 160n5
Darwinian, 26, 33n26
Davies, Paul, 24–25, 43, 126n18, 139n5, 171
Dawkins, Richard, 27, 32n20
decentralized possibility (Ferré), 132
demiurge, 71–72, 195
Descartes, 2, 34n31, 60–61, 70, 75–76, 144, 159n1, 160n8, 213
dialectical (Hegel), 77–78
dipolar, 79, 87, 177
dipolarity, 79, 177–78, 194
distributive explanation (Rescher), 40
divine character, 146
divine element, 64, 85–86, 102n2, 145
divine necessity, 4–5, 43–47, 54–55, 57, 90, 96, 99, 101
divine person, 43–44, 58–59, 96
divine reality, 45, 122, 168, 173
divine self, 53, 78, 99, 153–54, 156
divine simplicity, 44, 59, 74
divine thinking, 6, 166–70, 174–75, 182, 184–85, 187n4, 206
divine thought, 6–7, 61, 166–68, 173–75, 180, 182–86, 203–5
Dombrowski, Daniel A, 66n3, 102n3, 210n11

double-slit experiment, 114
dual-aspect idealism (Ward), 179
dualism, 75, 86

East Asian (concept of God), 192, 207n1
Eddington, Arthur, 208n2
efficacy (of possibility), 120–21, 193
efficient causality, 194
Einstein, Albert, 169, 178, 186n3, 188n12
Ellis, Fiona, 29n21
Ellis, George, 109, 124n10
emanation, 72, 176
entanglement, 55
entertainment (conceptual), 107, 111–12, 159
essence, 57, 61–62, 71, 75, 77, 91–92, 97, 101, 118–19, 123n3, 126n17, 160n12
essence of Christianity, 102n3, 209n7
eternal objects, 20, 117–21, 126n24, 127n26, 130, 144–45, 156–57, 159n2, 161n17, 208n3
ethically required, 57, 62, 94–95, 113, 136–37, 151, 172
ethical necessity (Leslie), 115, 136
ethical needs, 42–43, 53, 55–56, 136, 149
ethical requirements, 7, 19–20, 59, 61, 65, 82, 93, 100, 214
evaluative and theocentric understanding (Forrest), 95
evolution, 4, 18, 26–28, 33n26, 41, 46, 112, 194–96, 208n3
Ewing, A. C., 5, 7, 55, 65, 91, 94, 96–98, 214
existential unity (Leslie), 171–73, 180, 183
experience (human), 6, 12, 14, 18, 22, 29n2, 102n2, 110–13, 119, 125n13, 159, 172, 180
extensive continuum, 195
external relations, 193, 208n3

extreme axiarchism, 5, 53–54, 63, 65, 82, 92, 94–95, 100
extremes (Whitehead), 7, 44, 191–92, 196, 198
extremes of simplicity (doctrine of God), 44, 192

Faber, Roland, 7, 11, 12, 18, 21, 30n4, 31n12, 33n28, 67n8, 88, 103n9, 125n15, 139n8, 140n11, 167, 186, 194, 198–99, 202
Ferré, Frederick, 6, 9, 129, 131–32, 137–138, 139n7, 140nn9–10, 159
Fiddes, Paul S, 188n11
final causality, 194
final entity (God), 102n2, 145
fine-tuning, 2, 25
fire (breaths), 29, 41–43
first mover (Aristotle), 57
Ford, Lewis, 139n7
Forms (Plato), 20–21, 31n12, 42, 60, 64, 70–74, 79, 81, 108, 116–18, 127n24, 131, 145–46, 148, 193
forms of process (Whitehead), 145
Forrest, Peter, 5, 11, 55, 91, 94–96, 100, 169, 180
founded in value (God's existence), 90, 98, 137, 202
freedom, 2, 79, 83n4, 168–69, 176, 178, 185, 194, 198, 201, 205–6, 211n17
free will defense, 185
fundamental question of metaphysics (Heidegger), 14, 31n10
fundamental question of philosophy (Camus), 31n10, 122n1
Future, the (futurity), 18–19, 33, 107, 111, 119, 127n27, 130, 137, 139n7, 176, 179, 195, 197, 199

Galilean origin of Christianity, 197
Garland, William J., 30n8
Geist (Hegel), 77
God and Creativity, 201
God *in se*, 88–89, 98
God-or-Nature (Spinoza), 77

God's own possibility, 6, 61, 110, 150, 156–57, 160n12
God's will, 93, 196
Goff, Philip, 208n2
Good, the, 42, 56–64, 70–72, 89, 100, 146, 175, 178, 186, 206
Goodness and its instantiation (Polkinghorne), 91–92, 101, 154
Goodness as divine limitation, 120, 135, 137, 140n13
Gospel of fear/love, 209
Gould, Steven J., 27, 32n20
grandeur (of the world), 7, 168, 206–7
gravity, 24–25, 28, 40

Hamilton, Peter, 198, 201n12
Hart, David Bentley, 209n7
Hartshorne, Charles, 22, 32n14, 48n4, 66n3, 126n23, 188n10, 198, 210n11
Haught, John F., 22, 29n1, 32n13, 123n3
Hawking, Steven, 29, 34nn30–31, 36, 40, 41
Hawking-Hartle model, 41
Hegel, G. W. F., 2, 60, 63, 65, 70, 75, 77–79, 101, 213
Heidegger, Martin, 11, 14, 30n3, 31n10, 108, 158
Heller, Michael, 38
hell(s), 134
Herstein, Gary L., 127n24, 161n19
Hindu-Buddhistic traditions (Whitehead), 208n1
Homo Quaerens, 12, 22, 35, 46, 107, 112, 165
Homo sapiens, 12, 26, 28
Hosinski, Thomas, 49n10, 124n12, 160n3, 211n17
Humans as expressions/exemplifications, 13, 16, 27, 45, 157
Human uniqueness, 49n10, 124n12, 211n17
Hume, David, 38–39, 48, 64, 69

idealism, 2, 5, 54, 66, 69–83, 83nn4–5, 90, 179

Index

ideals, 21, 41, 90, 98, 112, 137, 139n3, 195, 197, 202
ideas (Plato), 21, 31, 60, 61, 73, 76, 78, 85, 118, 144, 148, 174, 193
Idea that thinks itself (Hegel), 63, 101
identity, 6, 166–67, 172, 174, 180, 182–83, 187n6, 201, 204–5, 207
ignorance (divine), 169
immanence of God, 64, 103n9, 137
immanent/imposed law (Whitehead), 196
immaterial, 71, 77
imperial ruler (God), 197
importance, 32n15, 41, 48n4, 62, 76, 79, 85–86, 103n9, 110–12, 115, 127n27, 136, 150, 173, 181, 183, 187n6
inability (of mind), 181–83
incarnation, 89, 145
inclusivist tradition, 77
independent existence, 21, 71, 159n2
independent of God (possibility), 150, 155
Indian or Chinese thought (Whitehead), 200
infinite minds, 47, 81, 84n7, 95, 100, 135–37, 173, 184
inflation, 40
initial aim, 202
inner relations, 193
instinctive faith, 24
intelligibility, 23–24, 26, 79, 149, 177
interfusion, 8, 156, 214
internal relationality, 82, 98
intricate divine thinking (Leslie), 6, 168–69, 173, 184–85
ipsum esse subsistens (Aquinas), 59

James, William, 15, 17–18
Jerusalem and Athens, 209n4
Johnson, A. H., 33n27, 67n8, 102n5, 210n10
Jones, Judith A., 32n14
Jüngel, Eberhard, 108, 158

kalogenic (Ferré), 132, 139n9, 140n10
Kauffman, Stuart, 109

kenosis, 166, 175–77, 204
Khora, 194
kingdom of possibilities (Leslie), 114–15
Kuhn, Robert Lawrence, 18, 30n4, 31n9, 35–36, 65, 67n10

laws of nature, 25, 32n18, 80, 109, 147, 182
Leibniz, G. W., 2, 15–18, 39, 60–62, 70, 75–76, 144, 150, 213
Leibnizian rule, 81
Lewis, David, 6, 36–37, 129, 133–38, 140n11, 159
lichtung (Heidegger), 11, 165
life of Christ, 102n3, 209nn7–8
limitation (of possibility), 25–26, 109, 120–22, 132, 137–38, 144
Lindsay, James, 12, 124n6
Locke, John, 69–70
locus (of possibility), 6, 39n8, 115, 120–22, 131–32, 144
logical necessity, 96
logical *vs.* temporal relation, 155
Loomer, Bernard, 45
love, 6, 17, 21, 77, 80, 102n3, 104n12, 166–67, 175–77, 183, 196–97, 204, 209n7
Lowe, Victor, 48n8, 208n2

Macdonald, Norm, 29n2
Mackie, John, 94
Malone-France, Derek, 130, 138, 157, 159n2, 161n17
materialism (materialist), 2, 20, 27, 44, 69, 77, 130–31, 138n3, 181, 208nn2–3
mathematics, 31n12, 41, 43, 125n15, 205
matter, 29n2, 31n12, 33n25, 37–38, 40–41, 71–72, 75, 77, 131, 171, 178–79, 193, 195, 197, 208n3, 210n14
mechanistic, 194, 207
mediating God, 93–94
Middle Platonic, 60, 71, 148, 151

misplaced concreteness (fallacy), 126n19, 193
Modal realism (Lewis), 37, 133, 134, 140n12
Moltmann, Jurgen, 108, 124n7, 158
morality, 32n15, 112, 125n15
Morris, Simon Conway, 27, 33n21
multiplicity, 22, 88, 103n9, 127n26, 145, 170, 203, 209n4
Munchausen, Baron, 154
music, 125, 205
mutual immanence: as fundamental philosophical doctrine, 21, 88; of God and World, 191–211; as key to metaphysis, 7, 88, 214; as metaphysical discovery, 88, 103n9; of Mind and Value, 85–104; of Possibility and Actuality, 143–162
mutuality, 5, 47, 63, 94–95, 98, 156–57, 183, 191–93, 202, 204
mutual transcendence, 3, 6, 55, 153, 156, 199, 203

Nagel, Thomas, 24, 29n1, 33n21, 44–45, 109, 186n2
naturalism, 130, 138n3, 140n10
naturalistic theism, 131
nature of God, 6, 45, 75, 77, 79, 86–90, 102n3, 103n9, 110, 130, 139n8, 146, 155–56, 160n7, 176–77, 202, 206, 209n7
necessary being, 104n15, 147
necessary mutual immanence (Whitehead), 205
necessity for relationality, 91
neo-Darwinian, 27
Neoplatonic, 58–59, 92, 176
Neville, Robert Cummings, 29n1
noesis noeseos (Aristotle), 71–72, 77, 101
nomological explanation, 69
non-being, 20, 116, 130–31
non-dual, 194
non-entity, 156
non-temporal, 64, 67n8, 144–45, 156, 201

nothingness, 4, 17–23, 30n7, 31n9, 37, 40, 46, 72, 114–17, 121, 130–31, 195, 199
novelty, 23–24, 26, 90, 103n13, 112, 117, 125n14, 126n17, 137, 139n7, 145, 158, 195, 197–200, 209n7, 211n17
Nozick, Robert, 14, 18
numbers, 19, 40, 80

objective values, 41–42
objects, 168
observer, 180, 183
observer-independent, 180
occasions of experience, 119
ocean (divine), 63, 81, 116, 137, 173
Ockham's razor, 94
Oddie, Graham, 29n1
omniscience, 146
One, the (Plotinus), 58, 72, 101, 176
ontological argument (Anselm), 58–59, 66n3, 73, 75
ontological principle (Whitehead), 20–21, 64, 86, 90, 130–32, 138, 143–44, 146, 149, 156–58, 159n1, 161n17, 212
ontological question, 4, 15–18, 21, 37, 46, 108, 199
order (cosmological), 16, 18, 22–26, 28, 41, 45, 108, 137, 145, 161n17, 174, 195–96
organ of novelty (mind), 90, 103n13, 126n17
otherness, 6, 78, 82, 166, 167, 173–75, 178, 180–83, 185–186, 187n7, 191, 198–99, 203–7
otherness (value of), 167, 175, 183, 204–5

panentheism, 6–7, 13, 138n3, 167, 173–74, 180, 183, 187n7, 188n7, 192, 198–99, 204, 210n11
panexperientialism, 123n2, 138n3, 208n2
panpsychism, 123n2, 169, 179, 208n2

Index

pantheism, 6–7, 167–68, 173–74, 180, 183–84, 186n1, 187n3, 192, 197–99, 204–5, 210n11
paradox, 155, 197–98
Parfit, Derek, 16–17, 37
Peacock, Arthur, 187n7
Penrose, Roger, 39, 148, 160n6
perfection, 32n15, 36, 53, 57–62, 73, 75–80, 85, 90–91, 97–98, 165, 169, 178
permanence, 19, 22–23, 65
personal idealism, 2, 5, 69, 82n1
personalistic theism, 92
personification of moral energy (God), 197
persuasion, 58, 102n7
philosophy of organism (Whitehead), 78, 85, 102n2
physics, 5, 10, 22, 25, 32n18, 41, 45, 80, 108, 124n8, 136, 158, 170–71, 179–80, 188n14, 193–94
pigtail (Munchausen's), 153–54
place of forms (God), 79
Plantinga, Alvin, 66n3, 139n3
Plato, 2, 20–21, 28, 31n12, 35, 42, 56–58, 63–64, 70–72, 85–87, 99, 101nn1–2, 102n3, 103n9, 113, 118, 127n24, 139n7, 147, 192–95, 213
Platonic-Augustinian model (Ward), 147–49
platonic haunting, 113–22
platonic realities, 19, 45, 74, 131, 150–51
Platonism, 21, 31n12, 46, 49n12, 59, 96, 131, 184
Plato's intellectual discovery (persuasion), 85, 102n3
Plotinus, 2, 42, 58, 72, 77, 101, 213
pluralistic idealism, 78, 83n4
poetic creation, 199–203
poet of the world, 203
Polkinghorne, John, 5, 32n19, 55, 65, 91–92, 100, 124n7
possibility-centric (ontological principle), 157

possible worlds, 63, 73, 76–77, 81, 108, 117, 129, 133, 134, 136–37
potency for mind, 179–80
potentiality, 20, 24, 57, 74, 78, 87, 103n11, 107, 109, 110, 116–19, 121, 123, 124n8, 127n26, 144–45, 156, 178–79
prehensive, 119, 193–94
presuppositional imperatives, 139n3
Price, Lucian, 7, 48n8, 125n14, 209n5
prime mover (Aristotle), 78, 85
primordial nature, 79, 87–90, 102n7, 130, 139n8, 156, 177
principle of axiology (Ward), 69
principle of determination, 89, 120
principle of limitation, 121
principle of perfection, 76
principle of plentitude, 135, 141n14
principle of sufficient reason, 39, 49n10
priority (question of), 6, 54, 108, 143
probability, 4, 40–41, 109
process philosophy, 2, 78–79, 83n5, 177
process theology, 2, 177
protestant theology, 79
Psyche (Plato), 85
psychophysical dipolarity, 122n2, 194
pure potentiality, 78, 156
purpose, 7, 27, 30n2, 57–58, 70, 76, 79, 88–89, 111, 125n14, 127n25, 134, 140n9, 146, 148–49, 197, 203, 207

quantum fluctuations, 40
quantum laws, 19, 41
quantum mechanics, 25, 41, 114, 170–71, 180
quantum tunneling, 41
Quine, W. V., 6, 129–30, 137, 138n1, 159

rationality, 38, 45, 73, 88, 203
Rawlette, Sharon Hewitt, 29n1
real potentiality, 119, 127n26
reasonless existence (God's), 89
receptacle (Plato), 194
reciprocity, 63, 65, 99, 198

Redhead, Michael, 171
reductive, 2, 69, 129, 132, 179
reification fallacy (Ward), 17
relational nature of ultimacy, 1, 8, 214
relativity (Einstein), 28, 79, 168n3, 169, 178, 188n14
relativized, 92, 158
relevance (of possibility), 4, 6, 110, 119–22, 144–45
Rescher, Nicholas, 16, 24, 29n1, 30n6, 40, 42
Rice, Hugh, 5, 55, 91, 93–96, 100, 167, 181–83
rightness, 120–21, 146, 202
Russell, Bertrand, 38–39, 48n4, 160n8, 208n2
Ryle, Gilbert, 75

sacramental (Ward), 178, 180
Saint Paul, 196
Scholium and *Timaeus*, 193–94
Schopenhauer, Arthur, 13–14, 31n10
Schrodinger's equation, 24
Semitic (concept of God), 191–92, 207n1
simple being, 44, 77
simplicity, 19, 44, 48n3, 59, 74, 192
Skrbina, David, 208n2
space and time (space-time), 40, 179, 194–95
specter of pantheism (Ward), 187nn6–7, 198
Spinoza, Baruch, 2, 60, 62–63, 70, 75, 77, 168–69, 186n1, 213
spiritual, 83n5, 174, 180
Stang, Nicholas F., 160n5
subjective aim, 90
subsistence (of possibility), 130–31, 137, 145, 153
Suchocki, Marjorie, 206, 211n18
suffering, 6–7, 21, 76, 102n3, 135, 167, 176, 183–86, 205, 207
superjective nature, 79
swamp (Munchausen's), 153–54

Swinburne, Richard, 43–44

teleology (teleological), 63, 80, 137, 179, 194, 203
temporality, 2, 46, 79, 177–78
theism (theistic), 43, 45, 67n10, 70, 79, 82, 92, 95, 131, 139n7, 140n9, 197–98, 210n11
theological mediation, 195–97
thinking (divine), 6, 7, 166–68, 170, 174–75, 182, 184–85, 187n4, 206
Thinking as being, 6, 136, 167–69, 182, 185
thinking of thinking (Aristotle), 71, 101
timeless, 41, 89, 115, 137, 144, 193
tragedy (tragic), 21, 23, 90, 111, 196, 206
transcendence, 7, 98, 118, 144, 191–93, 195–99, 204, 214
transpantheism, 7, 167, 197, 199
trinitarian, 103
truth, 22–23, 32n18, 35, 73, 84n6, 95, 103n9, 111, 117, 125n15, 137, 193, 197, 203, 209n7
Tyson, Neil deGrasee, 29n2

ultimacy of relationality, 1, 3, 8, 156, 213–14
ultimate actuality, 201–2
ultimate explanation, 30n8, 39, 43–44, 77, 97, 148, 158
ultimate irrationality, 88
ultimate notions, 1–3, 41, 158, 214
ultimate philosophical principle, 197
ultimate reality, 31n9, 45, 70, 74, 76, 83n5, 88, 148, 201–2
ultimate significance, 132, 207
unconscious, 71, 79, 83n5, 87–88, 103n7
unidirectional determination, 66
unilateral (unilaterality), 5, 58, 63, 65–66, 96–97, 100, 149, 153, 155, 158, 165, 167, 180, 192, 202, 206
union, 87–88, 171, 206, 209n5

unity, 22, 63, 73, 75, 78–79, 87, 90, 132–33, 169–73, 179, 180, 183, 200, 203, 208n3
universals, 19, 118, 200
unmoved mover (Aristotle), 196, 197
unspoken mutual immanence, 91–99

value principle, 7, 94, 96–98, 214
value realizations, 107, 122n2
Van Till, Howard J., 109, 124n11
Vilenkin, Alex, 41
void, 17, 37, 113, 121, 147

Wagner, Andreas, 33n26
Weber, Michel, 208n2
Weinberg, Steven, 32nn17–18, 44, 48n9
whole, the (Hume), 38
Wilmot, Laurence, 210n15
Wittgenstein, Ludwig, 15
Wolff, Christian, 108, 158
worldly mediation, 182
world of value, 65, 89, 103n11, 137
world-soul, 72
Wynn, Mark, 5, 55, 91–93, 100

About the Author

Andrew M. Davis, PhD, is program director for the Center for Process Studies at Claremont School of Theology at Willamette University in Salem, Oregon. He is author or editor of three books, including *How I Found God in Everyone and Everywhere: An Anthology of Spiritual Memoirs* (2018, with Philip Clayton); *Propositions in the Making: Experiments in a Whiteheadian Laboratory* (2019, with Roland Faber and Michael Halewood); and *Depths as Yet Unspoken: Whiteheadian Excursions in Mysticism, Multiplicity, and Divinity* (2020, with Roland Faber). Follow his work at andrewmdavis.info.

www.ingramcontent.com/pod-product-compliance
Lightning Source LLC
Chambersburg PA
CBHW050902300426
44111CB00010B/1348